Patsy McCarthy is an actor, teacher and administrator with 30 years experience teaching speech communication. She consults with organisations on communication issues and has worked in the USA and UK as well as Australia. She is currently senior lecturer in Speech Communication at the Queensland University of Technology.

Caroline Hatcher is currently a senior lecturer in the Brisbane Graduate School of Business at the Queensland University of Technology in Brisbane, Australia. She has a PhD in organisational communication and teaches in the area of speech and inter-cultural communication for business. Caroline has worked and consulted on communication issues in both the private and public sectors and has a special interest in the role of communication in change processes in organisations. She has lived and worked in the UK and Japan, as well as in Australia.

Patsy and Caroline have many other individual and joint publications in international academic journals and books. They have co-authored two CD Roms on speaking strategically in business.

T0332047

Speaking Persuasively

The essential guide to giving dynamic presentations and speeches

2nd edition

Patsy McCarthy
and
Caroline Hatcher

Routledge
Taylor & Francis Group
LONDON AND NEW YORK

First published 1996 by Allen & Unwin

Published 2020 by Routledge
2 Park Square, Milton Park, Abingdon, Oxon OX14 4RN
605 Third Avenue, New York, NY 10017

Routledge is an imprint of the Taylor & Francis Group, an informa business

National Library of Australia
Cataloguing-in-Publication entry:

McCarthy, Patsy, 1943– .

Speaking persuasively : the essential guide to giving dynamic presentations and speeches.

2nd ed.
Bibliography.
Includes index.
ISBN 1 86508 811 0.

1. Oral communication—Handbooks, manuals, etc. 2. Public speaking. 3. Self-presentation. I. Hatcher, Carolyn. II. Title.

808.51

Set in 10.5/12 pt Garamond by Midland Typesetters, Maryborough, Victoria

ISBN-13: 9781865088112 (pbk)

Printed and bound by CPI Group (UK) Ltd, Croydon, CR0 4YY

To our husbands, Paul and Paul,
who manage the pressures of busy partners,
and our much loved children,
Maya, Chaya, Joshua, and Gaju,
who have taken the long journey with us.

Contents

Acknowledgements

This book would not have been possible without the generosity of many colleagues and friends. We would like to particularly thank Clare Willis of Speak First (London), and Jeff Kinghorn (University of Houston) who took the time to read our early manuscripts and give us valuable feedback. Their encouragement helped to maintain our energy and excitement to complete the project. Our thanks also to Peter Mooney of OTMA LTD, London, for the opportunity of experience gained through his consultancy practice.

We are grateful to the Faculty of Business at the Queensland University of Technology for financial support through their Research Grant to study Australian business presenters. We are indebted to Ian Weber (QUT) for his resourcefulness in assisting us to assemble material for case studies in our book, and to Krista Berga (QUT) for her creativity and hard work in the early stages of compiling our material.

We are also indebted to our research assistant and colleague Shirley Lambert for her attention to detail and her generosity in providing assistance to help us through the labour of our final drafts.

Finally, we must mention our appreciation of Elizabeth Weiss, our editor, for the patience, direction and encouragement she has provided.

We wish to thank those publishers, organisations and individuals whose kind permissions have contributed to this book:

Columbia University in the City of New York
Sonoda Women's University, Japan

Clayton Utz law firm, Brisbane
Robin White–The Presentation People
Associate Professor Satoshi Hamashima of Sonoda Women's
    University
Times Newspapers Limited, London
Punch Magazine, London
Asian Business Review
The Australian newspaper
Parliament of Australia, House of Representatives
Michael T. Motley and Jennifer L. Molloy

The illustrations throughout the book are the work of cartoonist Fiona Mitchell.

AUTHORS' NOTE

The authors are sensitive to the use of non-sexist language and therefore have alternated the use of 'he' and 'she' throughout the text.

Introduction

*Because there has been implanted in us the power to persuade
each other . . . not only have we escaped the life of the wild
beasts but we have come together and founded cities and made
laws and invented arts . . .*

Isocrates

*There are three things that never return: the spoken word, the spent
arrow, and the lost opportunity.*[1]

WHO THIS BOOK IS FOR

A survey conducted in the United States revealed that the greatest
fear human beings face is the fear of public speaking. It is greater
than the fear of loneliness. It is greater than the fear of snakes. It
is greater than the fear of death. If you are one of those human
beings who wishes to convert the adrenalin produced by this fear
into excitement, this book is for you. It is your opportunity to read
and to understand simple ideas for practice. It is your opportunity
to stop fearing and start feeling good, perhaps great, about facing
a 'public' and speaking.

And this book is for you who realise that speaking is one of
the most powerful means of influencing others in business and in
life: you who realise that leading others is about understanding
and practising persuasive speaking. And for you who want to

make the most of your speaking opportunities, to make the best of your career or business ventures, to influence your professional or political credibility, or simply to further your study.

WHY WE DECIDED TO WRITE IT

In the past ten years we have seen presentations in our consultancy work and in our classrooms that have highlighted the need for a book to help executive speakers (and we use *executive* as a generic term for all those who are and all those who aspire to be) to make the most of their speaking opportunities. Our successes in transforming fearful and often uninteresting or even incoherent speakers into focused and interesting performers inspires us to write with confidence, to share with you a 'kitbag of knowns' to carry into your world of speaking opportunities. We speak of a 'kitbag of knowns' because there are some quite straightforward techniques which we can teach you to use so that you can become an expert and powerful speaker.

Recently, we were asked to help a group of scientists prepare for an important short presentation to government and this need for improvement was highlighted once again; we discovered a lack of expertise and a lack of experience which became a lost speaking opportunity.

The scientists in question fled into a boring presentation, reading sections of their written submission from their visuals. Their presentation was packed with material containing procedural, methodological and legislative language. It was most difficult, even for us as paid listeners, to maintain concentration. Watching a presentation like this can make a visit to the dentist seem like a high point in your day. Those precious ten minutes to persuade the Minister and his representatives of the superiority of the scientists' 'accreditation procedure' were ten minutes of frustration. Frustration enough, perhaps, to destroy the credibility of their case. None of us can afford to lose such an opportunity. With our help, these presenters realised that reading from visuals was really not the most stimulating way to ensure the Minister's understanding of and commitment to the procedures they were there to 'sell'.

As we watched the scientists, we thought of the many similar cases we had encountered in the past ten years of consulting to those who wanted to improve their executive speaking. Having presented, taught and consulted in various countries including the UK, the US, Australia and Japan, it has always been clear to us that the lost speaking opportunity is both tragic and pandemic.

We are reminded, particularly, of a marketing director of one of the world's largest construction corporations, who believed that showing seventeen slides of his corporation's buildings in twenty minutes was a suitably winning presentation. It was no surprise to us when feedback from the corporation's market research suggested that it was seen by its public as cold and faceless. This man had all of the abilities of a lively, interesting speaker, but he needed to be reminded of the important truth that his own persona, anecdotes and experiences were far more interesting than photographs of building after building. After our guidance, he had to work a little harder to share himself with his audience, instead of just pressing the slide projector button, but it was certainly worth the effort. Sometimes the high-tech help of modern organisations can suppress the humanity and spontaneity of the business speaker. This is a trap to be avoided.

An executive of another multinational company believed that if he spoke and showed a set of visuals at the same time, he would cover twice the amount of information. To complicate matters, the information he showed on the screen did not match what he was speaking about. As listeners, we caught little to nothing as we were torn between two different presentations—one visual and one aural. Luckily, he had come to our consultancy before presenting. After a careful re-working, his presentation at an international business convention held in London was sufficient to get him a mention in the following day's *Financial Times*.

This lack of awareness and skill is something we have seen so often, even in the highly educated. It highlights a huge gap in our education system that has not traditionally encouraged the development of this expertise. Concern about this lack of expertise is reflected in the debates that are currently going on in the education sector worldwide about the importance of graduate generic skills, such as speaking.[2]

Another challenge that many people, worldwide, are now facing is that of reaching out to others who are different from themselves. In countries such as the US, the UK and Australia, with their highly diverse populations, recognising and knowing how to speak effectively to mobilise different opinions and perspectives is a challenge for many presenters. Additionally, as our world increasingly acts as a global village, having expertise in giving presentations to people from many cultures becomes a requirement of professional performance. We hope that this book can fill this gap in speaking training.

The three short case studies above show some of the mistaken approaches to speaking which can be easily remedied if you have your 'kitbag of knowns'. In this book, we will use case studies as the means of exemplifying situations to be avoided or strategies to embrace. You can stand beside us as we re-experience many of the situations that have taught us invaluable lessons about the best means of influencing your audience.

YOU CAN LEARN TO SPEAK

One of the simplest rules for you to remember when approaching your public is that a formal presentation should be like an organised, enlarged conversation: speak to your listeners as you would speak to your peers over lunch or dinner. The power of speaking is in the personal contact it makes, in the immediacy it brings to an interaction. Use this aspect of immediate contact and do not sacrifice it under any circumstances. One of our past broadcast journalism students, who has since achieved fame, told us that the most important thing we had taught her was that mass media communication was really just interpersonal communication multiplied by many.[3]

A debate about who were better business speakers, the Americans or the British, sparked a recent survey of members of British American Business Inc. One hundred and nine senior managers responded to the survey. It seems that both the US managers (68 per cent), and the UK managers (70 per cent), rated the US managers as better speakers. Of other nationalities responding, the verdict was the same—all of them (100 per cent) rated US managers most highly. What did the majority of managers from all countries agree upon? Direct style and confidence were the main reasons cited. For a particular cultural group to be so clearly singled out by all respondents indicates that there is something in the cultural heritage of US managers that builds the qualities important for a powerful, personal approach. Fortunately, for those who find the personal touch difficult to achieve, management training was stated as the next main reason for this superiority, and this is undoubtedly comforting for those who wish to learn to speak well.[4]

Awareness of what makes good communication can make a great deal of difference to your credibility as a speaker. The situations we have experienced, and used as examples so far, emphasise this. It is certainly worth the effort to understand the basic rules of communication, which you can then use to take advantage of your speaking opportunity. If you have other problems which seem harder to work on, remember that most of our communication patterns have been learned as we have developed, and that we can, and usually do, respond to re-learning, and replace old bad habits with new successful ones. In other words—yes, you can learn to be a good speaker. The truth is that nobody is born a good speaker—good speaking is learned and takes a great deal of hard work. Some people show more of an aptitude and may even manage to do the hard work less consciously than others, but preparation and determination are the means to effective and eloquent ends. Even a great speaker like Winston Churchill, the British Prime Minister during World War II, was aware of this. His approach is well worth recalling:

> Once Winston Churchill went by cab to a meeting. When the cab stopped at the address, Churchill delayed getting out. The Cockney cab driver yelled, 'You've arrived, governor. You're 'ere.' 'I know, I know,' replied Churchill. 'I'm just preparing my impromptu remarks.'[5]

All good speakers get nervous. As a young actor, one of us was always comforted by the stock saying in the trade that if you were not nervous you would not be good. As a seasoned actor and lecturer now, she knows this to be the truth: you need the adrenalin of nervous energy to perform effectively. Even the great actor Laurence Olivier admitted to nervousness and, at one time, thorough stage fright. So, it seems reasonable that the rest of us should expect to experience nervousness when under pressure. It is important, however, that nervousness stays as adrenalin for greater alertness. It is important that it never translates into physical tensions which will hurt your effectiveness. You need an 'easy power' to capture your listeners. With physical preparation, you can be confident of a relaxed body and an empowered mind.

YOU CAN LEARN TO SPEAK WELL

Our aim with this book is to get you back in touch with the potential strengths of speaking. We say 'back in touch', because you must remember that speaking is, for human beings, a primitive strength, one that we have used as the dominant means of communication for many centuries. Before we could write, our contacts and our history were kept in the stories which we orally passed down. After all, remember that you learned, as a child, to communicate through speech and then moved to the added complexity of writing. Although complex ideas may need clear written communication to support, and sometimes replace, the immediacy of the spoken situation, you should not approach a speaking opportunity through the mode of written communication. We use a different form of language for writing; it is able to be more formal, more structured and more complex. You need to be a good writer of dialogue, as the good playwright is, in order to be a good speechwriter. Although you should be able to turn to speech with ease and proficiency as the form of communication you feel most natural with, we, as lecturers in Speech Communication, know that every time we ask students to prepare a speech, they feel more comfortable writing an essay and then reading it to us. Do you feel this way? Ask yourself why.

Perhaps it is because our education system gives us a solid grounding in writing, and has somewhat neglected excellence in the spoken word. Perhaps it is because writing can be more impersonal and you do not feel that you are placing yourself in the vulnerable position of personal interaction. It is also true that teachers have generally felt that they are more at ease criticising a student's writing than their speaking style. Somehow, criticism of speech seems to be closer to a personal attack. Perhaps it is because many of us believe that ideas equal information transfer in a simple equation, and the presence of a person confuses this otherwise unclouded issue. There could be many reasons for finding it harder to take the risks of working on self-presentation.

Remind yourself of the power of the spoken word in our daily lives and of the speeches that have changed history. With the future in media and telecommunications, this power can only grow. Instead of having only the medium of writing to use, you may be speaking to and viewing your email contacts on the screen very soon. You could certainly be teleconferencing more often or having your speeches videoed for other groups to watch. In the twenty-first century, you are unable to escape the strengths and limitations of your personal presence. With this in mind, prepare to pack your 'kitbag of knowns' with our help, and take the journey of reading our book.

Our strategy, then, is to share our knowledge and experience of the spoken situation: to get you back in touch with your past; to get you forward to your potential. We aim to strengthen your communication by helping you find the possibilities of the vibrant powerful speaker in you. You can learn, and we can show you, how to speak and to speak well; to feel natural and at ease within your organisation, in your political life, in your community life, in your family life and in your sporting life.

Although we have a simple aim, this cannot be a simple book. We are aware that versatility is the key to speaking well and to communicating well. As a speaker, you need to adapt to different contexts, to different situations, to changing fashions, to your listeners' belief systems. There are, though, some rules of communication, and some understandings of our self and of our physicality, that you can carry in your 'kitbag of knowns' into your speaking opportunity.

YOUR 'KITBAG OF KNOWNS'

This book, then, will introduce you to some of those 'knowns': to proven persuasive strategies, to listener analyses, to physical and mental preparation, to real-life case studies and specific examples of presentations, and to an exploration of the complex question of versatility. This book, then, is our open kitbag. If you practise the complex process of adapting our simple understandings to your speaking situations, you will be more powerful, more persuasive, more impressive as a public speaker. And more confident: you will face the opportunity without fear.

1

Getting down to business: Think before you speak

We are all it seems saving ourselves for the Senior Prom. But many of us forget that somewhere along the way we must learn to dance.[1]

WHAT DO WE MEAN BY PRESENTATIONS?

We recently worked with lecturing staff at a large university. They were given the opportunity to present proposals to enhance the quality of learning and teaching within their institution. These professionals approached this situation as an opportunity to give 'objective' information. With our help, they realised that they must seize this opportunity, sell their proposals and persuade their seniors. Their approach to the presentation—its preparation and construction—changed completely as they pursued a new, clear intention.

Our term *presentation* covers a wide variety of instances. We mean any opportunity you get to communicate your point of view to listening others. Any such opportunity should be seized, and should be used to enhance your credibility with those listening, within your organisation or without. The opportunity to share your ideas at a meeting is a presentation; prepare for these listeners with the same care that you would for those in a formal situation where you are the single focus of attention. The opportunity to discuss formally in a one-to-one situation is also a presentation. Joint goal-setting interviews, or discipline or exit type interviews when a person is leaving an organisation should

1

seem spontaneous, but they should actually be carefully prepared: read further into the communication rules which govern such interpersonal situations, as we will not concentrate on them in this book. You will find, though, that many of the rules we give in preparation for formal presentations can be used for interpersonal situations. When you present to a larger group, you will usually feel more pressured than in a one-to-one situation, and that is why we will concentrate on the more formal presentation of one to several in this book.

Most speaking situations have persuasive intentions, even if the speaker is not wholly conscious of them. Speakers who believe that they are presenting 'objective' information are unconsciously choosing words and positioning ideas so that they represent their point of view. The famous scientist Thomas Kuhn has argued that even scientists employ 'techniques of persuasion'. He says that the great scientist transforms what other scientists mean by fact and logic and induces conversion.[2] This suggests that even scientific reports that appear 'wholly factual' are really partially subjective and partially persuasive. With this knowledge in your kitbag, you will be more adept at recognising and revealing the persuasive parts of any presentation, and in pursuing your own points of view with clear and conscious intention.

For example, one of the groups of university lecturers mentioned in the opening of this chapter was putting a proposal to reorganise one of their current procedures. Initially, they felt that it should concentrate on information about how the system worked and how it could be changed. After we worked with them on effective persuasive strategies, they examined more closely the real purpose of their presentation and the importance of its persuasive features. They decided to change the structure and emphasis of their material. They now moved to an overtly persuasive approach which showed the disadvantages of the old system and the possible advantages of their suggested new system.

If you accept your persuasive aim, it can sharpen the focus of the choices you make on what to include in and exclude from your presentation. So, in order to persuade effectively, you must have the right attitude to the material. Before we discuss further this right attitude for success, let us consider how attitude affects anxiety in speakers.

ATTITUDES CREATE ANXIETY

Before you begin work on presentations, you need to examine your attitudes to speaking to an audience, because your attitudes can have a great effect on your speaking anxiety and, therefore, on your performance. Attitudes affect how you see yourself as a communicator and can dominate every aspect of your preparation. Almost everyone experiences some anxiety before a presentation, but your attitude to presentations will either generate more, or act as a brake on, unnecessary anxiety. Try to confront your nervousness, control it, turn it into adrenalin and work it into a more effective and energetic communication.

Some interesting recent research by two American professors, Motley and Molloy, has provided us with some important clues about handling anxiety. The key to confronting and then controlling public speaking anxiety is to examine how you think about a public speaking opportunity. This attitude to the objectives of the speaking opportunity they call 'cognitive orientation'.[3] To understand your orientation, imagine a continuum with *performance orientation* at one end and *communication orientation* at the other: those who have a performance orientation believe that speaking must be a perfect aesthetic experience for listeners; those who have a communication orientation consider it important to share their message with their listeners.

'*Performance-oriented* speakers are often unable to articulate what the critical behaviours for success are, but they invariably assume them to be more "formal", "polished", and "practised" than the skills in their ordinary communication repertoire.'[4] These speakers assume that their listeners are involved primarily in evaluation.

Communication-oriented speakers, on the other hand, assume that their listeners are 'focused with curiosity upon the speaker's message, and that success is measured by the extent to which the listener understands the message and its point of view. Thus minor "mistakes" are as tolerable as in everyday communication'.[5]

It is Motley and Molloy's belief that public speaking anxiety will be lessened if highly anxious speakers change their attitude or orientation to the speaking opportunity (see Figure 1.1).

After further studies to test this idea—that subjects with high public speaking anxiety would benefit from a treatment program to change their orientation—Motley and Molloy established a

Figure 1.1 Cognitive orientation

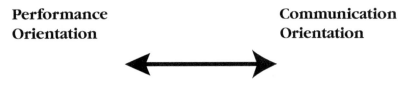

**Performance
Orientation**

**Communication
Orientation**

Heightens Anxiety

Reduces Anxiety

training program that successfully changed the orientation of the participants. These participants experienced a considerable reduction in public speaking anxiety. What they have done is to give us hard evidence that you *can* overcome your anxiety.

This research supports our belief that all of the work that you do to improve your presentation, and any of the evaluation you do of yourself as a speaker, must be done in the preparation stage: once you move into the presentation stage, you must treat the situation as one of *communication*. Your concentration must be on getting your message to your listeners. All else is irrelevant because you are deeply involved in a conversation. Your goal is to place your ideas before interested listeners in a presentation unhindered by interruptions. As a presentation is just an extended conversation, those listeners will want to feel you are speaking *to* them, not speaking *at* them.

In speaking to your listeners, you need to establish a warm rapport with them. The best persuaders seem to be speaking to each member of the audience individually. They show a verve and enthusiasm for their topic, for life in fact, which carries the listener along with it. This sense of excitement comes through in their vocabulary and their mental attitude, but it also is demonstrated to the audience by their physical actions. The term *immediacy* is used to express that charismatic physical expressiveness which causes an audience to feel the strength of the individual presence of the speaker and warm to it. You need not only to work on your mental attitude and your excitement about speaking, but also on your physical approach to it.

This is a second way to work on overcoming your anxiety and another way to gain an easy feeling: work on physiologically

Figure 1.2   Performance orientation   **Communication orientation**

Cartoon: Fiona Mitchell

preparing yourself. Relaxation exercises will help you relax physically and thus relax mentally. This approach, like the Motley and
Molloy approach, has proven success. In Chapter 4 we have
included a full relaxation exercise which you can use as preparation. If you wish to be a polished speaker, it is worth working
on all areas of your presentation at preparation time: you will
derive the physical and mental confidence you need to become a
powerful persuasive speaker in your preparation phase. It is the
work behind the scenes, with your trusty kitbag at your side, that
will lead to 'mind over fear'[6] and your chance of becoming a
powerful persuader. Because of this, we believe that Chapter 4 on
how to prepare is one of the most important in this book.

WHAT DO WE MEAN BY COMMUNICATION?

This book is about practice, but good practice is supported
by reflection, and reflection, of course, becomes theory. Early
communication theorists set up a model of communication that
spoke of the source of the message, the transmission of the
message and the receiver of the message. On reflection, this model
assumes that communication is a linear process: a message is
sent and received, and communication is achieved. We all know

intuitively that this is not how communication works. This is a too-simple perception of what is a more complex process. Come with us now as we examine some of our reflections on the communication process.

MIND OVER MYTHS

There are a number of myths associated with communication: that it is easy, that a message that is sent will always be clearly received, and a simple cause-and-effect process will ensue. Engineers even designed a model based on machines to explain this complex human process. In this model, words simply represent rather than shape ideas. The scientific approach to our conceptual understanding of ourselves has dominated in recent times, and this has influenced the study of communication. If we try to think of the process of communication as a puzzle with multiple parts, which can be put together in multiple ways to give different meanings, we would perhaps be coming closer to what we experience. Some of the major parts of the puzzle, missing in a scientific approach, are our emotional responses, which often rely on our previous experiences.

This leads us to one of the other important myths that has flourished because of the domination of scientific thought, and that is the *myth of objectivity*. This notion of objectivity arises out of a view of the world which takes as its starting point that information or facts are value neutral. As a consequence, it is simply a matter of transmitting value-neutral information to achieve good communication. With the rise of science, humanity has become obsessed with 'factual' knowledge. However, recent communication theorists, and scientists from many disciplines, question whether it is ever possible to achieve objectivity. Remember that when Newton's ideas were overthrown by those of Einstein, even the faith in 'scientific' facts was shaken. We certainly are very sceptical about the possibility of being objective.

One of the most accessible examples of the impossibility of being objective in communication can be seen in the efforts of the media each day in reporting the news. One media magnate recently went on the record claiming that his papers were completely objective in their reporting of certain incidents. He evidently still believes in the possibility of objectivity and in the righteousness of achieving it. If we examine the idea closely from a communication perspective, we realise that every word chosen and sentence written would have been written differently by another journalist. All words have emotional force and, therefore, each journalist generates an individual mood which accompanies the ideas. It is even more obvious that objectivity is elusive when we turn to the television news media and compare the 'objective' reporting of news from one channel to another. Talkback programs such as *CNN Talkback Live* in the US and *Right to Reply* on Channel 4 in the UK demonstrate the heated debate which is generated by the presentation of differing perspectives on our complex world. A program which provides excellent examples of this is *Media Watch* on the Australian Broadcasting Corporation, which examines stories that have been presented in the media in the week prior to its going to air. It especially examines the way the different outlets have presented particular stories, and reflects on the meanings and ethics of these presentations. By this means, it reveals the varying ways in which a news story can be constructed. By selecting some information, and omitting other pieces, it is clear that different versions of the 'truth' can be told.

Pictures do not lie? Even this truism is now questioned. Our attention was particularly drawn to the precariousness of reality by the now famous trial in 1992 in which Los Angeles police officers were accused of brutally beating the black American Rodney King. A home videotape of the beating of King by the police was broadcast on television sets around the world. The jurors in this trial in Los Angeles could be convinced, by an eloquent barrister who justified the verdict they desired, that there was a reason not to believe their eyes. This enabled them to give a verdict of not guilty to the police who savagely beat King. The home video pictures of a savage beating were not enough when the defence attorney used words to build his own pictures of King and the possibly ethical motivations of his 'honourable' defendants. With a knowledge of the media, we begin to see how our own eyes and ears can indeed deceive us. After all, camera angle, lighting and editing can all change meanings and cause the message to be structured differently for the viewer.

Through word and image, particular cultures have constructed particular ways of understanding which seem less acceptable to other cultures. In the west we were shocked when Saddam Hussein spoke of 'glory in defeat' at the end of the Gulf War, but we are capable of accepting a similar glory in defeat when we speak of Dunkirk or Gallipoli. We build powerful, cultural meaning on word and image, on oral and visual language, and we cocoon ourselves within those powerful, cultural meanings. It is our inability to search outside the dominant messages of our culture, even within a democracy, that the American academics Herman and Chomsky refer to in their book *Manufacturing Consent.*[7]

It is important to understand that we construct reality from words and images. This does not mean that concrete reality does not exist, but that our understanding of it comes to us through word and image. We are born into a certain construction of reality—our own culture—which is reproduced in our consciousness every day of our lives, in every word and in every image. There are, however, dominant groups that shape our consciousness: the words and images of our culture, our class, our education, our family and our peers shape our perceptions of 'reality'. These groups create the value and attitude systems by which we understand our lives, by which we respond to the words and images of others. The power of persuasive words and images should never be underestimated: they are central to the building of culture in large and small organisations; they are central to the building of culture in politics and in homes; and they are quint-essential to the building of languages of leadership.

We hope to have convinced you that the concept of objectivity is not a useful one for the successful persuader. Communication is, after all, a dynamic and value-rich process. Therefore, we believe that it is best to exploit this characteristic of communication, and to take the approach that practically all situations are per-suasive ones. With this attitude, it is then only a matter of deciding on the best means of persuading others as successfully, and ethically, as possible.

THE IMPORTANCE OF ETHICS

Persuasion is a very powerful tool. It is a fundamental human right which should be exercised to achieve your purpose. If you believe in the justice of your message, you have every right to present persuasively to your listeners, using every method available to you.

True, the ethics which govern your choices are important and you should consider them carefully. However, you do not have to pretend to objectivity in order to be ethical. Many presenters overlook the ethics of their choices and rely on the skills they possess to delude their listeners. Advertisers may often make choices which would not satisfy our ethical considerations. We would not accept the choice, in a television advertisement, of a girl in a bikini draped over the bonnet of a motor vehicle which is being sold to the public, as an ethical choice. It may appeal to some male viewers who could be the most likely buyers of the vehicle, but it is an overtly sexist choice which no longer appeals to many viewers, whether male or female. In business, executives often have to make choices about the omission or inclusion of information they will present to their employees. It can be difficult to balance exigency with ethics. However, by acknowledging the values that drive your message, you can contribute to your own ethical practice of persuasion.

Equally, the more you understand the techniques of persuasion, the more you will be able to decipher, carefully and critically, the persuasive messages you receive. You will be more prepared to recognise the messages you consider unethical and why this may be so. You will, after all, be more powerful as a speaker if you not only believe in the justice of your message, but also make an effort to understand how your listeners will react.

CO-ACTIVE PERSUASION

We take a co-active approach to communication.[8] We emphasise the power of readers to reconstruct the message from their own point of view. As the Australian journalist and writer Hugh Mackay says, 'It's not what our message does to the listener, but what the listener does with our message that determines our success as communicators'.[9] This is why it is so important, if you are to be an effective speaker—a persuasive, co-active speaker—that you understand exactly what your listeners' points of view are. You must understand where your listeners are in their thinking if you want them to move through those thoughts to reach a shared point of view. Professor Gerald Edelman, the Nobel prize-winning American scientist who writes about the brain, says, 'Unlike computers we understand ourselves and our world in individual, creative, dynamic and unpredictable ways. We create our outer and inner worlds in a context of unceasing novelty and change.'[10] Your persuasion should exploit the dynamic and creative capacities of your listeners.

You may have wondered why we used the word *reader* at the beginning of the last paragraph. Recent communication theory has emphasised the idea of a 'reader' rather than a 'receiver' of messages: readers receive the message and actively interpret it within their own frame of reference; they 'read' the messages they receive and actually reconstruct their own meanings. The word *reader* suggests activity, whereas *receiver* indicates passivity. Be sure to recognise the power of the reader, and realise, therefore, that listener analysis is an important step before you begin to prepare to communicate. This is why it is also important to observe your listeners carefully while you are speaking, and constantly to check understanding in an interpersonal interaction.

The words and images we use to represent our experiences generally determine whether we think about an experience as good or bad. We even perceive ourselves in relation to what others say about us or to us, or by the ways they appear to respond to us. For example, if enough people tell you that you look ill, you will probably be feeling so by the end of the day. Think of the power of a belief system which can cause you to die by simply telling you to do so. This amazing example of the power of perception comes from the Aboriginal culture, where members will die if 'the bone is pointed at them'. This punishment causes death merely because the perfectly healthy recipient believes that this ritual is fatal.

So, can you ever say that the way *you* view a situation is definitely the way the situation really is?

We are sure that you are truthfully answering 'no' to this question. It is important to realise that we play an active role in interpreting the world that surrounds us. The advice of songwriter and philosopher Leonard Cohen is very apt on the best way to approach your listeners: 'To discover the truth in anything that is alien, first dispense with the indispensable in your own vision.'

In this book, we emphasise the idea of co-active persuasion and the power of the 'reader'. This is, in fact, one of our interpretations of the way we understand the world, and it agrees with those communication specialists who suggest that individuals play an active part in 'constructing reality' from and through the communication process. If you are a powerful enough persuader, you may be able to convince others that your view is the way the situation is, and there are many notable examples from our history of the potential of great communicators to create and recreate how whole nations define themselves and their experiences. Your speaking goals may be less ambitious, but your need to succeed may nonetheless be very important to you.

OPEN UP YOUR KITBAG

Now that we have given you some 'knowns' for the journey, look in your kitbag—throw out anxiety, throw out objectivity, put ethics in a safe place so that you can always find it, and make space for the many resources you are about to pack which you will need in your career as an opinion leader to your peers. As we have said, this book is about co-active persuasion: so your next thought should be, and our next chapter is, about listeners.

TIPS

- All opportunities to communicate your ideas to listening others should be carefully prepared.
- Most presentations have persuasive elements. Recognise and pursue these.
- You can overcome anxiety by physical and mental preparation.
- Do not allow the myth of objectivity to interfere with your persuasive intent.
- Consider the ethical implications of your position before you start to prepare.
- Persuasion is a co-active process. Be prepared for what your listeners will do with your message.

2

Getting to know your listeners

It is the province of knowledge to speak and it is the privilege of wisdom to listen.[1]

Several years ago, one of our colleagues working in London for a management consultancy received a phone call from one of the world's largest multinational corporations. Its managing director asked her to meet with him. After a long trip across London, on an unusually hot English afternoon, she arrived; she was taken to the boardroom, seated at a long table facing four senior executives of the corporation, and told that she had thirty minutes to persuade them that they should use her consultancy. They wanted to know what she could do for them.

She was unnerved. She had come only in response to a request from the managing director and had expected an informal meeting with him. So she responded by spending the first fifteen minutes of her allocated thirty asking them what they felt they needed from her. She understood that good communication is focused not on 'What can I do for you?' but on 'What do you need from me?'

She was then in a position to offer them skills and strategies to service those needs. She spent the second fifteen minutes persuading them that she would do a great job for them. She convinced them, and she got the job.

A good speaker is a good listener, above all else. It is only by listening to your clients that you can know where they are coming

12

from; it is only by knowing where they are coming from that you can help them to where they are going.

LEARN TO CONSTRUCT MESSAGES STRATEGICALLY

You are probably aware, at this point, of the emphasis we place on communication as persuasion. If you want to achieve your purpose, if you want to have your listeners understand your way of seeing the world, you need to construct messages that start with their way of seeing the world. A good speaker actively engages in the construction of messages that allow shared points of view of the topic and its issues. If you get to know your listeners, you will have a considerably better chance of appealing to those aspects of the topic which make sense to them in terms of their values, priorities and concerns. Our strategy, then, is to help you to develop techniques that you can use to communicate persuasively by moving your listeners effectively to a shared understanding of your point of view.

This is the game that we call *strategically constructing messages for listeners*. How well you play will determine how well you can communicate, how well you persuade, and thus whether or not you achieve your purpose.

Your moves towards your listeners must be guided not only by what you want to achieve by what you say, but also by what your listeners might want to do with what you say. At this very moment, as you read this page, our purpose is to persuade you to think strategically about how to communicate. If you look back over the language we use you will see words like *game, strategically, engage, move* and *construct*. Our purpose is to urge you to see communication as moves and countermoves, as strategies to engage your listeners. Listening is an active process of making meaning out of what a speaker says. Consequently, speaking needs to be the active process of establishing and then exploiting what listeners are likely to do with those ideas.

One of the most important parts of the speaking process is the analysis of listeners. Good speakers, in their preparation, clarify the interests and needs of their listeners and determine what values, priorities and concerns their listeners have before they determine what it is, out of the vast range of possibilities, they could and should say to those listeners.

We do not intend this to mean, though, that you will always be able to achieve complete agreement. There will always be differences that are unresolvable, no matter how strategic you are. We do not mean either that you should say anything to achieve a shared point of view. What will help you most, however, will be sensitivity to how your listeners understand a problem as well as awareness of your own attitudes. Tough issues can be handled carefully in words and images that take account of your listeners' understandings of the world, and yet demonstrate how your intentions can be achieved to some positive effect.

LEARN TO ANSWER QUESTIONS STRATEGICALLY

'What's in it for me?'

Listeners listen, always, with one question in mind: 'What's in it for me?' This question should always guide your message construction. Our experience tells us that listening, far from being a passive activity, is a demanding one. Most listeners need to be given a great deal of encouragement before they make the considerable effort to tune in and to stay tuned to a speaker. Coming to terms with this is the first step in constructing a strategic message.

'What do I want to say?'

When speakers start to prepare a presentation, they usually ask: 'What do I want to say?' You will have particular points that you want to make and it may seem natural to you that if you say them you will achieve your purpose. However, knowledge of your listeners, knowledge of what they know and how they feel about those particular ideas, determines how you say them. Your goal must be to make a very large strategic move to aligning your listeners' needs and attitudes with your needs and attitudes. It requires your knowledge, time, creativity and determination; it requires your ongoing evaluation of how the two match.

'What is the most effective way of constructing and presenting the particular things I want to say to achieve my purpose?'

The only way to gain a clear understanding of how to be effective is to get to know as much as you can about both your topic and your listeners. The two are always related. It is the tendency to underestimate their relationship which leads to failures in communication. When a managing director who fails to value his employees' fear of change makes a presentation on a new corporate image, it can turn into an attack on the way things are done. If he uses their commitment to the past as his starting point and acknowledges their concerns, he could turn fear to energy. For example, he could frame the move to a new corporate image as growing out of old ways, and create a vision for the future out of past commitments. It is just as important for student presenters to understand their audience and its relationship to the topic to help frame their approach.

Answering the three questions that we have just discussed provides a good starting point for matching your listeners with your topic. There are also some other important pieces of information that you need. Lack of time and resources might prevent you from collecting everything you would like to, and sometimes you have to make an educated guess. You may also be able to draw on your experience from other situations to build a picture of the listeners for a presentation. However, in the ideal case, here are some tips on what would help you to guide your decisions.

LEARN THEIR DEMOGRAPHICS

To establish your listeners' values, priorities and concerns, you need to have an idea of their demographic characteristics: you may be able to learn their age, gender, cultural identity, including ethnic background, race, religious affiliations and group memberships.

Age

You should consider the age of your audience for any presentation. It is common to hear communication failures in families explained as a generation gap, but when the context moves from family to organisation this is rarely the explanation. We often imagine that the categories of 'employee' and 'management' will dissolve age differences but, in reality, the problems remain, and you need to acknowledge them. Consider this example. You are making a presentation on restructuring in your organisation. Employees who have been with you for twenty years have invested a great deal into the history of the organisation; new and young employees are investing great idealism into its future. The presentation will be 'read' by young and old listeners, and young and old meanings will be made. When you recall an important change that the organisation made ten years before, your ideas will matter only to those employees old enough to remember, and will be disregarded by those too young or too new. It is essential, therefore, that you balance your examples, and appeal to the different categories of your listeners.

Gender

While it is claimed that employees are employees no matter what their gender, a great deal of recent research has demonstrated that attitudes and values towards work are marked by gender differences.[2] When you prepare, you must take care to select ideas and examples that reflect those differences in thinking, knowledge and action. This is further complicated by the need for sensitivity to overcome gender stereotyping as well. The complexity arises because gender is only one of the many categories which determine a listener's attitudes to your topic and is sometimes, but not always, the category that a person identifies with. Sometimes they may be thinking more as a manager than as a woman, for example.

Your presentation may need to account for gender differences. Men and women share a broad range of experiences, but nonetheless, they are socialised differently. On numerous occasions, women managers have commented to us about their sense of exclusion from discussions, not by the speakers' intentions, but by forms of address and examples that imply that their listeners are men. Even humour can be gendered,[3] and so exclude some audience members. An awareness of the difficulty of catering for a mixed-gender audience has led some human resource managers to develop training programs designed for women. This can simplify the task for the trainer by drawing attention to the importance of targeting this group. However, you will seldom have the luxury of being able to cater for one category within an audience, and therefore you will need to manage the complexity of the category of gender carefully.

As an example of the need for sensitivity to gender, imagine that you are to give a presentation on telecommuting to a mixed-gender group. If your listeners comprise mainly women, current research on how they view their careers suggests that, as primary care-givers, their interest in and knowledge of leave and career development is strongly affected by the probability of breaks in their careers for child-bearing and rearing. This is in contrast with men, who are much less likely to have knowledge or experience about how career breaks would affect their development. For the men, you may need to build in a section on the implications of career breaks, to cater for this gap in their knowledge. You could also point to the possibility of alternative work attitudes and arrangements, if you wish to move the whole group to this new, more flexible work arrangement.

Learning about the composition of your audience in terms of gender will quite possibly have a significant impact on the selection of appropriate material, in terms of both information and approach.

Ethnic, racial and religious backgrounds

Most countries around the world have culturally diverse popu-lations. A recent article in the *Washington Post* described the struggle for the news industry in America to recruit black, Hispanic and Asian journalists to meet the needs of a culturally diverse American audience. Although meeting these needs for racial diversity has become a preoccupation in the industry, mainstream media outlets registered their concerns that it is not enough just to learn how to recruit an ethically diverse workforce. They must also learn how to keep them. It seems that the great majority of these journalists quit out of a sense of frustration, a sense that their point of view is not understood and valued, and that their limited opportunities for advancement are unreasonable. This case highlights the complexity of meeting the needs of a culturally diverse workforce.[4] It is clear that we must take account of diversity in our organisations.[5]

Sensitivity to diversity must also be translated to our presen-tations. The current debates between monarchists and republicans in Australia, which are filled with insensitivities to their listeners, provide a powerful example of the inherent difficulties. In this case, a British tradition and a Christian God are inadequate icons to move an Asian Muslim to a commitment to a constitutional monarchy. Better and more targeted arguments need to be made, and this can only be done by speakers who know their listeners. Effective communication includes, rather than excludes, particular ethnic or racial groups, and uses language which acknowledges particular religious backgrounds. It is of strategic importance for good speakers to recognise this, if they wish to gain a hearing on topics as diverse as equity issues, flexibility of work schedules and safety issues.

We recently heard a presentation on the importance of good communication, in which the speaker acknowledged that English is a second language for many employees. So, he suggested, 'we must build that into our planning for communicating important messages'. An organisation-wide decision was made to provide translations of important or urgent messages in the several common languages of the employees. In English speaking societies—societies such as the UK, the US, New Zealand and Australia, which can no longer take their Anglo-Saxon cultural framework as a given—getting to know your listeners and their differences, and reflecting this in what you say, is not just a challenge: it is essential.

Group membership

Despite a commitment to individualism, many western cultures understand their identity and prioritise their values via their group affiliations: sporting groups, environmental groups, political parties, parenting groups, professional and trade organisations, unions and consumer protection groups. Members derive particular ways of thinking about themselves and their world from such groups. Addressing a highly unionised group via appeals to the individual will generally be a foolhardy attempt that will most likely lead to resistance on the part of listeners. The solidarity characteristic of a union group will block these appeals. It is usually better to acknowledge group loyalties than to bypass them.

UNDERSTANDING ORGANISATIONS

Recent research conducted in the US, Canada and Australia reveals that employees' attitudes to management should also be part of our considered listener analysis. T. J. Larkin, an American consultant who specialises in planning communication about change in organisations, claims that studies throughout these countries indicate that employees are cynical and suspicious of management; moreover, one study suggested that 43 per cent of workers actually believe that management does not tell the truth. Another study suggested that employees believe that senior managers are neither candid nor accurate. On the other hand, up to 96 per cent of employees believe their immediate supervisors. Knowing the attitudes of these groups is an important part of our getting to know our listeners.[6]

The importance of this sensitivity to your listeners is demonstrated by our experience in one large organisation. When senior staff were attempting to implement a restructure, it was only when the newly elected union delegate was invited to speak alongside management that the reforms met with support. When the union delegate started to talk positively about change and its benefits, the unit which he represented gave its firm commitment. This unit believed that the union had their best interests at heart and would only support reforms that would advantage them.

How did management know that the new union delegate was a credible source? By the high attendance levels of employees at union meetings. How did they strategically construct the message? By getting to know their listeners and by successfully aligning their listeners' needs and attitudes with their own needs and attitudes.

What these demographics and studies of organisations can contribute to your presentation, above all else, is knowledge of the values, priorities and concerns of your listeners.

Know your organisation

There are also specific values and attitudes that different organisations expect of employees. Within each organisation there are particular ways of acting and speaking that are expected and valued by members, and ways that are not. Acting in a particular way may actually devalue you and reduce your credibility. For example, in many organisations, a commitment to team effort and cooperative action is valued. By using words like 'compete' and 'individual action', you can alienate your listeners and devalue yourself in such an organisation. By understanding the rules and regulations for acting and speaking within specific organisations, you can establish where your listeners are positioned on issues. Even if you wish to challenge many of their assumptions on those issues, you should aim to construct messages that start with your listeners' way of seeing them.

By knowing your organisation, you can determine what it is that will appeal to your listeners; by knowing your listeners, you can clarify their needs, match them to yours and move them to an understanding of your point of view.

Manage diversity

It is inevitable that there will be times when, by appealing to the interests of one sub-group of your listeners, you exclude another. It is realistic to assume that your listeners will be heterogeneous; what is crucial to remember is that the creation of ideas that are appealing to your listeners requires careful and sensitive handling. It is essential that you gain the commitment of the diversity of interests that your listeners represent.

Case study

If you know that there are both old and young people among your listeners, you must create ideas to appeal to both groups. Glen Small, the director of a small company which manufactures electronic parts for computers, provides us with an example of how a diverse audience can be managed. His task is to announce a company restructure. It will disadvantage the older, longer-term members of his company, and open up new opportunities for the young, innovative members who are part of the merger. His opening address needs to capture both sets of interests. He uses the following to frame his new direction:

> The electronics industry is a dynamic and competitive place to work in. For the last ten years AME has been a leader in the field. It was started by a group of bright, ambitious and hard-working professionals who took it to the forefront of the electronics industry. AME is now a catch-word in electronics excellence. These men sit before you today. They are battle-hardened and finely tuned to market needs.
>
> Beside them are the new young adventurers of the electronics field. It is a field exploding with new challenges and new technologies. The opportunities are waiting for us. Years of market experience combined with knowledge of leading-edge technology can take us to a bright new future. We can commit to this success by taking up the challenge. Restructuring can mean growth and benefits for us all.

By taking account of the demographics of his listeners and the way their organisation thinks, what it values, and how it understands itself, Small's presentation has a good chance of making contact. By determining common ground and points of view mutually shared with his listeners, his presentation achieves its purpose. Small provides an understanding for young and old.

KNOW YOUR CONTEXT
What are the numbers?

The number of listeners you have will often determine how you should approach your topic. When you have to deal with large numbers of relatively unknown listeners, you have to spend time developing first, credibility, and second, rapport. By contrast, when you have a small number of listeners, you can develop intimacy quickly. Equally important is the way the number of listeners impacts on your level of formality.

Large groups

Large numbers of listeners demand a structure and set of word choices that convey your acknowledgement of the formality of the occasion. This is not to suggest that you should be impersonal, but rather that this awareness of size will influence your choices in constructing a message. To compensate for the anonymity of the large group, you could prepare rhetorical questions which will solicit a response at a personal level from each of your listeners. Knowing the demographics of listeners will certainly help you to prepare suitable questions.

Small groups

Small numbers of listeners allow you the pleasure and privilege of interacting orally via questions and contributions from individual listeners. By choosing carefully, you may be able to engage your listeners in the construction of your persuasive message; by asking for opinions and attitudes about what you have said already, you may be able to use your listeners to structure links and transitions for your presentation.

In a training session we were conducting recently, after a short snappy introduction in which we used an example of our constant search for improving our own listening skills, we asked for some stories of difficult experiences with listening. Several people volunteered their stories and then, with their own personal experience in the forefront of their minds, we continued the training. Whenever possible during the session, we referred to those examples. In this way, with a small group, the research doesn't stop, even while you are making the presentation.

What are the listeners' attitudes to you as speaker?

One of the most important questions to ask yourself when you are preparing for your presentation is, 'What do my listeners think of me?' If they know you, you carry a level of credibility that will either allow them to accept what you say or to doubt you. We watched a presentation recently, given as part of the selection for a senior executive position. One speaker, an outsider to the organisation, spent a great deal of her presentation establishing her knowledge of the procedures and values operating in the organisation. This was crucial as she wanted to make suggestions on how to change the operations of the organisation. She had made the judgement—wisely, in our view—that because she was an outsider, the employer would need to be convinced that she knew the problems before she could offer solutions. By contrast, an internal applicant, who knew that his listeners knew that he understood the territory, could move quite quickly to future directions.

What are the attitudes to your topic?

Asking what your listeners think about your topic is also crucial to your preparation. You need to know whether there is agreement or resistance to your presentation. This will help you to determine how long you spend explaining your ideas, justifying your position, criticising alternative perspectives, and outlining the costs and benefits. By acknowledging that presenting an argument persuasively is more than just objective information-giving, you are acknowledging that you must allow your listeners to determine what it is you need to say to reach them. Finding out what they think is central to your preparation.

What are the politics of the situation?

It is also very important to question the significance of the situation to listeners. Often a presentation acts as a formal opportunity to re-present ideas that have been shared informally. It may be your opportunity not only to outline the points of your presentation, but also to stimulate excitement about, to motivate commitment to, an idea. If this is the situation, then sensitivity to your listeners' expectations is essential. If the presentation becomes a dry and repetitive enactment of former conversations, it misses the potential for heightened response. By contrast, if listeners expect the situation to be an opportunity to learn about the technical implications of your presentation, a lack of attention to detail may only alienate potentially positive listeners.

Unless you are sensitive to your listeners' expectations of the situation, all your good ideas, intentions and analyses are at risk.

What are the politics of the organisation?

Clearly, any presentation requires some risk-taking. However, you can reduce the risks, or at least decide carefully whether to take a risk, if you question the politics of your organisation and the implications of risk-taking. Perhaps a recent experience which reminded us of this will best clarify our point.

Case study

The CEO of our organisation visited our unit. He was coming to speak to us about his vision for the future of the organisation. There were some grave concerns that we, as a unit, shared about administrative decisions being made. Here was an opportunity for us to explain our concerns, expose our dissatisfaction and make our complaints. Or was it? Research into the politics of our organisation suggested that this meeting was not seen by our CEO as a place to solve our micro-level problems. We constructed a strategically sensitive message that highlighted our concerns, but we refrained from demanding action in a forum specifically designed by the organisation for looking for visions and hopes for the future.

The politics of organisational life demand sensitivity, intelligence, research and plain good strategy.

HOW DO YOU LEARN ABOUT YOUR LISTENERS?

Learning about your listeners takes a lot of time and energy, but it is worth it. Knowing the demographics of your listeners, their organisation and its culture makes the difference between preparing a presentation with a high chance of success and one which is doomed to be mediocre to poor.

Getting to know your own organisation is relatively easy. Getting to know another may not be. It takes ingenuity: you need to use any available contacts you have to explore the way it thinks. Talk to the staff; read reports, documentation, press and advertising material; discuss the organisation with business contacts; quiz your listeners at breaks in the proceedings, or in the form of questions inserted into your presentation.

It is only by beginning at the site of your listeners' expectations, knowledge and values that you can hope to gain their attention, maintain their interest and sustain their imaginations. By getting to know your listeners, by talking to people, by asking questions of and about them, by reading of their past achievements, and by observing their actions and reactions, you can plan and achieve a successful presentation.

APPEALING TO DIFFERING LISTENING AND LEARNING STYLES

You also need to be sensitive to differing styles of listening and learning. An understanding of differences—differences between professional groups, differences between groups with varying levels of education, differences of gender, of culture, of age—helps you to gauge preferred types of information, forms of information and argumentation styles for different listeners. For example, a trainer of intercultural communication recently reported that he had designed the format of his course to cater for the very different preferences in the learning and communication style of his Asian, Pacific Islander and Caucasian listeners.[7]

MATCHING LISTENERS AND CONTENT (THE FINAL CHALLENGE)

As you can see from the many examples we have offered, matching your topic to your purpose and to your listeners' needs and values is a complex process. One of our students recently presented a very fine seminar that demonstrated a subtle balance of managing content and listener needs while achieving his purpose. His task was to research and analyse the strengths and limitations of various forms of communication, such as the written word, spoken forms, and the new technologies. His audience was one of us, as his academic supervisor, and the students in the group.

After considerable research in the organisational literature, he came up with a rather unusual approach. He recognised that he had a largely student audience and wanted to find content that would appeal to them, so he used a number of research articles about the changing use of teen magazines, the Internet, CDs, mobile telephones and text-messaging by adolescents.

The focus on the forms of communication popular with teenagers provided a very interesting and up-to-date context for considering the advantages and disadvantages of each medium.

He was able find interesting visual aids showing changes in circulation of specific teen magazines such as *Dolly* and *Smash Hits*, details of numbers of subscribers to various competing websites and webpages, and graphs showing changing patterns of mobile phone and text messaging use. He also quoted from well-known editors and the former manager of the Spice Girls turned webmaster about why teenagers prefer different media. This teased out issues of preference, convenience, need, satisfaction and changing preferences.

This analysis provided the context for his argument that, if you want to communicate effectively in organisations, you have to realise that different competing media will draw the interest of some groups, and will gain their loyalty. He also argued that it is important to recognise that communicators must be sensitive to changing technologies and their seductions.

As the first point in a very impressive seminar, he recognised the importance of finding common ground with both his academic supervisor and his large group of young listeners. The rest of the presentation could then be delivered, based on more conventional literature. The student's imaginative leap, to start with his listeners' interests and move them to his position, paid dividends. He excited and stimulated them to think about the significance of the medium itself, and turned a potentially dry analysis into a lively, engaging, thought-provoking event.

PACKING LISTENING SKILLS IN YOUR KITBAG

Good speakers can become that way only by being good listeners first. Disciplining ourselves to take the time to listen first can be hard work. Our more automatic and probably more egocentric response is to think first about what we want to say. If we remember to think of our listeners first, and to seriously consider their interests and concerns as our interests and concerns, it will pay dividends. Such discipline will reward us with endless resources to achieve our goals, and the confidence to know that our case will get a good hearing because it starts in the place where our listeners have travelled.

TIPS

- Good listening is an essential skill for good speakers.
- Listener analysis is central to successful planning. It is the starting point for the planning of any presentation.
- Good speakers make it their business to get to know demographic features of their listeners—age, gender, group memberships and cultural background.
- Good speakers make it their business to get to know the cultural features of their organisation or of their situation.
- Good speakers never underestimate the role of the listeners' attitude to them.
- Good presentations start where listeners are and then move the listeners toward the speaker's point of view.
- Good speakers respect the way culture affects listening. Adjusting to the cultural perceptions and language limitations of listeners is critical to success.

3

Persuasive strategies: Calling up the past to make your point

You can persuade a man only insofar as you can talk his language by speech, gesture, tonality, order, image, attitude, identifying his ways with yours.[1]

THE PRESENT

Contemporary forms of persuasion are high art. The media is funded by the activities of those who exhort us to try and to buy all manner of things that the human mind can invent. A newspaper recently reported a story of people buying imaginary objects advertised in the media. These buyers would phone the company and receive a delightful description of an imaginary object for which they paid their money. They did not ever receive the object itself, just heard the description of it. Did this allow them the pleasure of buying without the burden of accumulating? Or did they just receive pleasure from the words of the imaginary object's description? Whatever their reasons, it is a potent example of the power of persuasion to elicit responses from us that cannot be explained in terms of rationality alone. And what is most interesting about this activity, and about most other activities of persuasion in our time, is that they rely heavily on Aristotle's 2000-year-old rhetorical strategy.

The term *rhetoric* is now frequently used to criticise the way people describe their intentions, a derogatory term to suggest that intentions of the speaker are dishonest and hide the truth.

However, as we have said, we believe that all attempts to describe the way 'things really are' rely on particular constructions of the meanings of those 'things'. 'Truth' is not as clear cut a concept as we have been made to believe. Therefore, it is important for us to realise that, without being dishonest, we have the potential to construct ideas in ways which represent them to our advantage rather than disadvantage.

THE PAST

Aristotle's traditional understanding of the term *rhetoric* is a very useful way to approach a modern understanding of persuasion. He attempted to describe the way social influence helps individuals achieve personal goals. He perceived rhetoric as the gentle art of persuasion, a study of what it means to be persuasive in any situation. Don't misunderstand us—Aristotle didn't invent persuasion. It has been around since people shared their first meal and lived together as a group. What Aristotle did was to describe how persuasion works. He had a very simple formula of three proofs or appeals which are used to make messages persuasive.

THE APPEALS OF *ETHOS, PATHOS* AND *LOGOS*

Ethos refers to the credibility of the speaker. It emphasises the fact that speakers are more effective as persuaders if they are believed by listeners to be credible sources. Listeners are immediately sceptical of speakers if their credibility and credentials are not readily apparent.

Pathos refers to the emotional appeal made by the speaker to the listeners; it emphasises the fact that listeners respond with emotion to ideas. When citizens are asked by government to go to war in a foreign country for the sake of 'the fatherland' or 'the mother country', the dominant appeal is to *pathos*. For this type of persuasion to succeed, strong emotional appeals to the citizen's love of country and heroic images of self are crucial.

Logos refers to the logic of the speaker's argument; it emphasises the fact that listeners can be convinced by facts, statistics and other forms of evidence to accept an argument.

These definitions will be expanded later in the chapter.

The mix

Aristotle believed that the most effective persuasive presentations have a mix of *ethos*, *pathos* and *logos*—of credibility, passion and logic—and he believed that the mix should be balanced. Of course, knowing the occasion and the audience will help you to determine the mix.

ESTABLISHING *ETHOS*

Your *ethos*—your credibility as a speaker—is established by the way you dress, the way you move, what you say and the way you speak—that is, by all you say and do. You must appear, through all your verbal and non-verbal messages, to be both confident and controlled. Your breathing, your voice and your facial expressions must appear confident if you are to be credible and your argument certain. If your listeners have prior knowledge of your reputation and abilities, this is, obviously, a great advantage to you.

But your credibility is also established by the words you choose. Do not say 'I will attempt to prove'; use positive and definite language. Choose phrases such as 'I will prove'. In our experience, speakers often use modifying words which make their arguments appear less certain. Be confident enough, or train yourself, to avoid these.

Ethos is also established by passing mention of your credentials: for example, 'as an airline pilot of twenty years' or 'as an accountant with considerable experience of taxation law'. Or you could mention your specific experiences: 'when I was working on a similar case in London', for example. However, whatever the instance, you must design this aspect to appear as part of the natural information of your presentation, and subtly heighten listeners' knowledge of your capabilities.

Case study

US media tycoon Rupert Murdoch, in a presentation on the future of global technology to the Asia-Pacific Business Congress in 1992 entitled 'Venice of the Southern Hemisphere', called on the past to make credible his point that the Asia Pacific is the future empire of global technology, and he is its future Doge (the traditional aristocratic leader of Venice). He needed to establish his *ethos* and so to move the congress forward from belief in him as a media tycoon of the 1980s to belief in him as a Doge of the future. His strategy was to move backwards to the empires of the past and to establish himself as a Renaissance man. He did this by drawing on one of the attributes of a good classical education, a knowledge of history and its great men. By using historical references, he effectively was telling his listeners that he was a man of substance and understanding who could be trusted. Here is a short section of his speech.

> The eighteenth-century Irish bishop and philosopher George Berkeley, reflecting on the successive rise to power of Babylon, Greece, and Rome, wrote and I quote: 'Westward the course of empire takes its way.' Anyway, it seems Bishop Berkeley's 250-year-old prophecy is still operating. The course of the empire is moving westward. The centre of global gravity appears to be making a further shift into the Pacific.[2]

Murdoch also uses indisputable historical facts to make his future plans seem natural and inevitable. Berkeley's prophecy makes Murdoch's destiny seem inevitable. Through these carefully orchestrated strategies, he firmly establishes his credibility. 'Venice of the Southern Hemisphere' is reprinted in full in the appendix. You may find it illuminating to read the speech of an outstanding communicator at work.

The appeal to *ethos* can make a significant contribution to the way your listeners will respond to your ideas. Just as Murdoch used a clever and imaginative appeal to heighten his listeners' response to him and to increase his stature and his place in history, you may be able to increase your credibility with your listeners by drawing on your strengths and expertise.

EXPLOITING *PATHOS*

Some presentations rely almost entirely on *pathos*. One famous example that still moves listeners when they view the media footage is Martin Luther King's 'I have a dream' speech. It was delivered at a rally of over 200 000 civil libertarians in 1963 in Washington, DC. Martin Luther King appealed to the sense of justice in all Americans and roused those civil rights' devotees who attended the rally to fight unceasingly for black rights. His ability to use the language of leadership in such a powerful way certainly contributed both to the improvement of civil rights for African Americans and to his own assassination. We cannot underestimate the power of emotion.

Political leaders are particularly adept in the use of this appeal. Paul Kelly, the editor of Rupert Murdoch's *The Australian* newspaper, said this of Prime Minister Paul Keating, with reference to his skill as a performer: 'Keating is an enormously passionate and emotional politician . . . It's not just intellect he's using. It's a whole range of skills, whether it's charm or intimidation.'[3]

Just as skilled performers like Keating, Clinton or Blair use more than 'just intellect' in their presentations to the public, so too do you, when making a business or professional presentation or giving a seminar, need to examine your argument to ensure that you have not omitted the appeal of *pathos*. If it will add to your argument, choose and use your words to add *pathos* to topics which might at first appear highly technical or limited to factual accounts.

Images are also a very strong means of encoding emotional appeals. We have all seen horrifying images of the dying in parts of Africa, and we recall those images at the very mention of names such as Rwanda or Ethiopia. Always remember to use images, either in pictures or words, to support your emotional appeals; your listeners are more convinced when they can 'see' things with their own eyes. Even the use of a simple drawing of a new office design can appeal to the complex emotion of pride or a sense of ownership in your listening employees.

Verbal images also have emotional power. Remember the old Chinese proverb 'The tongue can paint what the eye can't see'. We can still recall a student presentation on the dangers of drinking and driving in which the speaker described an accident she was involved in. She described her entry to the scene in great detail, outlining her actions after leaving her own car. She told us, in a quiet and deliberate way, that she and her two friends ran to the car of the other driver in the accident. They were confronted by absolute stillness. He was sprawled across the wheel, his face pressed on the windscreen and eyes staring. They felt paralysed by the horror of the moment. She managed to bring that horror to her audience as well, and to use that emotion to heighten our rejection of the practice of drinking and driving. Those images were just as powerful without pictures, because her language choices tapped our emotions and unsettled our thinking.

Case study

We recently watched a young architect present a proposal to an indigenous community group, on the design of an indigenous tourist attraction on a sacred site. He had based his design on the elements of earth, fire and water, which have great significance for this community. He used a scale model of the site that allowed the listeners to visualise exactly how visitors would proceed, geographically, through the three elements and be able to experience, through a variety of senses, each of the elements. For example, he described the pool where visitors could hear and feel the running water, and the fire pit where the heat of the blaze would rise to greet them. By using one of the elements as the theme for each of the three spaces on the site, he effectively demonstrated his respect for the indigenous people's view of the world and their commitment to natural forces. While the details of the project were adequately covered from a technical perspective, it was the young architect's appeals to the design's authenticity and the listeners' pride in their heritage that sold the design. Such a presentation, delivered to a different group, such as the local shire council, would undoubtedly have needed a little less *pathos* and more and stronger appeals to the project's practicality, profitability and viability.

Look for the balance of appeals that is required in all successful presentations, but remember to add appeals to emotion. Appeals to pride, to self-esteem, to altruism, and perhaps to fear, both verbally and visually, will enhance and support your message.

DEVELOPING *LOGOS*

Reasoning and use of evidence are also strong persuaders. The more you expose your listeners to your view of the facts, and the more you back these up with detail, the more chance you have of securing belief. You should never expose your listeners to abstractions without referring to specific examples or case studies to support your points of view.

Consider this case, one we believe to be a very persuasive presentation.

Case study

In 1991, a current affairs program, in attempting to promote the film *JFK*, interviewed Fletcher Prouty. At the time of President John F. Kennedy's assassination in 1963, Prouty had been Chief of Special Operations, Military Joint Chiefs of Staff. This powerful inside position certainly made him a very credible interviewee. He argued for a conspiracy theory behind Kennedy's assassination, adding enormously to the persuasiveness of his argument by giving many examples and detailed evidence to support his case.

One such example was the fact that normal security procedures for the visit of a President require all buildings to be evacuated and all windows to be closed on the route that the President's car will take. These normal precautions were not taken in Dallas on the assassination day. Speaking as a security chief, he claimed: 'Windows in the overlooking buildings were still open . . . It must have been planned that way.'

His references to security documents by date and detail, and the fact that these were now available by law and we could read them as proof, were all convincing arguments for the viewer. He referred, for example, to memoranda written by Kennedy, citing National Security Action Numbers 55 and 263. One of these was given particular emphasis, when he said, 'I worked on parts of it myself', along with senior Chiefs of Staff.

Obvious familiarity with, and use of, direct quotes from two Presidents of the day added most to his persuasive appeal. He quoted Kennedy who, referring to the Vietnam War, had said, 'I'll have a thousand men come home by the end of 1963', as proof that the pro-war lobby had reason to believe he was withdrawing support for the war. Prouty used this argument to justify his claim that the conspirators might have wanted Kennedy assassinated. He increased the impact of his argument even further, with a dramatic quote from Lyndon Johnson's reference to the CIA: 'We operate a Murder Incorporated.' By using that quote, he supported his argument that even senior political leaders knew of the licence the CIA had to kill. Prouty painted a very unflattering picture of the American political scene, and the possibility of uncontrolled elements within it. This made it seem plausible that a President might be assassinated from within the law.

Prouty's rhetorical impact resulted from a clever mix of many of the ingredients that we have discussed in this chapter. We were left, as listeners, either to disregard the evidence and believe a criminal had committed the assassination, or to accept that a conspiracy had occurred.

Prouty especially used appeals to *logos* along with his understanding of listeners' needs for consistency to persuade viewers that his position was reasonable.

Because viewers need to feel confident that government services are beyond reproach, this interview, with its use of documented evidence, high speaker credibility, and emotional impact, was a very powerful and persuasive one, even thirty years after the actual event.

USING A MIX OF APPEALS

Never feel coy about using the stories of your own successes, and never feel that you are being too daring in outlining solutions to problems by using analogies to your own experiences. A good speaker is prepared to take risks. Alan Alda, the Hollywood actor, became famous for his portrayal of a medical doctor in a military hospital during the Korean War in the television sitcom *M*A*S*H*; he provides a helpful model of the way a mix of the appeals of *ethos*, *pathos* and *logos* can be used to achieve successful persuasion.

Case study

Alda was asked by the Columbia College of Physicians and Surgeons to give the commencement speech to their graduating class.[4] He did not allow the fact that he had only *acted* a doctor in *M*A*S*H* to place limits on his use of appeals to *ethos*, *pathos* and *logos*. He used his own life experiences and his wonderfully humane intelligence to create one of the most memorable speeches those graduates will ever hear. We cite it as an exemplar of the persuasive presentation and have reprinted it in full in the appendix. To remind you of the possibilities of persuasion, and the way you can use your experiences, your expertise and your heart, consider this short extract from Alda's presentation, titled 'A reel doctor's advice to some real doctors'. After a brief introduction, he went on:

> I am not a doctor. But you have asked me, and all in all, I think you made a wonderful choice. I say that because I probably first came to the attention of this graduating class through a character on television that I've played and helped write for the past seven years—a surgeon called Hawkeye Pierce. He's a remarkable person, this Hawkeye, and if you have chosen somehow to associate his character with your own graduation from medical school, then I find that very heartening. Because I think it means that you are reaching out toward a very human kind of doctoring—and a very real kind of doctor.
>
> We didn't make him up. He really lived as several doctors who struggled to preserve life twenty-five years ago during the Korean War. In fact, it's because he's based on real doctors that there is something especially engaging about him. He has a sense of humour, and yet he's serious. He's impertinent, and yet he has feeling. He's human enough to make mistakes, and yet he hates death enough to push himself past his

own limits to save lives. In many ways he's the doctor patients want to have and doctors want to be . . .

If this image of that very human, very caring doctor is attractive to you—if it's ever touched you for a moment as something to reach for in your own life—then I'm here to cheer you on. Do it. Go for it. Be skilled, be learned, be aware of the dignity of your calling—but please, don't ever lose sight of your own simple humanity.

Notice how Alda draws on the 'real' doctor who preserved life for 25 years in Korea to make the transition from 'reel' doctor. He uses this evidence along with an appeal to *pathos* to encourage these new doctors to act like the heroes in movies—to feel motivated to strive to become the ideal doctor, a model of humanity like Hawkeye Pierce.

These appeals can contribute to your kitbag and can be used to great effect in your presentations.

BORROWING THE TOOLS OF PSYCHOLOGY

Modern persuasive strategy also borrows from behavioural psychology. Your understandings of certain psychological theories can also be used as strategic persuasive tools. Theories about how we make choices and how listeners can be motivated to make those choices can be used to help you to make decisions about what to include in a presentation.

Dealing with inconsistency

Over the last forty years, psychologists have helped us to realise the importance people place on holding a consistent world-view. While it may not always be possible, consistency theorists suggest that humans desire not to hold two oppositional values at one time.[5] This idea was used and understood, long before the discipline of psychology was even invented, by Shakespeare.

Case study

Shakespeare used this understanding to persuasive effect in Mark Antony's speech in *Julius Caesar* (Act III, Scene 3), which is delivered at Caesar's death. Caesar has just been assassinated and Mark Antony has set out to expose Brutus and the other assassins for the criminals he believes them to be. However, because Brutus has claimed he has delivered Rome from the grip of a 'tyrant', Mark Antony must be careful not to alienate the Roman crowd. So he carefully sets the nobility of Brutus and Caesar in opposition: either Brutus is an *honourable man* and was right to kill Caesar, or Caesar was an *honourable man* and Brutus was dishonourable. You will probably recall his oratory:

> Friends, Romans, countrymen, lend me your ears.
> I come to bury Caesar, not to praise him.
> The evil that men do lives after them,
> The good is oft interred with their bones;
> So let it be with Caesar. The noble Brutus
> Hath told you Caesar was ambitious;
> If it were so, it was a grievous fault,
> And grievously hath Caesar answer'd it.
> Here, under leave of Brutus and the rest—
> For Brutus is an honourable man;
> So are they all, all honourable men—
> Come I to speak in Caesar's funeral.
> He was my friend, faithful and just to me:
> But Brutus says he was ambitious;
> And Brutus is an honourable man.
> He hath brought many captives home to Rome,
> Whose ransoms did the general coffers fill:
> Did this in Caesar seem ambitious? . . .
> You all did see that on the Lupercal
> I thrice presented him a kingly crown,
> Which he did thrice refuse: was this ambition?
> Yet Brutus says he was ambitious;
> And, sure, he is an honourable man.
> I speak not to disprove what Brutus spoke,
> But here I am to speak what I do know.
> You all did love him once, not without cause:
> What cause withholds you then to mourn for him?

Notice that Antony constantly repeats the terms *honourable man* and *honourable men* in reference to Brutus and the other assassins. At the same time, he constantly refers to the excellent qualities of Caesar. The Romans cannot carry these two opposing ideas easily. They would experience a sense of inconsistency in carrying such contradictory positions in their heads and so they must decide which of the two men is honourable. They are persuaded to exchange their belief in the honour of Brutus for a belief in Caesar, and they must, therefore, label Brutus and his men as murderers and criminals. Do not forget that Antony has the most graphic of visual aids—Caesar's dead body—on the ground before him, and he uses it fully, exposing the traitors' stab wounds.

Getting agreement

Antony's speech, which Shakespeare so carefully crafted, also uses the 'yes, yes' technique. This technique starts with a small commitment and builds on that.[6] The speaker begins with statements that listeners are likely to agree with, and then, while they are in the mood to be saying 'yes, yes', moves to statements on topics that they might be less likely to accept. Antony begins by saying that he comes 'to bury Caesar, not to praise him', and speaks of the 'noble' Brutus, who at this stage is acclaimed as the saviour of Rome. However, Antony then reminds the Romans of the esteem in which they previously held Caesar:

> You all did love him once, not without cause:
> What cause withholds you then to mourn for him?

And eventually he comes out with a statement that reminds the Romans that treason has been rife: 'Whilst bloody treason flourish'd over us.'

The Romans, who would not have initially said 'yes, yes' to this reading of the situation, are now prepared to heartily agree that traitors rather than a saviour may have caused Caesar's death, and that Brutus and his followers may be assassins rather than heroes. Antony's appeal to *pathos* throughout this speech is also strong.

Case studies

You can use these psychological theories as persuasive tools. Here is an example of how one politician used his listeners' need for consistency to his advantage.

When Bill Clinton attended a Vietnam Memorial Service early in his presidency, he was aware of the delicacy of his past history as a youthful anti-Vietnam war-protester. The audience of Vietnam veterans likely held two images of the President—one a 'protest' image and the other of a leader celebrating veterans' contributions to securing US democracy.

Clinton dealt with the difficulty of holding two such opposing images in this way.

He managed to subdue the boos of the audience by reframing their thinking in his opening statement, saying: 'Just as war is freedom's cost, disagreement is freedom's privilege and we honour it here today.' Their derision turned to applause as they recognised that there was consistency in having Clinton come there to speak. Clinton represented the embodiment of the higher ideal of freedom of speech in a democracy. Their sacrifice was, after all, a sacrifice for democratic rights.

His clever framing allowed the veterans to continue to hold the two conflicting images, but to feel that there was a consistency in their joint belief in a broader ideal of freedom.

Here's another example of the way using an understanding of psychological theory can help a speaker.

We were once at a very dynamic and motivating presentation by the feminist speaker Naomi Wolf. We were members of a listening audience of approximately a thousand. Wolf managed to get all thousand listeners motivated to commitment to honour their feminist label by using the 'yes, yes' technique. Having asked us to raise our hands to show our commitment to equal rights for all human beings, equal pay for men and women, and a better world in which to live, she asked us to put up our hands to show our commitment to feminism. The label *feminism* is a hot issue. Many women are reluctant to use it about themselves. Wolf's use of this psychological technique as a persuasive strategy helped her to move her listeners to a 'yes, yes' position on that issue.

You, too, can use an understanding of this 'start-small' strategy as an effective persuasive tool. Keep it in mind when you want listeners to take that final, sometimes difficult, step to meet you at your point of view.

Tapping audience needs

During the 1950s and 1960s Abraham Maslow, along with other important writers such as Carl Rogers and Chris Argyris, provided us with further understanding of the way individuals respond to experience.[7] An important psychologist of the 1950s, Maslow suggested that human beings experience a variety of needs. Knowledge of those needs is a useful piece of information to carry in our 'kitbag of knowns' because it gives us some guidance on how we might involve our listeners.

Maslow suggested that while human beings ideally desire all

their needs to be filled, a hierarchy exists: our need for the basic requirements of safety and survival must be satisfied before we consider our other more complex needs.

He represents these needs as a pyramid, with our needs ordered in a hierarchy (Figure 3.1). At the base are the foundation needs of physiology and safety (food, clothes, shelter, protection from danger). Once these needs are fulfilled, humans scale the pyramid, looking to fulfil needs for love, affection and belonging; then for esteem, both as self-respect and respect from others; and finally, at the tip of the pyramid we want to achieve self-actualisation or a sense of personal competence, commitment and self-responsibility.[8]

Most workers have their needs for safety and reasonable pay satisfied through government legislation and awards. Therefore, we can target other needs that Maslow has identified. If, on the

Figure 3.1   Maslow's hierarchy of needs

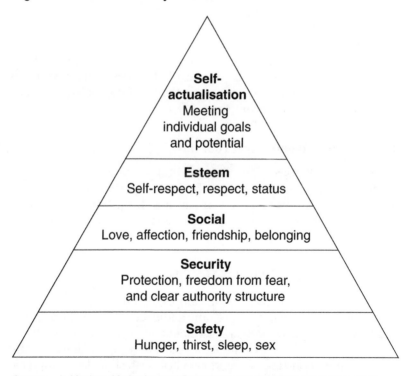

Source: A. Maslow, *Motivation and Personality*, New York: Harper & Row, 1954.

other hand, our audience research shows that insufficient attention has been given to some of those basic needs, it is clearly in our best interests to target needs lower on the hierarchy before tackling more complex needs such as self-actualisation.

In a presentation to your organisation on developing new competencies, you might start with a strong statement of how the company has always been committed to its workers, valuing their potential as much as their present skill. Your research might have revealed that morale is low and that workers feel that management does not value them. In this case, you might use language which shows how the company is a family, and thus demonstrate 'affection' for the group. Using Maslow's hierarchy as guidance, it is apparent that dealing with this may be an important priority. It becomes an important strategy to use with this group before you try to motivate them to take responsibility for learning new competencies, and committing their energies to the company—an appeal to self-actualisation.

It is worth reminding you here that it is most important to answer your listeners' standard question, 'What's in it for me?' This answer will provide the parameters for determining which strategies would be most useful. Understanding these psychological theories can change the shape of the presentation you are preparing, and equip you to take on the most complex of persuasive tasks with subtlety and style.

Using the ingredients to get your mix right

All of these strategies can be powerful ways to persuade your listeners to your point of view. By knowing what your listeners want, and by knowing how you can match this with your intentions, you can bring about dramatic shifts in how your listeners think and act.

EMPOWERING YOUR LISTENERS

We can learn from successful campaigns from the past about harnessing and empowering an audience. For example, the leaders of the Black Power movement in America in the 1960s understood how to use emotion and language to draw on the pride of their constituency, and also how crucial a clear, emphatic and imaginative slogan was to gain the commitment of blacks throughout America. The decision to use the slogan 'Black is beautiful' was a clever one, and a turning point for black American Civil Rights. This phrase gave black Americans a new-found sense of pride in the colour of their skin. This is an extraordinary example of the power of words to transform the 'meaning' of experience. This simple example demonstrates the capacity and potential available to us to empower our listeners, to heighten commitment, and to use not only the power of rational thinking but also our powers of imagination and emotion.

In this situation, the organisers were dealing with sympathetic listeners who wanted their rightful place in society. Therefore, it was important to dramatise the message—to overstate, rather than understate, what was intended—so that listeners would respond with a heightened belief in this new conception of the meaning of the colour of their skin. Remember this important technique when you are developing your persuasive argument with an already sympathetic audience.

Persuasion, then, can be a formative process for the listeners and speakers. The organisers involved their listeners, even mobilised them to build support, while simultaneously drawing energy from their responses. This is the power of thinking of persuasion as co-active.

This case provides a concrete example of the power of shared, focused messages that must be central to all your attempts at persuasion. You are probably making the connections between this discussion and that of Chapter 2 about the importance of listener analysis. You will also connect many of these suggestions with the discussion in Chapter 5 of the importance of structuring your presentation using clear, simple messages.

RECIPE FOR A PERSUASIVE PRESENTATION

When you have finished preparing your presentation, here is an easy and useful guide to help you assess whether it will achieve its purpose. We have developed it using Burke's 'pentad' or five-point guide.[9] Burke describes the process of persuasion as rather like a dramatic performance, with actors, scenes and scripts.

1. *Purpose:* Consider what response you want from your listeners. Ask yourself: What do you want your listeners to feel?

What do you want them to do? What do you want them to say? Write down the short-term and long-term goals that you want to achieve and prepare your presentation to serve these goals.

2. *The act*: Consider carefully all the rules of the type of communication you are hoping to use to persuade your listeners. This includes questions about whether the act should be a press conference, a workshop, a speech or a role-play. Is the speech for a big audience, a small audience, a televised audience or a live audience? Is it to challenge the audience or motivate them? All of these issues will shape your communication.

3. *The scene:* Ensure that your presentation matches the speaking situation. This is the big picture that surrounds your act. If resources are very tight in your organisation, presenting a clever, innovative but expensive proposal is tantamount to defeat. Alternatively, a proposal delivered in a time of rapid change will assume the momentum of the changes around you, and so you can be more radical in your proposals.

4. *The agent:* Create a credible and attractive image of yourself as speaker. Provide your listeners with good reasons to believe that you can deliver on your promises. If you can't do it on your own, call on all the resources around you—technical experts, research expertise—to build credibility for you.

5. *Agency:* Consider the style and phrasing of your presentation. Choose words and images which stir your listeners' imagination and motivate them to cooperation. Consider all of your personal resources, including your voice and body. Also, choose your visual aids carefully.

Case study: Persuasive strategies

There are few communicators who have shown a greater ability to persuade than ex-US President Bill Clinton. Right from his earliest campaigns, he showed the style the world has now come to associate with this extraordinary speaker. In his first Presidential debate in 1992, he was given two minutes to reply in support of his experience to lead the country. In just one minute and fifty seconds, his spontaneous response was perfectly structured, and not only used appeals to *ethos*, *pathos* and *logos*, but also used some other sophisticated language strategies and powerful non-verbal communication.

Here is the text of this special speech. We suggest that you read it before you consider our analysis of how Bill Clinton cleverly uses a perfect recipe for a persuasive presentation.

Figure 3.2   Bill Clinton is the great communicator

Moderator:
You have two minutes on the question of experience. He
[President George Bush Snr] says that is what distinguishes
him from the other two of you [Bill Clinton and Ross Perot].

Bill Clinton:
I believe experience counts, but it's not everything. Values,
judgement, and the records that I have amassed in my State
also should count for something. I've worked hard to create
good jobs and to educate people. My State now ranks first in

the country in job growth this year, fourth in income growth, fourth in the reduction of poverty, third in overall economic performance according to a major news magazine. That's because we believe in investing in education and in jobs. We have to change in this country. You know . . . my wife Hillary gave me a book, about a year ago, in which the author defined insanity as doing the same old thing over and over again and expecting a different result. We have got to have the courage to change. Experience is important, yes. I've gotten a lot of good experience in dealing with ordinary people over the last year . . . and month. I've touched more people's lives and seen more heartbreak and hope, more pain and more promise than anybody else who has run for President this year. I think the American people deserve better than they're getting. We have gone from first to thirteenth in the world in wages in the last twelve years since Mr Bush and Mr Reagan have been in. Personal income has dropped while people have worked harder. In the last four years there have been twice as many bankruptcies as new jobs created. We need a new approach, the same old experience is not relevant—we're living in a new world after the Cold War, and what works in this new world is not trickle down, not government for the benefit of the privileged few, not tax and spend, but a commitment to invest in American jobs, and American education, controlling American health care costs, and bringing the American people together. That is what works, and you can have the right kind of experience and the wrong kind of experience. Mine is rooted in the real lives of real people, and it will bring real results if we have the courage to change.

As Clinton could not, at this time, claim experience already as President, and as his opponent, George Bush Snr, had just pushed his own claim in this way, Clinton began with a quick rebuttal: 'I believe experience counts, but it's not everything.' He then went on to speak of the importance of values and judgement and his own record. He established his *ethos*, and with the support of *logos*, stated, 'My State now ranks first in the country in job growth this year, fourth in income growth, fourth in the reduction of poverty, third in overall economic performance according to a major news magazine.' As Governor of Arkansas, this detail provided proof of his own abilities as a leader, and also showed his capability to be on top of the figures that count in relation to his leadership.

Clinton then changed to the strategy of using 'we' to appeal to his audience to join with him on the road ahead: 'We have to change in this country.' This was a strategy that suggested a move from the past and President Bush to a new President such as himself. His use of a light-hearted reference to a book that his wife had given him, which said that 'insanity was doing the same old thing over and over again and expecting a different result', showed his practical 'down to earth' approach to life. It also showed his warmth towards his wife as an ordinary family man. As he restated, 'We have got to have the courage to change', his fist came up and down in a powerful gesture of conviction.

He then returned to the point of 'experience'. He shifted the way he used the term 'experience' to refer to his experience of the American people during the Presidential race, rather than his administrative experience as a leader. As he spoke of the ordinary people he had been meeting, and summoned the appeal to *pathos*, he also used the language strategy of consonant repetition by mentioning their 'heartbreak' and 'hope' and 'pain' and 'promise'. This emotional appeal was strengthened by the power of repetition and the emotional content of the words chosen. He then heightened this *pathos*, and created a link through more evidence, to establish *logos* to support his case, by saying 'I think the American people deserve better than they are getting'. Of course this statement also implies that he will provide something 'better' under his governance than what was already offered by President George Bush Snr.

The next section of the reply returns to *logos* with a vengeance, as he rolls out the facts and figures that indict Mr Bush and the current government: 'We have gone from first to thirteenth in the world in wages in the last twelve years since Mr Bush and Mr Reagan have been in. Personal income has dropped, while people have worked harder. In the last four years, there have been twice as many bankruptcies as new jobs created.'

This appeal to *logos* allows him to return to the theme of his reply that a 'new approach' is needed; that 'the same old experience is not relevant'. He then makes a perfectly balanced statement by contrasting what is *not* needed with what is required: 'not trickle down, not government for the benefit of the privileged few, not tax and spend, but a commitment to invest in American jobs, and American education, controlling American health care costs, and bringing the American people together'. Once again, there is a strong appeal to emotion, and the reply builds to a conclusion on a positive up-beat note. It is always important to leave the listener with a feeling of hope.

He finishes with a perfect return to the theme of his experience and a clear summary of the essence of his argument by saying: 'That is what works, and you can have the right kind of experience and the wrong kind of experience. Mine is rooted in the real lives of real people, and it will bring real results if we have the courage to change.' This final statement is accompanied by strong emphasis on the appropriate words to stress 'right' and 'wrong', and the important repetition of the word 'real'. It is again accompanied by the strong gesture of his fist and powerful eye contact with the camera, and therefore his audience.

It would be hard to find a more perfectly structured piece that uses every moment of the argument to strategically support a claim for leadership. At the same time, it is a piece that is pitched to the understanding of a wide audience, while also showing a sophistication that can be fully appreciated by educated listeners. The fact that this adroitness could be shown in a spontaneous answer of such brevity points to the expertise which marked Bill Clinton as one of the greatest communicators of the twentieth century.

PACKING THE TOOLS OF PERSUASION—A HEAVY LOAD FOR YOUR KITBAG

Your understanding of the strategies and techniques available to persuade your audience can turn a difficult and stressful situation into an exciting and stimulating challenge. Understanding how rhetoric works opens a kitbag of possibilities and directions for moving an audience along the road you are travelling to a mutually satisfying position on the many problems you face together in your organisations. Understandings from the past can truly be resources to use in your future.

TIPS

- Be creative in using the ingredients of persuasion, and make your presentation as persuasive as possible.
- Match your strategies to the particular audience you are addressing.
- Be sure to balance the ingredients and get your mix right.
- If you are making a presentation to listeners who may oppose you, try the 'yes, yes' technique or unbalance their beliefs about an issue.

- Be sure to establish your credibility as strongly as possible. Always use evidence, but especially so for the doubting listeners.
- If you have discriminating and knowledgeable listeners, marshal your evidence carefully, and thoroughly state your case while never overstating it.
- If you have sympathetic listeners, use evidence to dramatise your ideas. Use colourful language to capture their imagination and hold it.
- Use images, language and structure which empower your audience—which capitalise on the co-active characteristics of persuasion.
- Near the end of the preparation stage, use Burke's five-point guide to test whether you have taken care of all of the important aspects of persuasion.

4

Preparing to present

If you want me to talk for ten minutes, I'll come next week.
If you want me to talk for an hour, I'll come tonight.

Woodrow Wilson

DEALING WITH ANXIETY

Prepare mentally

See yourself sitting calmly in the room of your presentation and breathing deeply and freely. Now you are standing confidently and walking to the front of the room; you look purposefully out and smile at your audience before you begin.

This is the image you must keep with you at all times. You know that most people, faced with the idea of presenting to listeners, feel real fear. It is also comforting to know that you can overcome fear if you prepare for it. If you are prepared, listeners will not, cannot, hear your heart beating or feel your palms sweating; if you are focused on the purpose of your message and your desire to communicate that message, and if you appear confident, you will be assured of making contact with your listeners.

You have now at the least an educated guess about these listeners and their frames of reference, about the context of this presentation, and you have thought about persuasion for your context. You have now to prepare to know everything there is to know about the speaker; you have to prepare to know *yourself.* Let's begin that preparation.

Know your strengths

Begin by recognising your strengths. Write them down. We are sure that, if you are fair with yourself, you will realise that you could write a long list of your strengths and capabilities. For example, most people can generate a great deal of power with a warm smile, so, relax and smile, and you will feel good. Enjoy the smile, because you need to know how it feels. Imagine yourself standing in front of your listeners and smiling before you begin to speak. If you breathe deeply, and smile, you always have a good beginning (unless, of course, you want to set up a sombre atmosphere). So, begin by listing your strengths.

- It is highly likely that you know your topic well and can speak easily on it in conversation. If the topic is a new and challenging one, make sure that you have researched and become familiar with it. Ask the experts in your company for advice, or visit the library and search for that information which will most interest your audience.
- You are certainly capable of making the hard decisions and selecting only the best points to fit the time you have available.
- It is also highly likely that you can structure those ideas lucidly with careful preparation, and style them appropriately.
- You can think about the best phrasing for points which are difficult. If you practise speaking those phrases on audio-cassette, you can listen to your presentations; this will help you to remember useful words and images for when you speak to listeners. Remember, the audio-cassette is for the speaker as the word-processor is for the writer. It is what you use to make the drafts of your presentation, just as a writer makes drafts of a text.

It is also useful to list your fears. Ask yourself if they are rational fears which are worth worrying about? If your answer is 'yes', are there ways in which you can resolve them? If any of them are about your physical presentation or your voice, we can help you resolve them later in the book. Remember, though, that you will always make some mistakes in presentation—but you must be able to let go of those mistakes, you must not dwell on them. Allow your mistakes to wander off and the memories of your strengths to linger on.

Prepare physically

Good physical preparation has four keys. These are relaxation; posture; non-verbal communication; and vocal preparation. In this chapter we will help you with relaxation and posture. Later, as you follow us through the text, you can think about non-verbal communication and vocal preparation.

Relaxation

The increased demands of life in modern society, especially of working life, have led to increased, habitual, physical tensions. Yet we all want to feel as relaxed as possible, as often as possible, and we all prefer to listen to, and communicate with, people who are feeling on top of things. Two American researchers found that speakers with tense postures were less persuasive than those with relaxed postures.[1] Relaxation is certainly one of the keys to becoming more credible and more persuasive. Relaxation exercises not only improve our physical well-being, but also provide the beginnings for good posture and good vocal presentation. Take the time to work on relaxation. By skipping this step, you may reduce the potential you have to be a great speaker.

Exercise

Try this exercise to help you to get started. Concentrate on your breathing as you do the following relaxation exercise. We will give you a more detailed breathing exercise later when we deal with vocal preparation.

Get into loose comfortable clothes and prepare to relax. Find a warm, comfortable environment and lie flat on the floor. (Be careful not to push yourself too hard or strain yourself during these exercises, and be sure to stay warm.) Instead of keeping your legs flat on the floor, lift your knees, keeping your feet flat on the floor, and feel the alignment of your spine (it should be well supported in this position). Concentrate on feeling the length and breadth of your back as you lie in this position. Keep this image of the strength of your spine and how straight it feels in your memory, so that you can recall it and reproduce this feeling when you are standing in front of an audience.

Now straighten your legs again and continue the exercise. Concentrate and breathe in deeply through your nose, and feel the oxygen in your lower chest; concentrate and breathe out, relaxing, releasing any tightness in your body. Check, now, every part of your body. Concentrate on one part at a time. Think about your right foot and ankle and concentrate on releasing any tension there; work, slowly, up each part of each of your legs, then, slowly, to your stomach and chest and throat and shoulders; keep working, slowly, down each arm, and then concentrate and relax each part of your head and face.

Now that you have checked your individual body parts, you will have a greater understanding of physical tension, how it feels, and how to release it. So, this time, concentrate, breathe in, and feel the tension in your body as you (purposely) tighten all of your muscles: clench your fists and turn your toes towards your head and feel the increase of tension in your arms and legs. Now concentrate, breathe out, and feel the wonderful release as the tension flows out of your body: imagine that it flows out of the top of your head and out through the tips of your fingers and toes.

Lie still, continue to breathe deeply, and allow yourself to experience this wonderful outward flowing of tension. Do this exercise several times at any one practice to help you to relax. This stretching and releasing can become stretching and curling in conjunction with your breathing, and you can move as vigorously as you want on the floor. When you feel completely relaxed, listen to the sounds outside the room. Allow your mind to travel away from your body and then, slowly, back inside the room and then, finally, back to the sounds of your own breathing. Now you are ready to begin the voice exercises detailed in Chapter 8.

Be slow and careful with yourself as you prepare to get up from the floor. Before you attempt it, turn onto your side for about 20 seconds, then roll onto your stomach, then to your hands and knees and then back onto your heels. You will then, and then only, be ready to check that your body is in alignment for the important preparation of voice production.

KNOW YOUR IMAGE

Posture

It is important for you to be able to take up a relaxed and easy posture as you stand before your listeners. Standing upright, check that your weight is evenly distributed and that no undue tension pervades your body. Remember the feeling of relaxation you had on the floor, and keep this feeling in your body consciousness. Stand with your feet straight under your hips. Make sure that you unlock your knees and keep your spine straight. The spine should not have an S bend, but neither should it be hall-stand rigid. Drop your shoulders into a relaxed position. It is very important that your head (which can weigh up to nine kilograms) is well balanced. It is not only to allow a free passage of sound that head balance is so important; if the weight of your head is off-centre, you can get neck problems and headaches.

If you drop your head back, keeping your eyes closed, and then slowly lift it to an upright position, you should feel when it is in perfect alignment, weight carefully balanced. Keep this feeling. It is always a good idea to check your alignment (in fact, to do these exercises) in front of a mirror. If you are perfectly aligned and tension free, you should be able to rock back and forth on the balls of your feet without feeling as if you might topple.

As we have said, positive imaging is very important. To present effectively to listeners, you must appear confident. To do so, you must be capable of clearly recalling memories of the best and strongest images of yourself as a speaker. A good means of recall is to keep one of your best practices or one of your strongest performances on videotape and look at it the night before. You will appear more confident to listeners if you can also recall how relaxed you look when you practise and perfect your alignment in front of the mirror.

USE THE TOOLS OF PREPARATION

The tools of preparation are those 'knowns' and techniques which help you to prepare systematically without forgetting anything, and in a manner that brings the clearest focus to the task in hand. Tools always make a task easier and faster. In this case, one of your important tools is the map of your purpose.

Grasp your purpose

You should always write down, in one short sentence, the purpose of your presentation. For example, it might be 'to convince community members to join this group to fight against the proposed freeway' or 'to convince the board that two members of staff should be funded to attend the next overseas conference'. Your purpose statement should be specific and achievable; work on it until it is clear and focused. Do not have a vague topic like 'recycling' in your mind. You must know that you want: 'to convince listeners that we must have compulsory recycling of paper, glass, aluminium and plastic products to save our natural resources'. This purpose statement remains the driving force behind your speech, and you can keep recalling it, in order to make decisions about the material you need to use and how you want to structure it. All of your choices are made to support this specific purpose.

Case study

It is important that you aim for an achievable purpose. We once worked with the financial controller of a large British company, the purpose of whose orientation speech to new employees was 'to give a few lessons in financial procedures'. You can imagine how open these employees would be to concentrating on this complex message in the first few hours of their new job!

When we examined the purpose of his presentation, we determined that, in the main, it should be 'to motivate the young employees to have an interest in their new company and their specific job in it'. After we discussed this with the speaker, we realised that the company he was talking about was heir to many interesting anecdotes. This particular company had built airfields and pipelines in war zones. What a challenge it was to keep financial controls in these situations. Our speaker proceeded to prepare four points about why financial controls were so important. He used interesting anecdotes from company history to support his chosen points, for example:

> Imagine how difficult it is, with wharf strikes in London and war in the neighbouring countries that you need to pass through, to plan and financially control the delivery of pipeline overland through Turkey and safely to its destination in the Middle East.

By the end of our training session, the presentation was one that could—and would—achieve its purpose of capturing the interest of the new employees and motivating them to anticipate the exciting future of their new jobs.

Research your topic

- It is important that you know everything you possibly can about your topic; you must know all you can to support your argument in every way, and be ready to answer any and every question you are asked.
- It is important that your research is thorough to allow you to demonstrate your breadth of knowledge and, thus, your right to speak on it.
- Your greater knowledge will allow you to use a variety of persuasive strategies to strengthen and support your listener appeals. Find information in a library or get it from experts in the field, and remember that your own creative or reflective ideas are also an important part of your research.
- Find supportive visual information—slides, film or video material—which you can use to create atmosphere or illustrate content. Remember that this is also an important part of your research. (We will deal with the benefits of technology in detail later.)
- Find word-images and phrases to give life to your presentation and remember how important, and how supportive, simple statistics and real-life examples can be.
- Go back to the research phase, after you have completed the brainstorm procedure below, to fill in any gaps in your information that may be needed to support new aspects of the topic that you generate.

Brainstorm your topic

In brainstorming you generate, without being critical, all of the possible ideas which may be useful to your topic. After this initial flurry of activity, it is important that you gather your ideas and pull them together. There are a variety of strategies available for any particular topic, so don't limit yourself to your first choice: experiment with as many alternatives as you can think of. One very good choice, however, is to draw up a 'map of ideas' that represents your many ideas and visually lays out all the various ways that you could put them together. By choosing this approach to prepare, you are using all your stores of creative energy.

Suppose you want to present a plan to your human resources department to persuade the director that it is beneficial to have a member of that department attached to every organisational unit. You draw up a map of ideas that looks something like Figure 4.1.

Evaluate and select

Keep all of the ideas from your brainstorming and evaluate them before you select from them. You can only start to evaluate and select when you have the clearest of pictures of the specific purpose of your presentation. These stages are among the most important in preparation. You evaluate which of your ideas have the most impact in the light of your purpose. You select from your ideas those that you can link to produce a coherent argument. You can eventually select those quotes and anecdotes that you can use to produce a strong introduction and conclusion, always remembering that these are the most important few moments of your presentation. Be strict with yourself in evaluation and selection. It is important, even if difficult, to develop an outline. Sacrifice those ideas that will not fit your topic or structure, and clearly lead your listeners.

Select carefully

Remember that your listeners recall at a rate inverse to the number of points made. Research shows that the more points you make, the fewer the details they remember. To test this idea, two professors (named Erskine and O'Morchoe)

> taught one class only essential principles with little detail, and then compared their knowledge with another class which had been given a lot of details. The first class did better. Their conclusion was that too much material causes interference, and listeners remember less not more.[2]

Thus, remember your listeners and your listeners will remember you. Give them but a few points, but give those few points much life; give them anecdote and example (pegs on which listeners can hang their memories); give them entertainment (as long as it is pertinent); give them facts as illustration, not as the substance of your presentation. You can always write out details and large numbers of facts and present them as a follow-up handout.

Figure 4.1   Two ways to arrange your ideas about improving communication between staff and human resources department

Improving communication between staff and human resources department

Existing Problem
- lack of information
- poor communication
- low morale

Solutions
- different communication media
- give department a face in unit

Causes
- faceless department
- isolation of unit
- methods of communication
- active union
- many changes

OR . . .

Improving communication between staff and human resources department

Ideal
- the role of an effective Human Resources Department

What should it be like?
- face-to-face
- trust
- access to information
- proactive
- support
- sees staff development as central

Present Situation
- the role of Human Resources Department

How does it measure up?
- faceless
- memos/newsletters used
- lack of trust
- limited information
- watchdog
- reactive
- sees administration as central

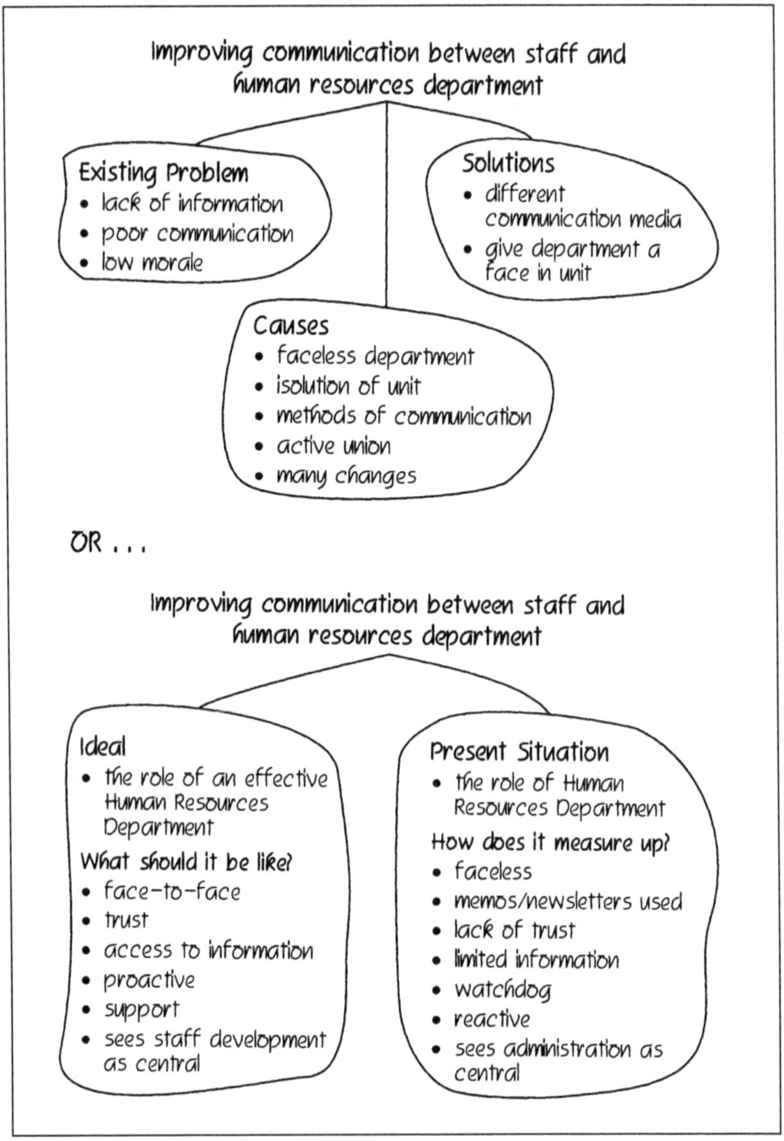

Develop an outline

The selection process starts the next important stage of your preparation. Gradually, you can develop and fill out the detail of your speech by drawing on your knowledge of your listeners, the situation and the topic. You will begin, in these important stages, to outline your presentation clearly. Your initial written outline may quite fully state your main points and sub-points, placing them in order. The steps of preparation are not mutually exclusive and you will find yourself going back and forth between your research, your selection and your structure to find the best solutions. Because preparation is not a straightforward process, you should respond to your good ideas as they arise. If you suddenly come up with a new angle on a topic, consider its usefulness; if it fits, do not be afraid to adjust what you have already developed.

Structure your topic

Deciding how to structure your presentation is perhaps the most difficult aspect of preparation, and we examine it in detail in the next chapter. We believe that the structure of your speech is most important, and you must carefully structure your message to take advantage of your speaking opportunity. Remember that the listener will always be looking for structure, and will struggle if you do not provide it. If you provide a clear structure, the listener can keep up with you as you progress through the speech. Generally, a speaking structure has three sections: the introduction, the body and the conclusion. The introduction and conclusion are very important parts of your speech, and you should put aside some of your best ideas from the selection stage to consider as possibilities to bring zest to your beginning and ending.

The introduction

Structure your introduction to capture your listeners' attention. Remember, your listeners will decide in the first thirty seconds what they think of you and whether or not you are worth listening to. Once you have their attention, you give them direction: outline the map of your ideas and, thus, the structure of your presentation. The old maxim is worth recalling here: 'Tell them what you are going to say, say it, then tell them what you have said.'

James Humes, the speechwriter of US Presidents, drives home this truth when he says, 'If being repetitive is a *vice* in an article it is a *device* in a speech.'[3]

The body

What is the right amount of information for a listener to comprehend? Because it is difficult for listeners to process too much information, you should select only two main points in a ten-minute presentation and four main points for a twenty-minute presentation. You can, of course, and should, present sub-points to support these main points, but limit them to three or four for each main point.

Remember, if you are speaking for more than twenty minutes, you need to add variety to your presentation by using a range of techniques, such as questions or visuals, to alter the rhythms of your interaction and so help your listeners maintain concentration. Work on this in your preparation. One of the most common faults in presentations is to include too much information. Winston Churchill fainted when he was making his maiden speech in the House of Commons. He later claimed that it was because he had decided to detail all of the world's problems in one speech and the effort overcame him. Later, as an experienced speaker, he emphasised the importance of one clear theme in a presentation. Know your theme and develop your material to support it.

The conclusion

Your conclusion must sum up, and strikingly, the theme of your presentation. A good presentation is one that listeners can later recount to friends in just a sentence or two. In a persuasive presentation, there will often be some action that you need to suggest to your listeners. Most importantly, a good conclusion does not linger; it is brief and to the point. We will give some examples to guide you when we look at structure in more detail in the next chapter.

BE CREATIVE

You now have the skeleton of your presentation, but how do you flesh out this body and bring it to life? What will give it life? What will make it engrossing? What will make it memorable for your listeners? What creative elements can you include? What words can you use? What images will you leave with your listeners?

To make your point, you could use:

- visuals in the forms of photos, pictures, slides, charts or graphics on overheads
- music or voice-overs of other experts to add to the aural experience
- role-play or dialogue.

Your creative ideas should always serve the purpose of your presentation, not distract from it. We once had a student who began her presentation on fitness by getting us all to run on the spot and then take our own pulses before she told us what rate a fit pulse should be. A number of listeners registered some shock at the pace of their pulse and became immediately more motivated to listen. This was a creative way of making certain that her listeners were aware that her presentation applied to their personal fitness.

Find examples, words and images

In this preparation stage, spend time exploring the possibilities of the language to get full value out of your presentation. For example, using an analogy can help people to think about an old idea in new ways. You must never speak in abstract terms: always use concrete example and analogy to make your point strongly. You might create a character and relate your topic to that character's life to make it seem more real for the listeners. A real character or a fictional character, whichever serves your purpose best, will bring your presentation to life. Create as many images as you can in words, as well as in visual forms. Word images, as we know from Shakespeare's plays, can be as powerful as visual images. Explore the possibility of a powerful sentence which emphasises your point, and think of repeating it to clarify your theme and to cement it in the memories of your listeners. If your presentation requires a certain style of language—for example, a simplification of terms for lay listeners—then consider those simple terms at this stage of your preparation. Consider also those phrases or words which will express your ideas clearly and pertinently, and write them down.

Humour can be a powerful ingredient if it is pertinent. A group of scientists we worked with came up with the idea of Dudley Do Right as the client who fulfilled his department's needs, and his brother Shelby Right (a play on the common Australian slang phrase 'She'll be right, mate') who constantly did not: Shelby did things the wrong way and he never followed the rules. These two characters added much humour and life to a difficult presentation, the purpose of which was to explain to corporate listeners how to conform with government legislation. We will concentrate in more detail on words, images, humour and visual aids in later chapters.

USING PREPARATION TOOLS WELL

Let us give you an example of the preparation process we used with a client to turn her written text into an expressive, persuasive presentation.

Case study

Our client had brainstormed her ideas, evaluated and selected the most important, and structured them carefully. However, by writing out her presentation, by concentrating on what she *had* to say, she had forgotten that much of her persuasion would come from *how* she said it. Of course the content is important, but the form in which it is presented will determine its impact. Our challenge was to be creative!

As manager of a large research centre at a university, our client had been invited to be the keynote speaker at a conference for about four hundred public sector accountants.[4] Her purpose was to persuade them that accounting for people was not the same as accounting for financial resources. In other words, financial and human resources cannot be managed in the same way.

She had determined that she needed to focus on:

- measurement of human resources as a new reform attempt in the public sector
- the complexity of understanding people as assets and how we might invest in them
- performance standards for managers and how to measure them.

Clearly, she had plenty to say about these complex issues. The challenge was to focus these accountants on her main message: measuring people and measuring numbers are not easily paralleled. We decided more brainstorming was needed.

We set out to help her find interesting forms in which to present these complex issues—quotes, analogies, anecdotes and characterisations that would give these issues life. This is what we came up with:

- the history/story of other reform attempts and the complexities and dangers
- a personal story about her experience of reform
- the use of the jargon of accountants to describe people so that they start to sound like machines or objects
- the introduction of characters such as managers with names and faces
- images that harness new ways to think about performance standards
- quotes that bring an idea to life.

All of these ideas enriched and enlivened her presentation: she turned an informative, comprehensive, written statement into a powerful, expressive, persuasive speech (being creative can do that for you).

This is how she used some of those ideas. She looked for a memorable way to describe her idea about the importance of people relative to other resources in an organisation. She found this old Chinese proverb:

If you wish to plan for a year, sow a seed.
If you wish to plan for ten years, plant a tree.
If you wish to plan for a lifetime, invest in people.

Its simplicity speaks eloquently; it highlights the value of people as resources and why people should be treated differently from other investments.

She also found an appealing description of the entrepreneurial spirit. It offered listeners a simple choice of two ways to manage people: control or facilitation. It reduced the ambiguity of the issue and demanded that the listeners think about the problem of managing people. This unconventional description was stimulating for listeners:

There are two different ways of approaching the management of people. They can be symbolised as either a man holding a large number of balloons or as a Christmas tree. For the man holding the balloons, 'Each of the balloons has buoyancy and lift. And the man himself does not lord it over the balloons, but stands beneath them holding all the strings firmly in his hands. Every balloon is not only an administrative but also an entrepreneurial unit.'

By contrast, the second approach could be understood as symbolised by a Christmas tree, 'with a star at the top with a lot of nuts and useful things beneath. Everything derives from the top and depends on it. Real freedom and entrepreneurship can exist only at the top.'[5]

She concluded simply, by throwing out the challenge to her listeners to make that choice. We are sure you will agree that it is a highly visual choice, and it offered listeners a simple way to conceptualise their decisions about how to treat human resources. They could either take control, continue to play a starring role, and risk losing the potential of their staff, as the latter metaphor suggests, or they could realise the potential of their staff, release their energies and their entrepreneurial spirits, and see them soar to new heights.

Techniques like these simplify complex topics and allow your listeners to use less energy in understanding and more in imagining and reflecting. A metaphor like this will linger with your listeners long after your presentation has been forgotten. It will stimulate their interest and provide talking points for later discussion.

GET READY TO PRESENT

Having gathered all your material together, you are finally ready to practise your presentation for that important situation. How should you deliver your ideas? We agree with the American speech writer James Humes: 'In speaking there are three axioms: *Bad speakers* read speeches. *Good speakers* read from notes. *Great speakers* read speeches.'[6]

We are aiming to create good speakers with our kitbag, which is why we have suggested that you work on an outline. For the great majority of us, our best option is to speak to an audience, not try to read to them. Speaking and writing are very different activities. Unless you are good at writing dialogue, that is, unless you are a good speechwriter, you will probably end up with an essay to read rather than a speech to speak. Reading an essay to listeners is one of the most common faults of the amateur speaker. At best, listeners have to cope with material and vocabulary that is difficult to listen to; at worst, they have to confront incomprehensible mumbling. Unless you are a good actor, you will definitely be a better speaker than you are a reader.

Trust yourself, and develop good notes which, after rehearsal, will allow you to speak spontaneously. If you must read, it is best to dictate your presentation in your normal spoken language and practise reading energetically, to perfect a confident and expressive style. Of course, if you want to develop the writing skills of a great speechwriter as well as the presentation skills of a great speaker, we encourage you. However, if you, like most of us, want to be an effective speaker for all occasions, but don't want to expend the energy needed to be a great speechwriter and speaker, you need to learn to plan, to take notes, and to trust yourself to speak from them.

If, for your first few times speaking, you need to rely on notes, allow yourself to use them as props until you develop your confidence. But remember, at all times, notes should be a life-raft, not the *Queen Mary*.

DEVELOP YOUR SPEAKING OUTLINE

Now that you have carefully considered your presentation, you must write and prepare a clear speaking outline—that is, an outline in point form. However, your speaking outline, which is your life-raft of notes, should be brief, and merely serve as a reminder to keep you on track. This outline should be on plain cards the size of postcards, so that you can hold them in your hand and still be free to use gesture. It is absurd to hide cards in the palm of your hand and pretend they do not exist. They need to be held at a comfortable reading distance so you can easily refer to them. You should need only a couple of cards once you become practised at outlining your prompts or points. Ronald Reagan, if we can believe ex-Australian Prime Minister Bob Hawke in his biography, was well practised at using these speaking cards:

> After the preliminary introductions and courtesies, Ron said: 'Well Bob, you are our welcome guest, would you like to open up the discussions? Feel free to raise any matters you like.'
>
> I responded with some observations and questions about the strength and durability of the United States economic recovery. The president, with an ease which obviously came from long practice, thumbed through a number of cards held in the palm of his hand, found the appropriate one, read a couple of generalised sentences and then, turning to the secretary of the treasury, Donald Regan, said: 'Don, this is your area, perhaps you would like to respond to Bob'.[7]

Hawke says he was 'astonished' by this behaviour. We can understand his surprise, because one does not expect cards in an interpersonal situation. Reading does give the impression that the speaker may not know or understand the topic they are conversing on. This is why we emphasise using the cards as prompts only, and appearing to speak spontaneously and knowledgeably on your topic. If you have quotes or statistics, you can put them on a separate piece of paper and lift them up from the lectern or table and read them to the listeners.

PREPARE HANDOUTS

Handouts can provide an important support for your oral presentation. Because a good oral presentation is simple and uncluttered and draws its strength from its capacity to capture the imagination and the emotions along with the rational self, it is not always suitable for handling detailed and complex material. When you are faced with the problem that your listeners need detailed material, you may choose to provide it in handout form. Of course, you should consider its placement in the presentation. Perhaps you could hand it out when you want to refer to that specific point, or just refer to the material and offer more detail at the end of the presentation in a handout form. Do try to avoid handing out your material at the beginning of the presentation, however, because it will compete with you for your listeners' attention.

REHEARSE

You are now ready to start rehearsal. Speak your presentation on audio-cassette, if you can, and listen to it with a critical ear. Tighten your structure, adjust your expression, or change your order if you need to. Leave it for 48 hours before you listen to it again, if you can, and then critique it again and tighten, adjust or change it again: you may have new thoughts, as you are now a fair distance from your initial attempt.

When you are confident, you could record your presentation on videotape and re-examine it. We believe, however, that an audio-cassette is preparation enough. Never listen to yourself or criticise yourself as you give a presentation, even in practice. Become used to being critical only when you are listening to the playback of your presentation, because when you face your listeners you must be able to concentrate on your purpose and forget the faults you are working on until your next rehearsal session. This approach is the key to concentrating solely on your message when you face an audience—you are now placing the focus on the communication orientation which Motley and Molloy's research proved to be so successful, as we mentioned in Chapter 1.

As you rehearse, take into consideration how you look and sound. Remember:

- You will be far more powerful as a speaker if you do not stand behind a lectern when presenting to listeners. A lectern forms a barrier which, although it may feel protective, actually blocks the strength of a strong physique and the expressiveness of your body language. For this same reason, it is best to stand to make a presentation, so that your expressive power is carried to the audience and they give you their full attention. Even at a board meeting, stand if possible—you could make the excuse of using visual aids to get you into a standing position. Once you get attention, then make sure you use all of your non-verbal strengths to sustain that attention.
- Your physical presence can help you: if you are physically approachable and comfortable, your listeners can be comfortable and focus on your message.
- If you use facial expression and gesture, you can add greater meaning and feeling to your presentation.
- If you use your voice well, you can heighten expression and explore the nuances of language. You can interpret for the listener by emphasising relevant, important words to give greater coherence to your presentation. And you can use rhythm patterns within your presentation, seeking variations to maintain your listeners' attention. Any change of pace is useful. Remember that you can also develop definite changes of pace from the way you structure your presentation—from interaction to slower pieces more packed with information, then back to anecdotes or lighter stories. Of course you can also use visual aids or video to radically change the listeners' focus and type of attention.
- If you develop good audio and visual aids to support your presentation in your preparation phase, and you use them in the most effective way to capture and maintain attention, you can add impact to your presentations.

Figure 4.2   Rehearsal is an essential part of good preparation

Cartoon: Fiona Mitchell

GROUP PRESENTATIONS

Group presentations require attention to all of the techniques we have suggested, but there are some particular strategies that will help you put a good team presentation together. Survey your team and assess where speakers will most be able to use their strengths. Ensure a consistent quality of presentation from speaker to speaker, and divide your material so that each speaker presents interesting information. Remember, however, that sometimes, in a group situation, you need to choose the better speaker rather than the greater expert, and use the expert as adviser. Our points in Chapter 5 on structuring presentations are as relevant to groups as they are to individuals.

It can be a difficult task, though, to structure a presentation carefully for three or four speakers, and for a half-hour or more in length. It is especially important not to overload the presentation with too many details, as this will tire your audience.

Here are some useful strategies to help you decide how to allocate speakers and material in a group presentation.

- Capture your listeners' attention with a strong introduction and conclusion, pulling together the various parts of the presentation.
- Carefully coordinate your theme so that the presentation works toward a common purpose.
- Ensure that you have clear and purposeful transitions that lead the listeners from one speaker to the next.
- If you have a speaker who is less experienced, the general introduction and outline of your group's presentation can be a straightforward section to handle. Alternatively, you may choose to place the inexperienced speaker in the middle of the presentation.
- Provide your listeners with help through a long presentation by exploiting their contrasting styles. For example, you can alternate male and female speakers, confident and less confident speakers, or those with humorous and more serious styles.
- You always have more power if you can stand up to present (in any situation). If this is difficult because your group is presenting across a boardroom table to just a few others, organise to minimise that difficulty: keep the group's chairs back from the table and have each speaker move their chair forward at the time of addressing the listeners.
- It is essential that you and your team watch your own speaker with avid concentration to mirror the response you hope to get from your listeners.

Presenting as a group, then, means following the same rules as for an individual, with the added complication of perfecting coordination.

An example of group planning

Your unit is to make a presentation on its performance for a review panel that is assessing your organisation. A group of three managers of the unit must coordinate their information to demonstrate that the unit is working effectively.

You might meet to plan your information and discuss honestly and openly the types of skills and weaknesses each of you has in presentation. Because you probably know each other well, you will know which team member has the best chance of opening and closing the presentation, concisely outlining the theme and building rapport with the review team. You might decide to place your serious speaker at the beginning of the presentation to establish respect for the situation, and use the presenter who can build in humour at the end, as energy wanes. It might also be possible to decide the order by arranging its sequence around the types of procedures the unit uses. This may mean ordering the managers' presentations to deal first with finances, then technology, and then human resources and communication.

All these decisions should be driven by strategies that will help you to make the most of all of the talents of your speakers.

ANSWERING QUESTIONS

You must also be prepared to answer the questions you will be asked in relation to your presentation. If there is a question you are afraid of, you must consider it carefully and prepare to answer it.

Before you begin your presentation, inform your listeners that you welcome their questions, but ask them to leave them until the end of the presentation. This is the best place for questions, because your train of thought can easily be broken by the interruption, and listeners may find their questions are answered anyway during your presentation.

Look directly at the questioner as they speak. Repeat the question for the rest of your listeners if you think it is necessary to ensure that all your listeners hear it, or if you need a little more time to arrive at an answer.

You can also consider question time as an opportunity to fill in any details or add emphasis to arguments that you had limited time to address during the formal presentation. Regard question time as an opportunity, not a threat.

If you are working as a group, you will also need to prepare for the answering of questions: you must know who will answer which questions and how, on the day.

In our experience, most speakers relax and handle questions well; question time usually gives them an opportunity to discuss ideas that their listeners have a special interest in, and the task becomes a reward. While it is not always possible to answer all questions, always promise your listeners you will find the answers.

OWNING THE BEST OF KITBAGS

Effective communication is based on exhaustive preparation. Preparation is your secret weapon. It is the resource that the great speakers use to make persuasion look easy. You will have a kitbag that is worth owning if you use the tools and follow the system we have outlined in this chapter. In other words, fill your kitbag with as much know-how as you know how.

TIPS

- Prepare mentally with positive imaging.
- Prepare physically with relaxation and posture awareness.
- Be sure to prepare a clear purpose statement.
- Remember to research, brainstorm and carefully evaluate and select the ideas for your topic.
- You need to structure your topic to maximise its appeals (turn to the next chapter for details on structure), and you need to clearly outline your topic to prepare for your presentation.
- Find creative ways of presenting your material through examples, words and images. Use visuals if possible. Prepare handouts if necessary.
- Go through a rehearsal stage, doing early drafts of your speech on audio-cassette.
- If you are doing a group presentation, you need to follow all of the tips above, but also consider the importance of your team structure.
- In all cases, prepare to answer any possible questions.

Structuring for listeners

I haven't the time to be brief.

George Bernard Shaw

LISTENERS NEED LEADING

We always like to begin a training session on presentations with a listening exercise. This not only emphasises the significance of listening, but also, very importantly, reminds speakers of the difficulty of listening, and the necessity to plan for listeners as part of preparation for a presentation. Listeners cannot read back over previous paragraphs as readers can, and so your presentation must lead your listeners to your desired goals. We cannot emphasise strongly enough that speakers must structure their presentations in such a way that listeners are clearly led from word to image, image to idea, idea to concept.

In this chapter we will spend more time working on the introduction and conclusion sections of speeches, as well as looking at the structural patterns you might use in the body of a speech. We will also introduce you to a secret but important ingredient which we have called the 'glue' of presentations. That great playwright and master of words, George Bernard Shaw, knew that concise selecting and structuring was time-consuming, and we use his timely reminder at the beginning of this chapter. His seven brief words highlight the vital importance of allowing time for preparation, and of doing it with our listeners in mind.

To demonstrate our central point in this chapter—the point that structure must not be cluttered or complicated, that structure must be clear and precise—we want you to do this simple exercise with a friend.

Exercise

Ask your friend to give you clear instructions on how to get to a reasonably distant destination. The instructions should be three or four detailed sentences which you are not to interrupt with questions. You are to listen to, then repeat, those instructions. We are certain you will find this simple exercise quite difficult. And the point? If it is hard to remember a set of short instructions clearly, it will be very hard to comprehend a longer presentation. If you are interested in further work on this aspect, we have included one of our favourite listening exercises at the end of the chapter (you will have to gather together a group of friends or colleagues for a full exploration of the exercise).

Let us now investigate some of the 'knowns' that will help you to achieve a suitable structure. It is time to bring the skeletons (for those presentations) out of the closet.

PRESENTATIONS NEED A THEME

Winston Churchill had read Aristotle and took to heart his idea that a speech should always have a theme. Churchill's colourful, or should we say melodic, way of emphasising this was to say 'A speech is like a symphony. It can have three movements, but it must have one dominant melody: dot, dot, dot . . . dah', and he would hum Beethoven's Fifth.[1] This great speaker is alerting us to the point that a good speaker should be able to sum up their message in one or two sentences, and structure their main points in support of that one- or two-sentence theme. We have already established why this structuring must not be complex: we are now to establish how. Let us call on our 'kitbag of knowns' once again as a starting point. We know the simple rule of two and four: prepare no more than two main points for a ten-minute presentation, no more than four main points for a twenty-minute presentation, and emphasise these points. Now marshal your other points into sub-points and use them as support. We, as human beings, organise our world into patterns for greater ease of understanding, and it is very important that you, as a speaker, do this necessary work of structuring for your listeners.

THE SKELETON OF THE PRESENTATION

Despite our experience in preparing presentations, we still find structuring for listeners difficult work. It requires time and effort to organise a simple and focused structure. All speeches should have a clear and definite introduction and conclusion. These are best left until towards the end of the preparation stage because they must make a strong impact, and you want to know the shape of the rest of the speech before you craft them. First, work on the two to four main points which make up the body of your speech. If you are speaking for more than twenty minutes, work on the principle that you should allow at least three to four minutes to fully develop any point you are going to make.

Now that you know the general structure required for an effective presentation, you need to choose a pattern of organisation for your points. Do not choose a pattern that best serves your listeners, or a pattern that best serves your topic, but a pattern that best serves both listeners and topic—a pattern that best serves your purpose. You can appreciate, as we do, why structuring is such a complex, time-consuming task. Arranging your ideas in a particular pattern can affect your opportunity for persuading your listeners to your point of view quite dramatically. It will allow you to focus on some aspects of a topic and perhaps underplay others. Let's examine your choices: your pattern could be chronological; spatial; causal; topical; theory and practice; or problem and solution.

Chronological pattern

A chronological pattern works well when you want to reveal the history behind your topic and a development of your points through time. Listeners find it easy to follow a logical, sequential time pattern. But you must be sure it is the best organisation for your topic; you must consider that a chronology limits the development of your topic to the extent that you look only at those points which are relevant to your time sequence.

Spatial pattern

This arrangement focuses your topic by organising points according to relationships to place. Representatives of a multinational company, for example, may wish to compare the procedures of the company in different places, either to point out that different regions require different approaches, or to point up the superior effectiveness of aspects of one of the approaches. In this situation, you may mention the approach in the USA and the approach in Great Britain as well as the approach in Germany. The spatial pattern best suits your purpose here.

Causal pattern

This arrangement of material organises your ideas according to what you consider to be the causes of a problem. When using this approach, you have to be very careful to avoid the 'laundry list' presentation (that is, an enumeration of a long list of causes or issues). There is nothing more boring than a laundry list in any situation: you have to stay eternally vigilant to avoid it. If your topic or problem has many causes to be considered, indicate this, then move into an analysis of the most relevant.

Topical pattern

This is a common and useful means of organising. You can say, for example, that there are four aspects which need consideration and then simply consider each of those four aspects in turn. Do not use more than four points, as this is another pattern which can lure you into a laundry list. You need to prioritise your points. Listeners will tend to be most attentive at the beginning of the presentation, as long as you have not lost them with a poor introduction.

Theory and practice pattern

This approach outlines the theory behind a situation and then moves to show its relevance through practical examples. It is sometimes useful to use your practical examples first, and then tease out your theory. This pattern is powerful for training presentations.

Problem and solution pattern

This pattern focuses your listeners on aspects of both problem and solution. Make sure that you state the problem clearly, and make sure that you balance the presentation. If you want to concentrate listeners on solutions, be careful not to deviate and spend most of your presentation describing problems; rehearse and time your presentation so that your problem description is clear and concise, and then you can move on to the solutions which need the most emphasis.

Case study

Here's an example of how you might structure a topic like population control.

Consider this page two headline: 'Population boom hits poorest countries'.[2] Many members of the United Nations and the world's governments were to make presentations to address this issue. As an example, we will explore this important debate and outline some possible structures to suit their presentations.

Some members of the UN would have the purpose of convincing listeners to enact a worldwide population growth control agenda; others would have the purpose of convincing listeners to act against an unethical 'worldwide social engineering project'.[3]

Let us look at the argument for worldwide population growth control and see how we would pattern such presentations to serve our purpose. In a business context, you could be a public relations officer attempting to get support for an overseas aid project that specifically addresses the problem of population control.

- Chronological pattern: examine the history of population growth; outline the smaller population of previous centuries; emphasise that this problem reached a critical point in the twentieth century, and in the twenty-first century may overwhelm our future.
- Spatial pattern: refer to the fact that population growth is a greater threat in Africa and Asia than it is in Europe and the USA; suggest a diversity of solutions.
- Causal pattern: examine the problems arising from population growth and assert that, as population growth is the cause of these serious problems, it must be addressed. Or, look at the causes of population growth and consider how these can be addressed.

- Topical pattern: examine many and various methods of preventing population expansion, and, depending on purpose, point up the benefits or ill effects of each of these methods.
- Problem and solution pattern: clearly outline the problem and then move to a detailed section on suggested solutions (this pattern chooses a balance between the two aspects of problem and solution).

We think that the problem and solution pattern will best serve our intention, our listeners, and our topic. We will use this pattern to model a full outline and a speaking outline for such a speech later in the chapter.

Special patterns

The motivated sequence is another well established pattern of organisation for the persuasive presentation. Developed by two speech communication experts,[4] the motivated sequence is a form of problem and solution and has five steps: attention; need; satisfaction; visualisation; and action.

Using our population example, these steps would be applied like this:

1. Attention: capture the interest of your audience for population control. The attention step is important to all presentations and we will examine it in detail later in this chapter.
2. Need: define the need that the speaker believes listeners share, for example, the need to overcome the problem of overpopulation.
3. Satisfaction: describe how we can overcome this problem. In this case, it may be how population can be decreased by birth control.
4. Visualisation: stimulate the vision of the better world which will eventuate after the need is fulfilled—a controlled population.
5. Action: emphasise what must be done, and done now. In our example, it is to activate possible controls which will be proposed. We will suggest these in our speech outline in the ensuing pages.

Consider the motivated sequence as another of your tools and another of your choices, and experiment with it.

DON'T FORGET YOUR AUDIENCE

Remember that you have to adjust your structure to suit your audience. There may be some persuasive strategies you need to keep in mind which will influence which structure you choose. Here are some pointers which will help you to adjust your structure for particular audiences.

- If you are speaking to an audience who will oppose your proposal, you may need to use the 'yes, yes' approach, or try to unbalance (consistency theory) the audience's beliefs. Remember to establish your credibility as strongly as possible. Always use evidence, but especially so for the doubting audience.
- For the discriminating and knowledgeable audience, you must marshal your evidence carefully and never overstate. A knowledgeable audience usually prefers to hear both sides. You will also need to address their possible objections.
- With a sympathetic audience, you can afford to use evidence to dramatise rather than prove. You can use a more motivational speech, you can use colourful, intense language and you can afford to overstate rather than understate to capture their imagination and hold interest.
- With an uninformed or less knowledgeable audience, research suggests that a simpler one-sided approach is more useful. Be sure your listeners understand your argument before you move to motivation.

All of these aspects influence your careful preparation. Depending on which pattern you choose, you change the emphasis on particular facts which may support your argument. The best way to work on your structure skills is through practical experience.

Exercise

Go back to your map of ideas which we suggested you should draw up as part of your preparation in Chapter 4. Choose a pattern which serves your purpose. Now that you have made that choice, structure your ideas around that pattern. Now it is time to move to the outline stage.

THE OUTLINE

How might we outline a presentation to lead our listeners? Let us return to our population topic and do an initial draft outline which we can turn into speaking notes later.

Purpose

To persuade our listeners to support proposals for sustainable population growth through worldwide family planning measures.

Theme

A grossly overpopulated world will threaten the well-being of all those on the planet: this is not just a problem for developing countries.

Main points

1. Problem
   a. Problems for population growth in developing countries.
   b. Problems from population stagnation in rich countries now placed under pressure from international migration.
   c. Problems from population drift to larger and larger cities.
2. Solution
   a. The United Nations be funded to introduce programs for family planning in developing countries.
   b. A program of education for men to motivate them to consider the advantages of family planning.
   c. The empowerment of women to make choices about planning through better access to quality health care, education, and increased economic power.

Within this problem and solution organisation we have a topical order. You could also structure chronologically, spatially, or by causation within these problem and solution sections. Figure 5.1 shows the notes we would make on postcard size speaking cards to serve as the life-raft for this presentation.

THE INTRODUCTION

Once you have developed a well-structured body for your presentation, you can start to work on your introduction and

Figure 5.1 Our notes looked like this

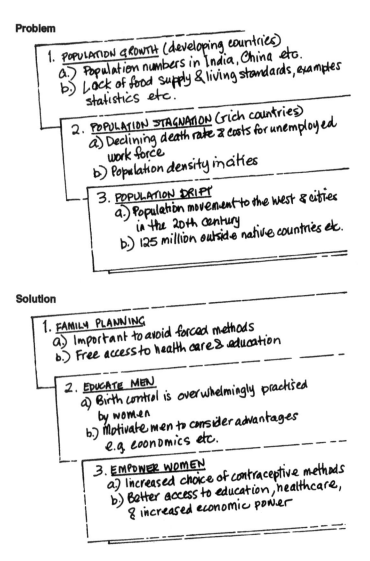

Problem

1. POPULATION GROWTH (developing countries)
   a.) Population numbers in India, China etc.
   b.) Lack of food supply & living standards, examples statistics etc.

2. POPULATION STAGNATION (rich countries)
   a) Declining death rate & costs for unemployed work force
   b) Population density in cities

3. POPULATION DRIFT
   a.) Population movement to the west & cities in the 20th century
   b.) 125 million outside native countries etc.

Solution

1. FAMILY PLANNING
   a.) Important to avoid forced methods
   b.) Free access to health care & education

2. EDUCATE MEN
   a) Birth control is overwhelmingly practised by women
   b.) Motivate men to consider advantages e.g. economics etc.

3. EMPOWER WOMEN
   a.) increased choice of contraceptive methods
   b.) Better access to education, healthcare, & increased economic power

conclusion. The introduction is very important because it is often the aspect of the presentation which causes the audience to decide whether you are worth listening to. It must, then, function to get the listener's attention and to give listeners direction. In some situations, if you and your topic have not been introduced to the audience beforehand, the introduction will have to perform the function of revealing the details of your topic and showing that it is worth listening to. You may also need to establish credibility early in your presentation and ensure that the listeners know a little about you. In summary, then, there are four functions of the introduction:

1. to get your listeners' attention
2. to outline the topic
3. to establish credibility
4. to give your listeners direction and so provide a map of your presentation.

Remember that a speaker does not just 'get' attention; the words 'grabs' or 'commands' are commonly used with 'attention', and this is what we exhort you to do. Be daring, and be prepared to do the work to compel your listeners to pay attention to you. There are many means of getting your listeners' attention: tell them why and how your topic relates to them; capture them with a quotation; make a striking statement; ask them a rhetorical question; tell them a story; tell them a joke; give them a shock. Whatever you do, add detail to make your statements concrete through the senses, and carry your listeners along with you.

A recent example of breaking through to reach the audience reminded us of the power of imagination in great communication.

Sir Richard Branson, the likeable and clever entrepreneur and owner of the international airline carrier Virgin Blue, showed us exactly how to grab attention when, as an introduction to a speech on a takeover bid on his company, he opened his presentation with a poker face. He started his speech, with a cheque in hand:

> After much deliberation, we've decided to sell to Ansett [another airline]. I'm afraid that in Australia, you just don't have the competition policies to attract smaller businesses . . . anyway, I'm off to England with my $250 million cheque and thank you very much.

The room stood still. His staff, the media and business watchers gasped.

Then, after a few moment's silence, a broad, warm smile came across Branson's face:

> I'm just joking! This Virgin bride is not for sale. I just wanted politicians to realise how people would actually think if Virgin Blue was no more.

This last statement was delivered as Branson tore up the cheque into tiny pieces, blinked back some tears, the audience cheered, and some of his staff rushed to the front of the room to kiss him for the cameras.[5]

Obviously, you can use the emotional responses of your listeners if you, and they, can handle it effectively.

Here are some other examples of this technique.

Case studies

At a conference presentation on organisational behaviour, the speaker asked all of her listeners to imagine they were bumper cars and to bump around the room, as bumper cars do, bumping into each other. She then asked them to stop bumping and to move smoothly. The conference was entitled 'Beyond Bullying'; the speaker was using the analogy of the bumper cars to demonstrate the roughness of bullying others, as opposed to the finesse of manoeuvring through situations. As you can imagine, this is a very effective action to get listener participation.

Another good example of an introduction intended to give listeners a real start was a presentation by an executive of a security organisation at a trade exhibition in England. This gentleman began by walking up to delegates' desks, rifling through their papers, then swishing them to the floor. When the room looked completely ruffled and the listeners completely startled, he said, 'How would you feel if you walked in and found your office or your study looking like this?' Of course, the solution to this problem was to install one of his organisation's security systems.

Imagine the presentation we heard from one student speaker who began with a role-play of three people eating dinner.

Suddenly one of them falls to the floor, obviously having a heart attack, while the others sit stunned. The speaker, a nurse in the organisation, comes forward and asks who of us in the room can help this man because the other people sitting at his table do not know how to assist. Most of us are forced to confront our ignorance of first-aid and the helplessness we would face in this situation. The shock and reality of the role-play motivates us to listen doubly carefully to the speech and her message to attend a first-aid course as a matter of urgency.

We will describe one more introduction in the creative and daring category, especially as this introduction was an outcome from a somewhat nervous and conservative group we encountered in training, and it surprised and encouraged us greatly. It followed a workshop where staff of a large organisation were preparing presentations for management on quality service. We challenged them to come up with introductions that would capture management's attention. Although we did not see the actual presentations, one of the staff present was 'knocked over' by this introduction.

One member of the group walked across the stage, as if floating, with a balloon held above her head, while the other members looked skyward in amazement, saying: 'Look, there's a hot air balloon, it looks as if it is in trouble. It is going to land right here on the oval.' The balloon holder floated to her knees and looked up dazed to ask: 'Where am I?' 'You are 5 metres from P block,' her colleague replied. 'What?' 'You are 10 metres from A block.' 'Where?' Her colleague eventually replied: 'You are in a balloon basket on the oval in front of the main building of the company.' The dazed balloonist then said: 'You must be from professional services.' 'How did you know?' was the surprised reply. 'Because you always give us belated, accurate and not very useful information,' was the answer.

The group successfully drew management's attention to the key concerns of their presentation, and thus to the changes they felt were necessary to improve the quality of the communication coming from their section.

Some alternatives

If you are concerned about the creative difficulty of coming up with such a daring introduction, or if you are worried about the personality required for carrying it off, remember that, for the sake of originality, it is worth learning that the risk is worth taking. There are, though, some gentler means of introduction for the beginner, and more fitting means for the style of some presentations.

For example, as the first step, in order to get attention for the presentation on population boom which we used earlier in the chapter, you might:

• quote the overwhelming figures on infant mortality in developing countries

- describe life on $1 a day
- state the numbers of people migrating to the wealthier countries, and raise questions about this trend.

As these ideas suggest, there are many and various, softer options.

Note that Winston Churchill's opening to his first speech as Prime Minister was just a few well-chosen, well-spoken words, but they are remembered by all of us in English-speaking countries: 'I have nothing to offer but blood, toil, tears and sweat.'[6]

Case study

One of us was recently asked by the Equity Department of our university to speak in a mock debate on the affirmative on the topic that SNAPs (Sensitive New Age Persons) make better managers. As is so often the case, there was little time to prepare. I went, in haste, to the dictionary of quotations and found the words of Thomas Fuller, spoken 250 years ago; 'Soft words are hard arguments.'[7] This would just have to do as a theme for my presentation and as the attention step in my introduction. It went something like this:

> We are going to prove to you today that Sensitive New Age Persons make better managers. Why do they make better managers?, I hear you ask. Because they will create a workforce which is more productive and less stressed. They, at last, have learned the truth of what Thomas Fuller said more than 250 years ago, 'Soft words are hard arguments.'

This attempt managed successfully to lead the audience into this debate without resorting to some of the more daring but effective techniques we have illustrated.

Making the most of your introduction

In our experience, introductions are often not introduction enough. Speakers spend too little time creating a context for the body of their presentation and too much time making the assumption that listeners are acquainted with the topic and its situation. Speakers should spend the time and take care to actually introduce listeners to their topic and its situation, and to direct their attention to the main points in the body; they should not be afraid to launch their presentations with daring, nor should they be afraid to take risks to be original.

The lessons are:

1. Be creative.
2. Be as daring as you can comfortably manage.
3. Capture your listeners: do not ever ease in while your listeners ease out.
4. Once you have prepared your introduction, it and the conclusion of your presentation are the only parts you should know by heart. Remember that they are dialogues (shaped to be spoken, not written to be read).
5. Time your introduction. If you are speaking for ten minutes, your introduction should be about one and a half minutes long—long enough to preview your presentation before your transition to the body; short enough to clearly mark its own end and prepare listeners to make a commitment to your ideas.

THE CONCLUSION

The conclusion should be concise, punchy, and reiterate your theme. The biggest mistake you can make in conclusion is to linger too long (a conclusion for a ten-minute presentation is not lengthy: you have about thirty seconds).

The conclusion to the Sensitive New Age Persons debate (remember that it was instigated by the Equity Department of the university) went something like this:

> The only solution is to offer a prayer to the goddess: Please send us SNAPs. For those who have no choice and must survive in the workforce, and those of us who have a choice and want a career—send us SNAPs. Save us from being left between the two extremes of being somewhat bored and—if the research be true—often sozzled in the suburbs, or, on the other hand, caught into the syndrome of the superwoman. Send us SNAPs to help us find the sanity that is somewhere in between. For truly, 'Soft words are hard arguments'.

These words, with the action of kneeling in prayer, made a strong ending to a humorous approach to a serious topic. It enforced the theme that SNAPs would secure a more productive and less stressed workforce in which women could participate more comfortably.

We earlier mentioned Alan Alda's impressive speech to the College of Physicians, included in the appendix. The conclusion to this presentation, 'A reel doctor's advice to some real doctors', is one of our personal favourites:

> Well, that's my prescription. I've given you kind of a big pill to swallow, but I think it'll make you feel better. And if not—well, look, I'm only human. I congratulate you, and please let me thank you for taking on the enormous responsibility that you have—and for having the strength to have made it to this day. I don't know how you've managed to learn it all. But there is one more thing you can learn about the body that only a non-doctor would tell you—and I hope you'll always remember this: The head bone is connected to the heart bone—and don't let them come apart.[8]

That is the conclusion to a very moving and entertaining longer speech. It uses the analogy of the medical prescription in its language to appeal to the specific listeners, young doctors. It fulfils its task of congratulation and leaves them with a punchy line that sums up the essence of Alda's message on the importance of a 'human kind of doctoring'.

Of course, if you are capable of it, there is nothing that compares to the crescendo: it is incomparable as a conclusion to a motivational presentation. We have quoted the best we could possibly find; perhaps the best crescendo there has ever been. It is the conclusion to American civil libertarian Martin Luther King's now famous 'I have a dream':

> When we allow freedom to ring—when we let it ring from every village and every hamlet, from every state and every city—we will be able to speed up that day when all of God's children, black men and white men, Jews and Gentiles, Protestants and Catholics, will be able to join hands and sing in the words of the old Negro spiritual, 'Free at last! Free at last! Thank God almighty, we are free at last!'[9]

Notice how carefully structured these final words of the speech are. Notice the use of repetition and the use of structuring into three-part messages—'black men and white men, Jews and Gentiles, Protestant and Catholics' or 'Free at last! Free at last! Thank God almighty we are free at last!' Martin Luther King had the ability to make a speech which was both creative and coherent. Let us now look at those techniques which will help you to achieve coherence in your presentation.

THE GLUE

What do we mean by *the glue*? The idea of glue helps us to imagine the adhesive qualities of the many connectives you need to make a coherent presentation. The parts of your presentation must be glued/connected/woven together to clearly lead your listeners *through* to your ideas, *to* your intention. There are four aspects of the glue you need to understand and must learn to use: signposts; transitions; internal previews; and internal summaries.

Signposts

We have just given you an example of signposting. These are simple, helpful directions for the listener. 'There are three main points. Firstly . . ., secondly . . ., and, lastly . . .; the most important point, however, is . . .' They can be simple questions: 'Why does this occur?' 'How can we solve the problem?' Signposts show the listener where you, and they, are going; they point out your organisational pattern as it happens.

Transitions

Transitions are the bridges you build for your listeners from one part of your presentation to the next: 'Now that we have explored . . . let us turn to . . .; we have spent a lot of time talking about . . . it's time now to discuss . . .' These bridges help the listeners to understand the relationships of parts of the presentation to each other, and of each part to the whole. Transitions are, therefore, very important to orientate listeners to your map of ideas or the strategic plan of your topic.

Previews and summaries

Internal previews and summaries give the listeners a similar opportunity to one they enjoy when they can look back over what they have read, or skim forward into the next paragraph. Provide these previews and summaries within each major part of your presentation: say what you are going to say in this particular part, say it, and then summarise what you just said. Simple, but vital. Here is an example from our population topic mentioned earlier:

> [Transition] Now that we have seen how serious the problem of world population growth is, let's look at some solutions. [Internal preview] I will concentrate on three solutions in particular—possible United Nations programs for family planning; a program of education for men; and ways of ensuring the empowerment of women. Let us look at each in turn. [Signpost] Firstly, family planning . . .

An internal summary invites the audience to pause for a moment to recapitulate what has been said so far, and then summarises the earlier points.

For example, we have outlined a simple map of a structured presentation: (1) *the introduction*; (2) *the body*, which consists of clearly marked points in clearly marked parts; (3) *the conclusion*; and, holding the good structure together (4) *the glue*, which consists of (a) *signposts*; (b) *transitions*; (c) *internal previews*; and (d) *internal summaries*.

LISTENERS NEED FURTHER HELP

In other chapters of this book, we have detailed ways in which you can further help your listeners: the words you choose can create the images they see; the experiences you choose can help to focus and direct the emotions they feel; the concrete examples you choose, or detailed statistics you don't, can help your listeners to a clearer understanding. The arrangement you choose, and the research you do, can help make your points more relevant and your presentation more powerful.

Exercises to promote structure

Practice listening with the Rumour Clinic

For this exercise to be successful, you need at least five or six people. You can have multiple observers, but you need at least one person to note the additions, deletions, and distortions of the message that occur during its transfer.

Keep one person inside the room and send the four or five others outside to a point where they cannot hear your conversation, and then pass this message to your remaining friend, the first listener:

> I could tell that the three men were doing something secretive. One was a well-known city lawyer, but the other two were slightly shabbily dressed and seemed nervous. The lawyer handed the first man some money and the second man a large envelope. I did not see what the men handed to the lawyer before they walked away, but it was something small and apparently valuable.

Bring the outsiders in, one at a time, to hear the message passed on by each previous listener.

You will be shocked, we are sure, to notice that the message changes quite drastically from its original, as it is transferred from one listener to the next. Even the most highly educated listeners, who may be used to complex material, find that they confuse elements of the message. This shows the difficulty of listening, and emphasises the point that if you do not lead your listeners and structure simply and clearly, your listeners will not comprehend or remember what you have said.

Answer the questions posed by the six honest men

Look back over some speaking situations you have been in, or imagine yourself forward in a future situation, and practise an organised approach by following Rudyard Kipling's simple direction:

> I keep six honest men,
>   They taught me all I know,
> Their names are what and why and when,
>   And how and where and who.

- *Who*: put down any important information about your real or projected listeners here.
- *Why*: put your purpose down clearly here.
- *What*: make your theme statement here.
- *How*: make a plan of your structure here.

We are sure you will not forget the final questions of *where* and *when* (nor forget to check every aspect of the venue if it is not a place you are familiar with). Also do not forget to plan the most suitable *where* and *when* for your audience if you have the choice.

Practise glueing

Take some of the ideas from the presentation you have outlined and experiment with connecting words: practise making transitions from one idea to the next.

Practise making an internal preview and an internal summary.

Now ask yourself which areas would benefit from signposting? Do you have any points which should be clearly marked *firstly, secondly,* and *finally*?

PUTTING THE SKELETONS INTO THE KITBAG

It is always worth working on interesting introductions and conclusions and, of course, practising possible outlines for past or projected topics. Even if you are already a good speaker, this approach may help you to improve your standard. If you are a novice speaker, this approach will help you to focus your preparation and be confident of your ability to present and to present effectively. If you have followed this chapter closely and taken the time to do some of the exercises, your kitbag shall surely be a little heavier, having to carry all of those bones around. But we are sure that you will be able to produce some very serviceable skeletons when they are needed.

TIPS

- Always prepare with your listeners in mind—your structure must be clear and able to be followed with ease.
- Unite the thoughts of your presentation around one clear theme.
- Make a clear one-sentence purpose statement to identify and maintain focus.

- Your presentation should have an introduction, a body and a conclusion. It is best to prepare the introduction and the conclusion at the end of your selection stage when you have the best material to choose from.
- Be daring and creative at the beginning of your introduction to capture the attention of your audience.
- Do not leave any points in mid-air. Each point should be developed and clarified. Therefore, follow the rule of two points for a ten-minute presentation and four points for a twenty-minute presentation.
- Examine the six possible patterns we have suggested and decide which best suits your intention, your audience and your topic.
- Work from a general outline and develop a speaking outline (a life-raft of notes) with your main points on cards, in prompt form, to steer you through on the day.
- Make sure that your speech is carefully glued together with signposts, transitions, previews and summaries.

6

Using language

White House speechwriter James Humes described his approach to his work in these words:

> *I'm a translator. Not French into English, but the bureaucratic into the poetic, the legalistic into the eloquent, the corporatese into the conversational, the complex into the simple.*[1]

Imagine that you have just arrived at a meeting to hear an important presentation by your CEO about the future of your organisation. You sit down full of apprehension about your future. You concentrate on what the CEO has to say. You know it has implications for your career. You harness your energy in anticipation. You would be very disappointed if your CEO chose to speak to the group in language which was distant and cold, particularly if you were an expectant and possibly fearful audience.

Now, by contrast, imagine an important meeting that is one of four important meetings you will attend today, a busy day. You find it difficult to tune in and stay tuned. You find it even more difficult to make a contribution, let alone make a commitment. At times like this, it is very difficult for a speaker to involve you and the other busy members of the audience.

Whether the situation be one where it is hard even to get a hearing, or one where your audience is motivated to hang on every word, it is important to use the full power of expressive language to capture and hold your audience.

REALISE THE POTENTIAL OF LANGUAGE

We have observed that when inexperienced speakers are preparing, they often invest all of their energy into determining the content of the presentation, into *what* they want to say. By focusing on this aspect, they lose the opportunity to bring those ideas to life through clever language choices. Therefore, this chapter invests all of its energy into language, by providing some guidance on *how* to say what you want to say.

Language is slippery

Many misunderstandings arise and many speaking opportunities are lost because words have different meanings for different listeners. Meanings move and change with different contexts and with different situations. Thus, explaining the real meanings of words becomes complex and difficult work.

Words have two different kinds of meaning, the denotative and the connotative. The denotative meaning is the one we find in the dictionary. It is the literal meaning which describes an object, action or feeling. As speakers, we assume that many of the words that we use will be understood at dictionary level, at the denotative level. Yet as listeners, we know that many meanings are misunderstood because speakers assume that their listeners know as much about the topic as they themselves do. For example, a recent informative presentation that we attended on using electronic mailing systems was not as effective as it could have been when, in question time, it became apparent that many listeners did not understand many of the meanings of the terms that the speaker had used throughout. The speaker had undoubtedly forgotten just how many new terms she had used as she explained the new system. The listeners had been reluctant to acknowledge their 'ignorance' in 'public'.

The connotative is the more complex and more challenging level of meaning. It is the figurative meaning, the implications, the emotional and experiential connections of a word. This meaning may not always even be at a conscious level of understanding. For example, most contemporary organisations are keen to develop a mission statement. Let's consider the connotation and denotation of the word *mission*. The denotation of the mission statement is that it is a description of the goals that the company aims to achieve. The connotations are richer and much broader. Imagine all the missions you know of: grand representations by governments to venture into space or by religions to civilise barbarians. Now imagine your own mission statement. Unless you work for a fairly unusual organisation, it is unlikely your mission will be so grand. But the decision to use the word *mission* to describe business activity is a good strategy. Other possible choices, such as goal, direction, or purpose statement, do not invoke the same commitment and sense of excitement. That choice of word may make all the difference to the way we approach an exercise of writing the goals of the company. It is clear that finding the right word can make all the difference.

Many great speakers who have become powerful leaders have demonstrated to us that they valued language as an important tool for achieving their purpose. John F. Kennedy chose to use the word *pledge* rather than *promise* in his Inaugural Address to demonstrate what he perceived as the binding nature of his agreement to become President of the United States. While both words have similar denotative meanings, the connotations of *pledge* are more powerful: *pledge* is connected with heartfelt commitment, law and duty. *Promise*, on the other hand, is used more commonly in everyday interactions and is somewhat more light-hearted. Another example is Winston Churchill's coining of the now accepted term *summit* to represent the meeting of great leaders for the most important of matters. Apparently he came up with the idea while looking out of his Moroccan hotel window at the grandeur of the surrounding mountains. His inspired choice has influenced later generations to continue to think in terms of geography to describe our important political meetings because the term captured the importance of the meeting so well.[2] This is a great example of the importance of combining creativity with clarity in choosing words.

Language is powerful

Language can harness your listeners' energy in a way that recourse to hard facts cannot. While images of the ongoing unrest and killing between Israel and Palestine remain uppermost in our minds, many still recall the powerful image of the quest for peace of the late Prime Minister of Israel, Yitzak Rabin. Rabin made a powerful presentation in 1993 when he met with Yasser Arafat to shake his hand and so attempt to end nearly fifty years of terror in Israel and Palestine.[3] He started his speech by proclaiming the opportunity for peace that such an agreement between Israel and the Palestinians offered. He contrasted peace with violence and war. By linking war with violence, he managed to shift the meaning and experience of war to a personal and emotional level, and to rob it of some of its abstract and impersonal connotations. Look for the language and ideas which give his presentation such power as you read this section of the speech.

After acknowledging the difficulty of the peace process for both countries, Rabin began:

> We have come from Jerusalem, the *ancient* and *eternal* capital of the Jewish people. We have come from an *anguished* land. We have come from a people, a home, a family that has not known a single year, not a single month, in which mothers have not *wept* for their sons.
>
> We, the soldiers who have returned from battles stained with blood; we who have seen our relatives and friends killed before our eyes; we who have come from a land where parents bury their children; we who have fought against you the Palestinians, *we say to you today in a loud and clear voice—enough of blood and tears.*
>
> Enough!

Of course, in such situations emotions run high. However, both leaders believed that it was time for peace. Rabin chose his language carefully. He knew that, while he had to remain a statesman, he also needed to harness the emotional commitment of his countrymen to peace.

He described, in a style reminiscent of a chant, a seemingly endless list of Israeli experiences. He started his sentences repeatedly with 'we' to identify himself with the experience of the ordinary Israeli. He then brought this to a sudden close, with the short sharp words, 'we say to you today in a loud and clear voice—enough of blood and tears. Enough'. The effect of 'enough' came not only from its short consonants and syllables, but from its contrast with the long and doleful sounds of the words 'ancient', 'wept', 'eternal' and 'anguished'.

This final phrase echoed around the world again in November 1995 at the time of Rabin's assassination. This news clip was chosen by most television producers to capture the essence of the man of peace, and to highlight the irony of the violence of his death in stark contrast to his own exhortation—enough of blood and tears. Enough! The loss of this powerful leader, and with him his language of leadership, made many fear for the future success of the peace process in the Middle East.

Rabin could easily have chosen to be straightforward. He could have chosen the facts and kept them brief. He could have said: 'We have had enough of war and suffering. There has already been too much death. Let's make a peace agreement now.' While the content is right, it lacks emotional impact.

Most of us will never be called upon to make a presentation to which the whole world could respond, but most of us can learn from the power of his oratory and the powerful rhetorical choices he made to achieve his purpose.

USING LANGUAGE CLEARLY

It is very important to use clear, accessible language, especially when you are explaining difficult or complex ideas. Avoid clichés and meaningless phrases.

To assist you to explain difficult ideas, use concrete language. This will help you to be as clear in your explanations as possible. Recently, one of our students was preparing a technical presentation on a highly sophisticated device which allowed different computers to work in tandem. He came up with the concept of describing their operation as 'talking to each other in a common language when it is mother tongue to neither'. This concrete language choice helped the management and marketing staff understand the complexity of his device.

One of our clients was presenting a case for an increase in staff training. We suggested to her that until her listeners started to think of management as real people, with real abilities, real strengths and real weaknesses, they would clearly not realise the specific aspects of training that staff needed. She built in our suggestion. She asked them to imagine their most impressive managers and then she introduced them as Sue and Bill. These two managers became the motifs for all the arguments she mounted in her case. She asked her audience to consider the implications of improving perform-ance in concrete terms—in terms of real people—not in abstracts. Her audience responded very positively to her use of these

Figure 6.1   Avoid clichés and meaningless phrases

Cartoon: Fiona Mitchell

characters and, judging by questions asked at the end of her presentation, had started to consider the serious flaws in the logic of saving money by limiting training programs.

These examples demonstrate the importance and the potential of careful language choices which make your presentation not only understandable enough, but concrete enough, real enough, to draw a personal response from your listeners.

USING LANGUAGE HUMOROUSLY

Humorous language can be a useful device for gaining attention, maintaining attention, and building rapport with your audience. But use it carefully, because it is possible to offend your listeners.

One of the safest ways to use humour and not abuse any listener is to target yourself. Pick an element of your topic that you want to emphasise and point to your own weakness. In a recent training session that we observed, the trainer claimed, with a straight face, 'I have never been guilty of keeping quiet in a meeting to save my job. I am always absolutely honest about what

Figure 6.2   Humorous language can be a useful device

Cartoon: Fiona Mitchell

I think.' Silence. The listeners were still. The statement was outlandish. Their response was tentative, then committed laughter. Everyone in the room read the wry smile and feigned innocence of the trainer as an entree to acknowledge their own strategic decisions to be less than honest at times. By her admission of the need to put herself before her organisation on some occasions, using humour, she demonstrated her common experience with her listeners. By using a comic style, she opened up the topic of strategic communication and managing impressions in an unthreatening way which eased her entry to the more difficult aspects of communication management.

Adapt and personalise old jokes, one-liners and stories, and use them. Adapting quotes and one-liners provided the framework for a very well-received after-dinner debate for an Australian Labor Party fund-raising function that one of us was involved in. Calling on the wit of Oscar Wilde, amongst others, provided both humour and sharpness in a serious comment on the use of a quota system to give women a start in politics. Wilde's 'Women are a decorative sex. They never have anything to say, but they say it charmingly', and Benjamin Franklin's 'Women die as poets sung, /his heart's the last part moves, her last, the tongue', provided ample opportunity to demonstrate the barriers facing women in a light-hearted and entertaining way.[4] We have included this speech, 'Do women still need a leg up?', in the appendix, to provide an opportunity for you to think about how you might use humour.

In a student presentation on industrial design, the speaker started by telling the story of standing on the curb and witnessing an accident. When he rushed over to hear the dying words of the victim, he was requested, in whispered gasps, to send an urgent fax back to the office. The speaker responded to these gasps by telling the victim that all was well because he had 'just invented a public fax which will solve all your problems'. The absurdity of the suggestion that a dying victim could have all her problems solved by good communication made his audience chuckle. He had successfully gained our attention, charmed us with the absurdity of the situation, and introduced us to the idea of the public fax system, all in one humorous story.

We advise you add humour to amuse, not to abuse, listeners. However, you may wish to use sarcasm, exaggeration and cynicism to add humour. These techniques are much loved by many politicians. They can sometimes be used to great effect when referring, in-house, to your competition. Wartime ex-British Prime Minister Winston Churchill was renowned for his imaginative and effective use of language. He was a master of the art. One of our favourites is his definition of compromise: 'An appeaser is one who feeds the crocodile, hoping it will eat him last.'[5] Ex-Australian Prime Minister Paul Keating's taunt to the Opposition that 'being attacked by you is like being hit with a warm lettuce' is one memorable example from an extensive repertoire.[6] This style of humour may not amuse you, but it is useful to be aware of it, as it is handy to have it in your kitbag.

You can use humour when you are facing a difficult topic which requires tact or leads the listener through sensitive ideas. We were asked to make a luncheon presentation on National Secretaries' Day. We were intensely aware of how much secretaries, poorly paid and relatively undervalued, have been stereotyped merely as female attendants to the 'brains of business' or as maternal figures, and we were committed to challenging these stereotypes. We were also aware that the senior staff of our organisation would be present at the luncheon and that it could be difficult: any challenge to the stereotype could be taken as a criticism of their management.

We decided that the only way to handle such a sensitive topic was to use humour. As so many important issues are handled by secretaries with so little acknowledgement, we scripted a role-play with secretaries answering phone calls in the absence of management and solving important problems for their clients. We acted out a conversation with Rupert Murdoch, who wanted to buy our large city office site for his new developments, and we found a solution for a serious fault associated with a city bridge design. One secretary answered her phone like this:

> Good afternoon, Faculty of Engineering. Can I help you?
> No, I'm sorry, the Dean is overseas at a conference.
> The end of July. No, Professor is at a Senior Staff Conference. Could I take a message?
> Yes . . . Victoria Bridge, yes, swaying . . . yes, immediately . . ., yes, avoid catastrophic accident.
> Just a moment, I believe we do have a file on long-term super-structure inclemency fatigue. Hold a moment, I'll see if I can help you. Yes, here it is . . . I think you'll find it is the fourth pier on the left as you're coming from the city side. Yes, 0.0053 megamils above the water line.
> Yes . . . well I think you should try inserting the hydrophile steel energiser injections at 0.0053 megamils intervals on alternative mainframe stress lines. Keep accurate rigour flume readings during the tide turn at 13.20 hours, and relax the strummels on the overdecking at the Melbourne Street end . . .[7]

And so the secretary went on to handle this complex engineering problem.

Both the secretaries and management responded positively to the unsaid truths about the unequal distribution of rewards and respect in organisations. Laughter rang out as the secretaries proudly acknowledged their competence to handle the many complex situations they faced each day, and their bosses could gently admit that outward appearances can deceive us into failing to recognise talent when it is clothed in the garb of the traditional secretarial image.

Complex material which is apparently rather dry can also be difficult to handle. By being imaginative, you may be able to ease the burden for your listeners by explaining these ideas in a novel or humorous way. A recent presentation by an accountant on tax planning was enlivened by his use of the image of a monkey swinging through a tax jungle. He extended the image by suggesting that, with the support of a guided tour with an expert, the jungle would take on a whole new meaning and the fruits of the labour would be many: 'Instead of lurching from disaster to disaster, you will swing smoothly from treetop to treetop.' He added a sense of fun to what was otherwise a serious business. While the audience were amused by his technique, they were also stimulated to listen carefully to his simplified explanation of the role of the accountant in guiding them through the complexities of making investments.

USING LANGUAGE VIVIDLY

Successfully selling your idea can often depend on how vividly the images of your ideas are formed in your listeners' imaginations. Compare these two ideas and consider which image is the more encouraging:

> When you throw litter on the beach you spoil our community. It costs the Council a lot to employ staff to clean up. This is added to your rates. Littering is everyone's responsibility.

> Every time you throw your Coke can or your stubbie, or leave your McDonald's wrapper on the beach, you spoil our beautiful pristine coastline. The Clearwater Council now employs four full-time workers at a cost of $100 000 a year to collect our rubbish. This adds an average of $1 a week to our rates. The next time you are tempted to drop that stubbie on the sand, or you see others leaving rubbish about, take a stand. Our beaches will be more beautiful and our rates will be cheaper if we all take responsibility.

A vivid image of your point of view encourages listeners to engage with your ideas. Paying attention to your language choices can be rewarding for you and your listeners. What about this startling image: 'When you are up to your armpits in crocodiles, it is difficult to remember that your primary purpose is to drain the swamp.' You could use it to jolt your audience out of their daily rut and encourage them to pay attention to the important issues.

BUILDING YOUR RESOURCES

Collect stories and quotes that could help you to build humour into your future presentations. Keep your eye out and your kitbag open for books of jokes, famous sayings and stories, and keep a file of newspaper cuttings and witticisms that you come across on radio or television.

USING RHETORIC STRATEGICALLY

There are some other simple language techniques which you can build into your presentations which will support your good ideas. These include using rhythms, repetition, images, metaphors and analogy. It is worth asking yourself, as you near the end of your preparation, whether you have used some of these techniques. It will require your conscious attention to the detail of your language if you do this, but the rewards will be evident on the day of the presentation.

Rhythm and balance

Experience tells us that most speakers believe that the only place where there is rhythm in speech is in poetry. However, it is possible to create interesting rhythms in ordinary speech with some simple techniques. The energy and effort are rewarded by the responses of listeners who remember catchy phrases.

Pairing words of opposite meaning can achieve this rhythmical effect. Two common examples are those famous or perhaps infamous phrases of the 1960s and 1970s, 'Make love, not war', and the feminist catchcry 'The personal is the political'. Pairing opposites like this simplifies ideas and is memorable.

British Prime Minister Tony Blair used this strategy to make his point: 'Power without principle is barren, but principle without power is futile.'[8]

One of our clients, when describing the land use of a national park, chose to describe the way Australians use their parks as either to 'love them to death' or 'ignore them'. By contrasting these two very different uses of the parks, the phrases helped her to highlight the problem of trying to maintain pristine rainforests while at the same time encouraging people to use them.

We were overwhelmed recently by the effect of this strategy, when one of our students quoted from a letter she had read on the Internet, purported to be from a student from the high school where the Columbine massacre occurred in the US:

> The paradox of our time in history is that we have taller build-ings, but shorter tempers;
> Wider freeways, but narrower viewpoints
> . . .
> We've cleaned up the air, but polluted the soul;
> We've split the atom, but not our prejudice;
> . . .
> These are the times of tall men, and short character; steep profits, and shallow relationships;
> . . .
> It is a time when there is much in the show window and nothing in the stockroom; a time when technology can bring this letter to you, and a time when you can choose . . . either to make a difference or just delete!

This dramatic piece shows the strategy at its best.

Similarly, management consultant and writer Rosabeth Moss Kanter described the way business should do business as 'more with less'.[9] This could be used in a presentation as a theme for your organisation.

Do not be afraid to frame your ideas in simple terms. Balanc-ing the complexity of your argument with the clarity of your ideas is one of your greatest challenges. Using this approach of pairing opposites or contrasting terms not only helps listeners to under-stand what your ideas are: these phrases may become the most quotable quotations that your listeners take away with them.

Repetition

You can also repeat sounds or words regularly to add interest and impact—and to add rhythm and balance—to your presentation. Bill Clinton, speaking with admiration about Nelson Mandela, used the words 'unbowed, unbroken and unembittered'. Clinton's simple repetition of sounds is not only lyrical but powerful. He emphasised the strength of Mandela, who refused to buckle under the weight of the state. Al Gore turned to repetition at his accept-ance of the Democratic nomination: 'I believe we must challenge a culture with too much meanness and not enough meaning.'[10]

Andrew Denton, the Australian television personality, added humour when he described football in the following way: 'the liniment is imminent and the tournament of the disfigurement of the ligament is upon us'.[11] A simple message can be underlined using repetition. One community organisation fighting a freeway proposal was looking for a slogan to stop the development. They found it in simple repetition: 'The wrong road in the wrong place for the wrong reason.'[12]

Imagery

Images—vivid images—can gain and sustain attention and stimu-late your listeners' thinking. Because of our desire for comfort and a lack of ambiguity in our lives, most of us, most of the time, fall into the obvious ways of thinking about a topic. Presentations frequently demand imaginative thinking and daring responses. One of our clients, faced with considerable opposition to her human resource management reforms, took this challenge seriously. She used the language that accountants are most comfortable with, the language of numbers and statistics, to talk about the people they were dealing with. She engaged her captive accountants on their own territory:

> How should we measure human achievement? Not just in output, in bottom-line terms. We are talking about human achievement. But I'm on dangerous ground here—yours is the world of figures—the measurement of quantities.
>
> I want to draw on my experience to suggest that such an approach has difficulties and dangers. It is important not to put too much weight on simple measures.
>
> After all, do we want to see ourselves in such neat terms? Perhaps I can suggest that not until death do we want to become a simple statistic.[13]

Notice the careful choices like 'bottom line', 'weight', 'simple measures' and 'statistics' that contributed to her image of the danger of talking about people as if they were numbers.

Working with engineers took on new meaning for us after we listened to a presentation made by the managing director of a large mining and engineering organisation. He explained to his listeners that the word *engineer* has been associated with images like engine drivers on railway trains and mundane mechanical activities. He suggested that this word–image association limits our appreciation of the profession of engineering. 'Instead,' he said, 'I always think of the origin of the word from its French derivative *ingénu* which, of course, is also the origin of our word "ingenious".' His new association has changed our thinking irrevocably.

Metaphor and analogy

Rupert Murdoch, CEO of News Corporation, one of the largest global media organisations in the world, has worked hard over the last two decades to sell his vision of how a world linked by technology has the capacity to change history. He needs the commitment of world business, of world governments and of other media organisations to make his vision a reality.

In the beautifully crafted presentation to the Asia-Pacific Business Congress which we referred to briefly in Chapter 3, Murdoch demonstrated his sensitivity to the importance of language to motivate his listeners. Consider this image of a yacht sailing on the open sea as a strategy to motivate this region of the business world to commit to his vision:

> There's a precise analogy to sailing—you can sail along slowly, being content with slow but sure progress. Or you can spread your sails and catch the winds; it takes intelligence and quick reflexes. But it's faster. And more fun.
>
> On top of which, there's this further point: when the wind blows strongly enough, it will capsize you anyway—even if your sails are furled. And some of Australia's protected and obsolete industries are already shipping water.[14]

His analogy is a rich and complex way to conceptualise his vision of our global future. There is room in it for both sailing and sailors. He uses the sailors to represent the approaches to problems: they can either be cautious or take risks. The sailors who take chances are characterised as intelligent and skilled, the cautious ones as plodding. Characteristics of yachts are used to heighten the dangers of being cautious—the boat may capsize under a strong wind anyway, or if the technology is old, the boat may 'ship water'.

Murdoch rouses his audience with the possibilities for the future in a way which stirs the imagination more powerfully than would—than could—any appeal to reason. Remember that if you want to get some tips from Murdoch, 'Venice of the Southern Hemisphere' is reprinted in full in the appendix.

Women leaders often find it difficult to position themselves as capable leaders. Here's how one woman used an analogy to present the strength of her leadership.

A visual aid of the image of Boadicea, the brave British warrior queen who fought against Roman oppressors, supported this opening statement:

> Deciding how to position oneself is always the most challenging task for any potential candidate for a leadership position. I have always identified with Boadicea as a role model for the sort of leader I want to be. She was a strong leader. She was someone who always led from the front. She was also a master strategist, many times managing to outwit the military might of Roman forces who far outnumbered her, and she was committed to giving voice and action to the will of her people.[15]

USING STORIES STRATEGICALLY

Listeners love stories. For most of us, the pieces of a speech that we take home with us to share are the stories told and the remarkable, quotable statistics. Speakers, then, should use them as strategies for committing pieces of their presentation to listeners' memories. You can use them for many different effects, such as to open a presentation, to form a bridge between speakers or to illustrate a point. They must, of course, be relevant, they may be humorous, and they must be short.

They can refer to the situation, a similar situation, a strongly contrasting situation, or even the venue. Here's an example to illustrate how useful it might be to put energy into finding a story. It could be used to highlight the importance of innovative and divergent thinking for business. You could tell the old story of the shoe salesmen who were sent to Africa to expand the business. The punchline, framed as two telegrams from two different salespeople, could go something like this:

> SALESPERSON 1: I am coming home stop there is no market here stop nobody wears shoes stop.

Salesperson 2: The market is ripe here stop there are fantastic opportunities stop no one owns shoes yet stop.

This story offers the perfect opportunity to comment on the role of imagination and initiative in the development of technical or business innovation without turning the comment into a lecture for everyone involved.

PUTTING LANGUAGE IN YOUR KITBAG

In this chapter, we have given you many strategies which will help you to develop an interesting presentation. Sometimes, in our rush to get our ideas ready, we can overlook the way the language available to us can liberate our thinking about a topic and give us a fresh approach to a problem. Coming up with an imaginative way to describe a problem or event can make the difference between success and failure for your efforts. Even in our everyday lives, it is worth reflecting on how we describe a situation. Once we start to really listen to how we are describing an event or an organisational procedure, we may start to realise that our present language limits our thinking. We have offered a selection of language devices that, if you carry them in your kitbag with you at all times, can help to enliven, charm, or even inspire the most difficult of audiences.

Exercise

Here's an exercise to get you thinking about the language of your everyday organisational practices.

Choose a procedure that you would like to change in your organisation. Write out a description of how that procedure works, one you could use for your co-workers.

Now, think of an analogy which you could use to show why it is not necessarily the best way to do it.

List all the characteristics of the analogous objects, just as we did in the Murdoch example above. By thinking about the topic in this new way you will probably find new characteristics of the procedure that had not occurred to you before.

Try also to think of a humorous or dramatic story that you could tell about an event surrounding this procedure.

You might also play with the title of the procedure, trying to find words that start with the same letter, or phrases that describe it in dramatic ways.

This would be a good way to develop your awareness of how to improve your language choices.

TIPS

- Pay particular attention to the language you use when preparing a presentation.
- Be daring with the language you choose—creative choices will repay you many times. Don't forget that the repetition of either sounds or words can capture the listener's ear.
- Use metaphors to help you generate new ways to think about a problem. Your language will set you free.
- Collect quotes, stories, newspaper articles, photographs and cartoons—resources that you can call on when you need to do a presentation. It will save time and worry if you have them at the ready.
- Remember to include at least a couple of quotable quotes in every presentation, so that your audience can take a little of you and your presentation away with them to their next meeting or business luncheon.

Using non-verbal language

*People can understand gestures because of an elaborate and
secret code that is written nowhere, known by none, and
understood by all . . .*

Edward Sapir[1]

As we proceed through our busy lives, most of us are hardly
conscious of how people communicate. In fact, just working out
what our co-workers and friends are saying to us seems task
enough. Just occasionally, we are brought to a halt as we feel
puzzled by a whole range of signals which seem confused and
even contradictory. At times like these, we start to be aware that
so much of our communication comes, not through the actual
words that a speaker is using, but through all the other signals the
human race has developed to give meaning to their experience.
This complex set of signals, which includes those produced by the
voice and the whole body itself, are non-verbal or non-word
codes. Those codes can give us even more information than the
words we use.

Consider this extraordinary description of Bill Gates, Chairman
and chief executive of Microsoft Corporation, which was reported
in an article about Gates's brilliance as an entrepreneur. The interviewer gave us a strong sense of the electric atmosphere generated
by Gates:

Most alarming of all, while talking he rocks incessantly. This rocking is not a minor tic, it is a violent motion. He sits forward in his chair, his forearms resting on his thighs and his hands clasped. Pivoting on his buttocks, he swings back and forth so hard that the soles of his shoes slap in a continuous noisy rhythm against the carpet.

His pale, staring eyes look down or directly at you. Occasionally he bangs the table as if to check that the contents of his head have reached the external world. Sometimes the rocking is not enough to disperse the energy and he suddenly stands up, does a quick five-pace circular walk and sits down again.

This is intimidating stuff, but it can be contained, the rock can be stopped. If a question demands something of him that he is not expecting he collapses back into the chair, completely immobile. Easiest of all is to stop the rock with something personal.

'You got married recently . . .' or 'I know your mother just died . . .' and, instantly, he freezes into the paralysed collapse and the harsh, loud voice fades almost to a murmur.[2]

Bill Gates has become a legend in this age of the information superhighway. His eccentricity has been one of his trademarks. From this description, it is clear that it is a little difficult to miss the non-verbal messages Gates is sending. However, most of us are constrained by codes of behaviour that may have us dismissed from our jobs for such lack of conformity to the ideal of the controlled and poised executive.

CRACKING THE CODE

Edward Sapir wrote the epigraph used at the beginning of this chapter in 1928, and it still rings true today. Perhaps we tend to think of an 'elaborate and secret code' as something subtle, but certainly in the case of Bill Gates this code could hardly be overlooked. Since the 1920s, a considerable amount of research has been dedicated to non-verbal communication: it has revealed the power of our voices, posture and gestures, and it has proved Sapir right. Non-verbal codes carry a higher percentage of the message than verbal codes, and they are more trusted by listeners than the actual words we use: 'when verbal messages contradict nonverbal ones, adults usually believe the nonverbal message'.[3] A way to help us think about non-verbal codes is to consider them as a language: a language whose structure and meaning we may not always consciously understand as completely as we understand those of verbal language, but whose impact affects us just as significantly.

We learn, sometimes consciously, and at times quite unconsciously, about non-verbal language through verbal descriptions. When, as a culture, we say someone is 'afraid to lose their head', we refer to someone who holds their neck stiff to maintain their control; when we say someone is 'anxious to get ahead', we refer to the posture of reaching forward from the neck. There are many examples which reveal how we have internalised and reproduced our awareness of posture and gesture and their links to personality in verbal language.

Researchers suggest that whenever human emotion is concerned, non-verbal communication is involved. We are animals who still carry around the imprint of our preverbal language, the language of Sapir's 'elaborate and secret code'; it allows us to sum up others quickly, and it still determines our feelings of fight and flight, of power and vulnerability. Every reader of this book will realise that any assertion that rationality rules in business is a ruse. We are highly intuitive animals, prone to making many decisions in business based on emotion and, thus, on the information we receive from primarily non-verbal communication. We usually protect our decision by immediately finding rational bases for these emotional responses or by talking about a 'gut feeling'.

There is no easy formula to follow to answer the questions surrounding the meanings of our non-verbal communication. We do know that these meanings are strongly influenced by the culture which has shaped us. By culture, we do not mean only ethnicity, but the many cultures of class, education, religion, the media, our parents, our peers—whatever and whoever has influenced our personality and shaped our individuality. Yet, despite this cultural diversity, research into theatre practice has revealed that there is a universal non-verbal language of emotions which forms a base for the non-verbal languages that develop in different cultures.[4] Thus, we can expect a degree of shared understanding of non-verbal messages between all speakers and listeners, but a much smaller degree of understanding for the subtle nuances of messages unless speakers and listeners share the same culture.

Remember that, as both speakers and listeners, we are constantly making cultural and individual meaning:

> There is a property of behaviour that could hardly be more basic and is, therefore, often overlooked; behaviour has no opposite. In other words, there is no such thing as non-behaviour or, to put it even more simply; one cannot not behave. Now, if it is accepted that all behaviour in an interactional situation has message value, i.e. is communication, it follows that no matter how one may try, one cannot not communicate. Activity or inactivity, words or silence all have message value; they influence others and these others, in turn, cannot not respond to these communications.[5]

We cannot avoid sending non-verbal messages. However, we can exercise greater control over the messages we send. We must, therefore, first crack the 'elaborate and secret code' of those messages—get to know them—before we can control them.

One thing is certain. Our reaction to non-verbal language is often instinctive and immediate. How often have you said or heard the statement 'there is something about her' before hearing the descriptors 'I don't trust her' or 'I like her'? How often have you assessed almost immediately if the speaker addressing you is interesting to you or not? First impressions are important; we must appear immediately worthy of attention. First things first, then: we must crack that system of codes that influences such assessments. Let's get cracking. After all, the content of our presentation is really just the tip of the iceberg.

APPEARANCE

The influence of appearance has been emphasised, if not overemphasised, by the power of media images in western culture. Understand western image politics and you will understand the power of your individual appearance.

When Margaret Thatcher, the first woman Prime Minister of the United Kingdom, came to power, her advisers changed her clothes, her hair, her voice, her image. She appeared more tailored, far less feminine, far less fussy than before the election. She wore clothes in strong colours, especially 'royal' blue; she wore jewellery in the classical style; she wore her hair in a smooth coiffure. To avoid any gender stereotyping, her advisers changed

her voice, removed the strident tones and added the more androgynous tones of her deeper register. There were no risks taken with
the first woman Prime Minister in a western democracy! They
'lowered the pitch of her voice by forty-six hertz—half the difference between the average male and female voice',[6] and her
changed voice contributed to her new control at Question Time.[7]
They even hired advertising agency Saatchi and Saatchi to coin the
phrase 'Iron Lady', which emphasised her new androgyny. They
realised that the politics of Thatcher's image were dependent on a
detailed attention to her personal appearance, including the
'preservation of her blonde hair by regular tinting and elimination
of a gap in her teeth by dental capping'.[8]

People in the public eye often have makeovers. You have
probably seen photos of the considerable changes in the image of
that other female success story in western politics—Hillary Clinton.
As a young woman at university, Hillary's appearance fitted that of
the young woman activist of her era. Her dark shoulder-length hair
was ungroomed and she wore thick-rimmed glasses and little make-
up. This is a very different image from that of the well-coiffed,
blonde, non-spectacled, expertly made up and classically dressed
high-profile woman who has become the Senator for New York.

We read messages from one another's bodies. Experts on body
language have concentrated on exploring the more controllable
aspects of posture, gesture and facial expression. The truth is,
however, that very definite cultural stereotypes have developed,
which cause us to make certain assumptions about people's characters based on their body shape, facial physiognomy, even
colouring.

Naomi Wolf's *The Beauty Myth* attempted to expose definite,
cultural stereotypes that we have accepted about women and
beauty.[9] That blonde women are vulnerable and dark-haired
women are dominant is one of the more obvious stereotypes that
influence our readings and misreadings of women in western
culture. It is interesting that Bertolt Brecht, the famous German
dramatist who attempted to expose the underlying agendas of his
audience, dared to cast a heroine who, according to the British
critics of the day, was plain and had fat legs. This unusual action
immediately drew attention to our expectations of beauty and, of
course, its automatic link with the images of those we are
supposed to look up to.

In his 1995 book *The Perfectible Body*, Kenneth Dutton looks at the western ideal of physical development and notes that the cult of the undeveloped body accompanied the counter-culture of the 1970s and was 'just as emblematic of underlying values as that of the muscular hero figure'.[10] He notes the specific political connection between the swing back to the right in the 1980s in America and the re-emergence of the muscular hero—such as the characters represented by Stallone, Van Damme and Schwarzenegger. There is no doubt that there is a politics of appearance and it is just as well to realise this, and to respond to it as sensitively as you can.

You may not be able to change the basics of your appearance, but you can adjust aspects of your physical presentation and so send positive messages to your listener. You may be overweight and embarrassed by your size. But the overweight person who accepts their physique and is fit and healthy, who dresses in an attractive way, and who demonstrates that they love communicating with others, will present an attractive self-image.[11]

You are able to modify some aspects of your personal presentation either to support or to subvert those messages sent from your image. What is dubbed personality is really presentation skill. Margaret Thatcher was blonde, but no one would read vulnerability from this attribute in her case. The other aspects of her non-verbal communication, which her advisers so carefully emphasised, ensured that she could not be stereotyped as a fussy, feminine, grocer's daughter, but would be seen as a classical, powerful, androgynous leader.

William Hague seemed to face a far more difficult image problem in his race for Prime Minister in 2001. It was said that where Tony Blair had really trumped William Hague was in the battlefield of public perception. There were complaints that in image politics the battle for style over substance had certainly been won. The worst descriptor that Tony Blair had to overcome seemed to be that of a 'boy scout' image. Poor Hague, on the other hand, was referred to as a 'nerd' with 'an awkward public manner' and 'completely lacking in charisma' with disparaging references to his vocal quality, which we discuss fully in Chapter 8 on voice.[12] Jeffrey Archer, the Tory MP of some fame and infamy, was moved to comment vociferously to the television reporter when speaking of the opportunity to become Prime Minister: 'Is it an immediate qualification to be tall and good looking? William has had to suffer in the cartoons and in photographs because he is bald at a young age. Does this mean however clever you are, if you are bald don't

Figure 7.1   William Hague faced an image problem in the 2001 British election

apply for public service. What a ridiculous situation!'[13] I suppose that the burning question to ask ourselves is: could Hague have overcome these physical attributes, which seem to be less appealing, in the way he presented himself?

Hollywood was so interested in the controversy that surrounded the media coverage of the response of a young mother to the unusual manner of her child's death that US actor Meryl Streep came to Australia to depict her in a film called *Evil Angels*. There was a lesson to be learned about audience response to appearance here. After the death of her small baby in Central Australia, the mother, Lindy Chamberlain, claimed that the baby had been taken by a dingo. In her case, some Australians came to a 'guilty' decision very

Figure 7.2   Tony Blair won on the battlefield of public perception

quickly because Lindy appeared 'stony faced' and 'did not cry' on television when telling her story of these events. These outward non-verbal actions convinced some members of her audience of a malevolent force within. We believe that her conviction was very much influenced by these non-verbal messages; she was later pardoned. It is easy to see that if you do not show the non-verbal responsiveness that people expect, they are prone to distrust you.

Therefore, you can see that it is important to decide to put some energy into working on your non-verbal image; you must make controlled and conscious choices about the messages you are sending and readers are reading.

IMPROVING YOUR APPEARANCE
Fitness

In recent years, most of us have become aware, whatever our body's appearance, of the benefits of fitness. A fit body reflects someone who exercises and who pays attention to posture and relaxation. Our first tip, therefore, for an appearance of health and well-being, for an aura of energy which is important to a strong presentation style, is fitness. A fit body breathes better and, when you are interacting, your breathing needs to be relaxed and your body free. Because of the vital importance of breathing, we discuss it in detail in Chapter 8 and outline exercises there for a better breathing technique. It is of vital importance because, in the words of one of our expert colleagues: 'If you control the breath, you control the thought; and if you control the thought you control your emotions; and if you control your emotions, you control your behaviour, and thus . . . the situation.'[14]

Breathing

Breathing is a code that reveals a lot about you to your audience: if your chest is tight and your breathing shallow, listeners read anxiety. That anxiety could then cause *them* anxiety, lessen your credibility, or allow them the opportunity to dominate the interaction. Our executive clients are often sceptical about the importance of breathing until they see themselves on film or video and see the camera pick up the tightness that our training has taught them to read. To enjoy a strong breathing style, keeping fit is essential; and to enjoy a skilled presentation style, knowing your image and how your readers see you is essential.

You are what you wear

Good grooming is also essential to a strong presentation style but—and this is our second tip—you can go one better. You may realise which clothes and colours most suit your personality and colouring. Colour experts will give advice on which tonings will suit you best to bring out your vibrance. You can then choose clothes and colours that control your image—to support or subvert the non-verbal messages people are receiving. For example: a shy, petite or submissive woman may choose to subvert her image. Strong colours that she normally avoids will add zest to her presentation skills and make her presence more dominant in an important situation.

Examine the image you want to communicate and spend time matching clothes; examine the situation you have to communicate in and spend time matching clothes. It is important. Do you want to communicate 'powerful', 'professional', 'significant'? Do you want to communicate 'relaxed', 'approachable', 'comfortable'? John Molloy's *Dress for Success* matches clothes to situations and speakers to readers.[15] One example of how this matching proved successful remains in our memory:

> This approach worked for Phil Dusenberry, chairman and chief creative officer of the New York advertising agency BBDO. When pitching the Apple computer account ... Dusenberry says his team 'left our six piece suits at home and dressed down—in sports jackets—for the presentation'. The folks at Apple wear jeans and open-collar shirts, 'and we didn't want to come off as slick New Yorkers', Dusenberry says. It worked. BBDO landed the account.[16]

These decisions can powerfully influence the readers of your image. And remember that these decisions are critically influenced by the fashions of the day. Try to overcome any blocks you have about paying attention to fashion or appearance. Attention to your appearance is part of your professional preparation to do a good job and so you need to do it well. However, as the Apple example demonstrates, there are no set formulas to follow, because changing time and changing situations influence what determines an appropriate image and personal presentation style.

The importance of being adaptable and aware of looking right in the business community was the subject of a recent newspaper article.[17] In it, we are told that 'dressing down has failed to deliver value internally and externally'. On the other hand, the jury is still out on where corporate dressing is headed. In some of the large international firms, which were the first to adopt corporate casual, there has been a return to a suit and tie policy. Bill Gates is now wearing a suit in many business appearances, so the 'slick New Yorkers' would have to think carefully, and do their research again, to decide upon the appropriate dress for the occasion. As dress is an important personal and organisational marketing tool, knowing how to dress appropriately for the occasion and the times is essential.

OTHER ARTIFACTUAL COMMUNICATION

The artifacts that you own and wear—jewellery, watch, glasses, handbag and briefcase—send important messages about who you are and how you think. Choose accessories like glasses that do the most for you in your image of a 'professional'; and choose differently to do the most for your image of 'approachable', especially if you are doing media interviews. Although Oscar Wilde expected a laugh when he wrote 'A well-tied tie is the first serious step in life', he knew there was an element of truth in it. Men still have the opportunity to use the tie to introduce different nuances of tone to their dress. Study magazines and television and ask yourself how meaning is made from each image by the choices of clothes and artifacts: collect this knowledge and understanding of how image is read for your kitbag. Remember that Margaret Thatcher's advisers even changed the style of her jewellery because they knew that it was an important code of communication.

POSTURE

Posture is one of the main indicators of your power and confidence. It is, therefore, of particular importance for it to carry the meanings which most support your message. You are able to do a great deal to relax your body and correct your posture. As consultants, we often have to work to correct posture problems. It is worthwhile to check your posture, recognise any weaknesses and work on them—and this will benefit your health as well as your image.

Have you heard of the Alexander Technique? This was the name given to the ground-breaking work on body awareness and posture done by the Australian-born actor Frederick Alexander, who became famous in England earlier in this century. His influence is still very strong today amongst those who work on the voice and body. It was so influential that all primary schools in England used once to incorporate some Alexander work in the daily curriculum. In a nutshell, it works on keeping the body free, open, relaxed and aligned, with the spine always rising. Alexander believed that the freedom of the body contributed to the freedom and openness of the mind, and this idea is supported by many educationalists. His technique became so well known that it was commended in the Nobel Prize-winning address of one of England's famous physicians.

An Alexander exercise

If you drop your head back and slowly lift it up until you feel the weight of it is perfectly placed in alignment in a spine-rising position, this will help body awareness. Check in the mirror that you are not craning the neck and thrusting the chin or pulling the chin in. Imagine a string pulled directly up through the top of your head.

Stand erect with your head and body clearly aligned, your muscles relaxed, and your breathing uninhibited. Place your arms by your sides and get used to the feeling of them hanging loosely. This is the best position of repose to allow you to move into gesture when you are speaking to an audience. Using these techniques, you will achieve good posture: you will be read by your audience as relaxed and open, with an aura of strength and confidence (Figure 7.3).

Posture problems

Assess your posture in the mirror or on video, and check for some of the common problems we list below. Before you begin, realise that your head is very heavy. It is important to keep it in alignment (with its weight well balanced) both for appearance and to avoid neck pain.

Do you show any signs of the problems depicted in Figures 7.4, 7.5 or 7.6? These are common posture problems which make you look powerless and are often compounded by slumped shoulders.

On the other hand, also avoid the dominance of the posture shown in Figure 7.7. In this case the chin is tilted above alignment position, which reads as overconfident or arrogant and is often compounded by raised eyebrows and eyes looking down judgementally.

Of course, a stiff posture, as well as being strained, can look defensive and unapproachable. One position, which has been humorously described as the stalagmite posture, has shoulders back and arms held stiffly at the sides. Avoid becoming a stalagmite. Another posture to avoid could be described as 'the dancer'—the person who cannot stay still, and moves from one leg to another or in little steps in a constant pattern of movement. Other ineffective postures are those of arms folded, which creates a barrier across the body and squashes the breath, or arms pulled

Figure 7.3 The body is relaxed, the head is balanced and the spine is rising

Cartoons: Fiona Mitchell

Figure 7.4 Posture is poor and hips are slumped

Figure 7.5 The neck is craned and the head is off-balance

Figure 7.6 The head is thrown back and the throat can be strained

Figure 7.7 Chin held high, eyes looking down the nose

Cartoons: Fiona Mitchell

behind the back, which looks too military, and also affects the breathing because the chest muscles are stretched.

Demonstrating confidence and relaxed power is all-important in presentations. The Alexander Technique is a great way to fight posture problems. You can improve through practice in front of the mirror, and look in your library to read more about it. Go back to your relaxation exercises and use these to focus your work on posture problems. If you are aware that your posture negatively affects your image and causes you health problems, then you should seek out an expert to work with you as soon as possible.

FACIAL EXPRESSION

People read a great deal from your facial expression. If you have a characteristic facial expression—a frown or a smile—your facial muscles begin to set into those positions and that frown or smile can be read as a permanent expression. Make the effort to smile, and suffuse your face with warmth and colour when you walk before an audience or a camera. It is easy to allow your nerves to deaden your expression; take the time to look alive and vital. Non-verbal research—published as long ago as 1969 but still true today—revealed that relaxed expressions are read as more persuasive than tense ones.[18] So relax your expression, smile, and breathe deeply before your presentation.

One of the most versatile faces in politics was that of Bill Clinton. This is obviously one of the secrets to his great success. The still photographs in the world's papers reveal a face that can carry great warmth and empathy, humour with head thrown back in laughter, tears of despair, and of course intense seriousness, as well as nuances of any of these more extreme feelings. There is no doubt that this facial responsiveness is one of the reasons that Bill Clinton is described by all who meet him as overwhelmingly charismatic. The more responsive we appear to others, the more they feel that they know us and can trust us.

EYE COMMUNICATION

Eye-contact suggests confidence on the part of the speaker. It carries a strong message to the reader, a message of self-assurance at least, and a message of power at most. European cultures, particularly, relate levels of trust to eye-contact.[19] You may think you do look at your audience with power, but check this with colleagues you can trust or with yourself in close-up on video. In training student speakers and in working in business consultancies, we find that 90 per cent of speakers do not use their eyes to full effect. It seems that lack of confidence produces flight, and people withdraw behind their eyes in any way they can, allowing them to become vague and not focused on the listeners. There are many rationalisations to support this withdrawal—'I looked away in order to think', 'I had to refer to my notes', 'I had to look at the slides.' If you want to be a speaker of influence, you must learn to use your eyes and feel at ease with their power.

Old clichés can hold a great deal of truth, and 'the eyes are the windows to the soul' is certainly one of these. We can learn a lot about the meanings that are generated by the eyes from a study of our favourite film and television actors. The good actor uses the power of the eyes to great effect. A study of the work of chameleon actors like Laurence Olivier, Meryl Streep, Sean Penn or Marlon Brando would reveal that the eyes can carry many moods. Eyes can be warm, smiling, confident, steely, staring, sultry, withdrawn, shielded, nervous or lifeless. I am sure you can think of many more adjectives to describe eyes you have seen. For the next month, spend some time concentrating, when you speak to others and when you are watching film and television, on the way people use their eyes effectively, or ineffectively, to communicate a mood or to establish credibility. The most important aspect of this exercise is your realisation that you must use your eyes to display expressiveness and gain full contact with your audience, whether that be one or many.

MOVEMENT AND GESTURE—KINESIC INDICATORS

Kinesics is the technical word for all aspects of gesture and expressive movement that the speaker uses. Your use of the kinesic code is a strong indicator of your personality and an important component of your presentation skills. Gesture should, of course, appear spontaneous and always help the viewer to focus on the meaning of your message. Small and fidgety movements or gestures, especially if they are repeated, become mannerisms and will irritate an audience, whereas strong generous gestures are living communication. Shakespeare had a great understanding of non-verbal as well as verbal communication, and

Hamlet's advice to the players is still sound advice: 'Suit the action to the word, the word to the action.'[20]

Practice is the most important aspect of gesture: practise until you perfect a natural and spontaneous repertoire of gestures, but practise during preparation time. Do not concentrate on gesture in your actual presentation. Just as we mentioned in Chapter 4 that working to free your body can help to free your voice, so, too, working to make your voice more expressive will help to free your body movement and gesture.

VOCAL NON-VERBALS—PARALANGUAGE

Paralanguage refers to vocal quality and use of oral grammar (yes, pauses and vocal changes are similar to commas, semi-colons and full-stops). We react, as we do to other non-verbal language, to paralanguage; we read the qualities of the voice and form opinions of the qualities of the person, just as we judge a letter by its clarity and use of punctuation. For these reasons, it is important that you have a free and expressive voice which is true to the mood and intentions of your message.

One of our friends, a medical doctor, made the surprising comment to us one day that he did not believe he would have married his wife if she had had a sing-song voice, as he found this such an irritating quality. He drew our attention to the deep, powerful quality of his wife's paralanguage and reinforced our belief in the importance of the voice to the response of the listener.

One of the best examples of paralanguage or vocal quality producing images and attitudes for listeners is the radio. Do you have an image of your favourite announcer on radio? Can you imagine their attitude from their vocal image? Do you infer gentle and mild, or strong and athletic, or hard and driven? Whatever your interpretation, realise that it is produced by vocal quality alone. Another good example of the power and importance of the voice to produce an image is the way we respond to an unknown voice on the telephone. Never fear—if you are feeling apprehensive about the quality of your own voice, we will be focusing on that in our next chapter.

MANNERISMS

Sometimes through habit, and sometimes through nerves, we develop body language characteristics which become mannerisms which can hold us back as communicators. Many executive speakers have mannerisms that should be avoided, or at least kept to a minimum. Mannerisms such as non-verbal fillers—ummms and aaahs—can be avoided by breathing in those empty spaces or by being silent. Silences are codes of control: use them as power tools to drill your message into the minds of your readers. Mannerisms such as moving from foot to foot or wandering, fiddling with pens or ties or jingling coins in your pocket, can be avoided by conscious relaxation of your body and especially of the chest and arms. Do not cling to the lectern or the chair while speaking to an audience. Mannerisms, such as repetitive patternings of your voice, also become irritations and need to be avoided so that listeners do not become distracted by them.

We recently watched a speaker whose left hand and left foot kept up a rhythmical movement along the side of the lectern in the most distracting manner—so distracting that we had to look away. His verbal presentation was magical, but it was impossible to follow with the non-verbal distraction.

While Bill Gates may be able to get away with his unusual style, another executive may become a source of amusement for such extremes of behaviour and thus detract from their credibility.

On one consultancy in London, we observed a very unusual mannerism in an executive speaker, representing the sort of extreme distraction that can intervene and obscure communication—the lifting of both hands up towards the face and then the clenching of them in a prayer position. This gesture was more appropriate to an archbishop celebrating High Mass in a grand cathedral than to a business speaker. He was young, his colleagues were all senior to him in age, and he may have unconsciously developed this mannerism to appear more mature. Unfortunately, he came across as pompous, and he certainly distanced himself from his peers. He was able to oust this gesture from his repertoire of gestures when he became aware of it, and this made a great deal of difference to his image as a speaker, and to his reception by his listeners.

One particular situation where this becomes critical is when you must present for the media. The camera will pick up small mannerisms of your face, such as repetitive eyebrow raising or lowering, or continuous blinking or not-blinking, which become large distractions in close-up. In general, you need to be relaxed and poised, your weight evenly distributed, your body perfectly aligned and ready to move into expressive gesture. Mental and physical discomfort or tension often cause repetitive gesture, and awareness of this tendency helps to control it.

PROXEMICS

Proxemics, as it is known technically, is the way we use space in interactions. Proxemics is an important code of non-verbal communication. Your use of space indicates the power relationship of your situation and the degree of intimacy or friendship of the interaction. How you position yourself indicates the degree of liking or disliking that you bring to the interaction in relationship to your listeners. Presenting in your own space gives you the advantage, always. If you wish to relax the others in an interaction, allow them the advantage and make the presentation in their space. You will probably have noticed that higher-status individuals occupy larger spaces—larger offices, larger cars, larger homes. This occupation of space is one of the non-verbals most culturally determined. Most western cultures, for example, do not live as closely together as do many eastern cultures and are, consequently, not used to interactions in close proximity.

But, when you present, regardless of culture, it is best not to be at a distance from your listeners. Sometimes this will not be possible, as for a really large audience you will have to go up on a podium to aid visibility. If our presentations are performances in our organisational life, then they are like theatre performances, and we must use the stage space to create the greatest impact. Do not hide behind props. Move with zest, or move in a way that gets you closer to one group of listeners to capture their attention, and then move again to interest another group. With large groups, play to the whole house. With large spaces, so as not to be dominated, work the space, take in the whole area with your eyes, expressions and voice, and use larger gestures than in more intimate spaces like the boardroom.

US communication consultant Nick Morgan recently reminded us of the importance of the 'kinesthetic connection' we need to make with our audiences in an article in the *Harvard Business Review*.[21] He believes, from his wide experience with business speakers, that most do not make the 'visceral, personal and emotional' connection needed to inspire trust and action. This is because they do not fulfil their audiences' need to experience a presentation on a physical as well as emotional and rational level. In his view, as in ours, the podium and the PowerPoint can draw the speaker away from their own power with an audience. One hundred years ago orators used large gestures for large audiences. With the advent of television, these are no longer in fashion, but an audience is also used to the televised close-up and wants to be able to see the speaker and feel their presence. Morgan suggests, as we have done, that you should 'walk the walk as well as talk the talk' in presentations. He exhorts you to use gestures, use the space, including the personal space of the audience, and take every opportunity to connect with them. Therefore, plan your presentations on a physical as well as content level, and then stay alert to the audience's physical presence and respond according to their needs.

USING NON-VERBAL CODES

Your video camera is your closest friend when using non-verbal codes. If you do not have one, use the mirror. Remember that you need to make bigger gestures and bigger expressions when you are working in front of an audience than you need for a camera. Therefore, it is important to note that if you are lifeless on camera, you will be dead, live. Exercise, then, in preparation, practising big gestures and expressions.

In our experience, executives who practise this exercise do not look over-expressive at all. They are just beginning to look lively. Most speakers are more likely to subdue rather than to extend their non-verbal communication. Whether this is due to the pressures of modern society or to an overcivilising process is hard to tell. Whatever the explanation, the fact remains that, for many of us, the expression of spontaneous emotion in communication, especially in front of an audience, is hard to achieve. Those who do achieve it are generally rated by their listeners as good speakers. Good speakers are also those speakers who can adapt to meet the needs of every situation. They have the ability to use powerful non-verbals, but they have the capacity not to walk across that fine line so that they overwhelm others.

Exercise

Experiencing the versatility of your non-verbal language

Think of a topic about something you either love or hate and make a presentation of three to five minutes fully expressing your appropriate strong emotion. Support your topic with explanations of why you feel the way you do, and focus on expressing your approval or disapproval as energetically as possible. Make an effort to 'ham it up', then check it on video.

Case study

Kerry Packer, an Australian media magnate, has been involved in ongoing collisions with the media laws. One confrontation is the source for this case study. His appearance before the Print Media Inquiry in 1991,[22] which was broadcast Australia-wide, was an example of powerful non-verbal communication. He had to convince the inquiry that he would not exercise undue control over the Australian media by the purchase of 15 per cent of the Fairfax media empire. His posture and his every gesture communicated the control he was there to deny. Look at the still shots taken from that presentation (Figure 7.8). They reveal a great deal about Kerry Bullmore Packer.

As he has not often appeared on television, there is little to no public expectation of the overtness of his non-verbal power. Yet his history—he is the son of Sir Frank Packer, once one of Australia's most powerful press magnates—and his posture and gesture, seen in still photographs, suggest the great reserves of power within him.

Packer used the Australian vernacular freely throughout his presentation, yet displayed an eloquence rarely seen or heard in Australian executive communication. He used the full range of his voice to fully express his attitude towards the inquiry (tinged with contempt), and he opened his large, powerful body and displayed absolute invulnerability to his detractors; he moved forward to make a point strongly and lounged back straight after to show his absolute belief in the strength and righteousness of his position.

He used his hands in powerful gestures, rhythmical repetitive gestures, as he reiterated his position as a bidder for Fairfax, a much-contested newspaper empire; he pounded his hand on the table to give determination and force to his statements. A current affairs commentator

Figure 7.8   Notice the open body and the expressiveness of the hand gestures

Source: Reproduced with permission of the Fairfax Photo Library, photographer Peter Morris.

that evening used the words 'amazing performance'; and even his detractors were forced to pay attention to him.

Performances like this, by virtue of their strength, cause a strong
reaction from the public, and polarise judgements. There was probably no
winning position for Kerry Packer in this situation. Even if he had the
ability to resort to them, humble non-verbals would not have served him
well in the eyes of his shareholders, employees or the public, who expect
him to be a man of power. The performance he gave was exactly what
would be expected of a powerful leader in private enterprise, and any
other would probably not have been believed. It certainly did not non-
verbally deny the assertions made by the inquiry that he might expect to
exercise control over the Fairfax group.

However, as a rich and powerful media magnate, Packer showed
apparent honesty and conviction in the immediacy of his non-verbal confidence. It was likely to have made this one of his more successful exposures
to public scrutiny. While the reasons for Packer's continued success as an
entrepreneur were apparent, the facts for a case against his versatility were
exposed. Could this powerful persona be capable of the role of a humble and
accepting listener? He balanced this power with excellent verbal examples
of his own tolerance: he recounted to the committee that one of his
best-known media journalists had once put a program to air which was quite
damning to Packer, but he had not lost his job for this. All the same, members
of the audience would have found it difficult to believe that anyone who
crossed Packer, or seriously disagreed with his point of view, would not incur
the same powerful opposition that he displayed to the inquiry.

MAKING THE MOST OF YOUR NON-VERBAL LANGUAGE

Versatility is your greatest strength as a communicator. Although
our case study has described facets of a powerful leadership style,
it is also important for you to develop the other side of the coin
and show, through your non-verbal behaviour, that you are a
sympathetic listener. One of the oft-quoted responses by employees when questioned about good leadership is: 'I like my boss;
s/he listens to me.' This should also be an important component
that you pack into your kitbag.

ORGANISATIONAL NON-VERBALS

The non-verbal communication of your organisation is another
powerful tool that you can use. It comes not only from your logo,

or symbols which represent you in the marketplace, but also from your employees and your environment—offices, vehicles, furniture, fittings, paintings, colour schemes.

Logos and symbols can be important and public ways of communicating and associating messages. Flags, at once symbols of nationality and individuality, send messages of identity. If you are representing your organisation, use every symbol that your public will read as associated with you to reinforce your verbal message.

The name of an organisation itself is an important way of carrying its image to the public. When the Exxon company changed its name from Humble Oil, the cost to the company was considerable. More than 300 million kinds of printed materials had to be changed. The company decided, though, that the impact of the new name on the competitive market was worth the expense.[23]

Imagine the power of the image in the advertisement of the BHP oil rig in the middle of a vast ocean, supported by the auditory strength of music, and the oratorical strength of the words on the screen: 'BHP—THE BIG AUSTRALIAN'. The oil rig was the insignia of an organisation with a spirit of adventure that challenged the power of the seas. It was a memorable image that gained its strength from the associations it brought to the minds of Australian viewers. Consequently, when a merger with the huge South African-owned company, Billiton, was announced in 2001, it sent shock waves through the Australian populace. American-born CEO Paul Anderson empathised with the Australian audience and attempted to present the merger of BHP and Billiton in a way which would reshape that image and allay their fears:

> There was a very valid expression of almost a grief that we've known BHP as The Big Australian and now it's going to be the bigger global Australian. And that's not the same BHP we've known for years and years.[24]

These are examples of the grand images of large companies, but they should remind you that every choice, even that of the room you will meet your employees or clients in, will contribute to your image and that of your company.

INTERCULTURAL AWARENESS

It is important to realise that non-verbal subtlety is often culturally specific. It is, then, one of the codes we need to study most, if we are to move across cultures successfully. There are many examples of the way different cultures use non-verbals. For example:

- In some cultures, strong eye-contact is read as rude, in others it is important to use direct eye-contact if you are to be trusted.
- On different cultural terrains, rules of touch apply; in some countries young men walk around arm-in-arm or holding hands, in others this would be taboo.
- In some cultures, some non-verbal symbols are read as offensive although they are not so in others.
- In some cultures, such as Japan, being unable to produce a business card is tantamount to not existing as a potential business partner.

Here's a case study that shows how important it is to be flexible in dealing across cultures. Recognising the rules of engagement in all contexts is so important.

Case study

During 2001, a tragic accident occurred off Hawaii, when a US submarine, the USS *Greenville*, collided with and sank a Japanese high school fishing training vessel, the *Ehime Maru*. Four young high school students, two teachers and three crew were lost. This tragedy has demonstrated, very publicly, the importance of recognising the different ways in which demonstrations of respect, apology, and building and rebuilding relationships can occur in different cultures. During 2001, the US was embroiled in months of media, political, military and legal scrutiny over who was to bear the blame, cost and compensation for the Japanese loss. The photo of US envoy Admiral William Fallon and diplomats (p. 132) meeting with the bereaved victims of the sunken vessel has a few rather surprising features. You will already probably have noticed that the group is very large, unusually large for a formal interaction. Media coverage normally shows us single leaders shaking hands, or a leader meeting with some individual or other. This photo shows the US Navy's attempt to match their communication with the cultural demands of an apology, Japanese style. As a society that values the group experience, and places less value on individualism, the presentation of the apology to the whole bereaved group, by the group of people who were responsible for it, makes perfect sense. The second thing that might have surprised you is the way the usually straight-backed, powerful, uniform-clad admirals are bowing deeply to what look like quite ordinary citizens. As one Japanese professional suggested to us: no negotiation and healing can proceed in the Japanese way, without that non-verbal as well as verbal act of apology.

This short case study demonstrates the complexity of getting our intercultural communication right.

UNDERSTANDING AND RECOGNISING CULTURAL RULES

The many cultural rules about what is appropriate to express makes reading communication across cultures quite difficult. In collectivist cultures, such as Korea, China and Japan, maintaining harmony is considered a very important priority. Even across these three cultures there are significant variations, of course, but generally, expressing emotion, particularly negative emotion, is considered most inappropriate. This makes understanding the

Figure 7.9   US admirals bow to Japanese cultural expectations

nuances of communication very challenging for both western and eastern cultures, although, of course, those from eastern cultures have some advantages here. By contrast, individualist cultures such as the US, the UK and Australia, where independence is valued, encourage expressing emotion through vocal, facial and gestural codes. Nonetheless, this general non-verbal style can appear overly expressive to some listeners.

A common human response to any difference is our tendency to stereotype cultures and compare them with our own as the norm. This presents a challenge for us all. For example, in Britain, large gestures are interpreted as highly aroused and dominant. Consequently, many British people interpret that the large gestures of the Italian, using the arms from the shoulder down, mean that Italians are in a constant state of high excitement. Equally, an Italian reading of the limited gestures of the British, using mainly hands and wrists, may well be interpreted as closed and cold.[25]

Trying to juggle the tendency to put meanings from one culture onto another is a great challenge for cross-cultural speakers, who are under such focused scrutiny during a presentation. One of our colleagues in London, who regularly trains Finnish and Swedish business executives to sell their ideas and services to British businesses, has considerable difficulty getting some of her clients to open up, to be more expressive and to relax. The Finnish tendency to hold emotion inside, and to mask it with facial neutrality and a still body, limits their effectiveness when speaking to a British audience. Our colleague works on warming up and loosening up such non-verbal communication.

You can see how a subtle difference in gesture can carry a significant difference in meaning. There is no doubt that this non-verbal language is an 'elaborate and secret code', complex and difficult to get to know.

PUTTING YOUR BODY IN YOUR KITBAG

Nor is there any doubt that any of these elaborate and secret non-verbal codes are the strongest communicators of power to readers. Dominance and submission, sincerity and insincerity, respect and disrespect are, just as in the animal kingdom, communicated by appearance, by posture, by gesture, by facial expression, by vocal expression and by visual symbolism. Good speakers must make entrances with confidence and energy, must attract readers with presence and control, must have and hold silence and warmth in their stature, hold eyes with strength, and must move their bodies and voices to gain and sustain attention despite their fear and tension. This is an altogether challenging but essential step in becoming a good communicator. Remember to put your body in your kitbag and then bring it out for all to see.

TIPS

- Non-verbal languages can be controlled. You must start cracking the codes.
- A fit body, relaxed breathing and good grooming will help your image.
- Find the most relaxed, comfortable and open posture in order to communicate your power to your readers.
- Realise the importance of facial expression and powerful eye-contact.
- You must be able to use gesture freely and emphatically.
- What you wear will affect the way others respond to you. Choose accessories carefully. These are part of the message.
- Use your voice with versatility to carry the meanings and the feelings in your content.
- Avoid mannerisms—repetitive gestures and ummms and aaahs will detract from your image.
- Remember that your non-verbals not only carry messages about you as an individual, they also represent your company to others and, therefore, should be well planned.
- Keep an open mind about what others mean, especially if you are operating across cultures.
- Remember that different cultures express dominance, passion and determination differently. Observe those around you carefully to learn how to read and use suitable forms of dominance, advocacy and emotion.
- If you are communicating across cultures, you need to research the non-verbal differences.
- Be patient and expect that you will make mistakes in inter-cultural communication. The important thing is to learn by them rather than blame others.

8

Getting to know your voice

Her voice was ever soft,
Gentle and low, an excellent thing in woman.

Shakespeare[1]

When you leave a voice mail, you're leaving a lot more than just the
content of the message.

Jill Margo[2]

YOUR VOICE HAS AN IMAGE

Shakespeare, in his usual wisdom, saw the image that the voice carries to the listener. He realised that humans define personality through vocal quality. In this case, he saw specifically how his society defined femininity. In the sixteenth century, women were expected to have a soft, gentle and low vocal quality. In the 1990s, luckily, we culturally redefined the categories of femininity and masculinity, and this has created new rules for the use of the voice.

It is surprising, though, that we think so little about our vocal image, yet so much and so often about the way we look. We are often shocked when we hear the sound of our own voice on audio-cassette or video, not only because it sounds different from outside our head, but also because we avoid listening critically to ourselves. We often believe 'this is my voice, and there is not much I can do to change it'. You may not be looking for a transformation of the degree of Eliza Doolittle, but the principles that George Bernard Shaw explored in *My Fair Lady* remain relevant: it is not so difficult to change your voice if you are prepared to exercise, listen to, and carefully recondition bad old vocal habits.

It is important to realise that our voices are expressions of our inner feelings—a submissive voice reveals shyness within, a loud voice may reveal anger or hide shyness. It is also important that you recognise that our stereotypes of masculinity and femininity, although politically more correct than those of the sixteenth century, still influence our vocal tone in western society: men may still swallow their voices back into their throats in an effort, conscious or subconscious, to keep their voice sounding as deep and as masculine as possible; women may still bypass the deeper resonances of the chest, consciously or subconsciously, and use the lighter resonances of the head in order to sound lighter and more feminine. However, recent research has revealed that women in the latter part of the twentieth century had deepened their vocal tone about 10 per cent in comparison with women in the previous decades. The researchers studied a group of 66 women aged 18–73 and compared their results with a similar study made in 1945. They believe that the results point to a change in cultural and social views.[3] It is likely, then, that with further redefinition of the categories of masculinity and femininity, and with time, both women and men will liberate their voices and be less constrained by stereotypes.

LISTEN TO YOUR VOICE

Your body carries within it memories and experiences. Your voice reflects these moods and thoughts, and must be able to carry them out freely. But your voice is so closely connected to your moods and thoughts that it can become locked into one that can dominate it: shyness, apprehension, anger or cynicism, for example. Your voice can lose its versatility. Just as the roles we play in life can lock us into narrow behaviours, voices can become inflexible too. Listen to your voice. Is it versatile? Can you move easily out of your role-voice as bank manager, doctor, lawyer, student or teacher to speak with the local motor mechanic, shop-keeper or child next door? Is your voice flexible? Do you need to exercise it to manage effective communication with a wide range of listeners who may use different vocal styles?

Your voice can become locked in minor ways which can then inhibit your personality and prevent you achieving wide and versatile communication. We are not suggesting, though, that if you are locked into a shy voice you need only to exercise vocally and immediately become assertive. We are suggesting that you need to consider the causes of your shyness within, and positively image your voice in conjunction with physical and vocal exercise, or your voice can become limited in a serious way. Remember that trauma or other psychological events can have a serious effect on your ability to communicate freely. If your voice is locked in a serious way, the exercises in this chapter may be less effective. In this case, we suggest that you read Chapter 6 of Patsy Rodenburg's book *The Right to Speak*[4] and make an appointment with a good voice teacher or speech pathologist for further advice.

BE AWARE OF DIFFERENCE

It is important that you realise that cultural differences affect voice. A Japanese student in one of our lectures recently expressed surprise at the loud voice of a strong feminist character in an Australian theatre production; real strength in Japanese culture is expressed with soft and contained communication. In many cultures, lightness of voice has been connected with femininity. In eastern cultures, women's voices are often particularly high in timbre; eastern vocal role models influence the way women use their vocal instrument.

In American English, loud, deep and fast speech is interpreted as the voice of a powerful person. By contrast, in German, dominance is signalled by a deep tone, soft volume and breathiness, at least in men. British speakers often interpret Americans as very excitable and extroverted and, like all cultures, use their own slower speech and softer volume as a measure of what's normal and appropriate.[5]

In Western culture, voice teachers influence students to 'free the natural voice'[6] and certainly, a free and fully developed vocal tone which has warmth and shows confidence puts the least strain on both the speaker and the listener.

There is now greater acceptance of a range of different accents and greater desire for individuality in voice quality, and there is less emphasis on the 'beautiful' voice and the 'right' accent. Patsy Rodenburg, in *The Right to Speak*, has examples from many cultures, both western and eastern, of the extent to which we are judged by our voices in terms of education, class, culture and ability. She writes, 'You may not believe it is true, but there is such a thing as "vocal imperialism".'[7]

Understanding vocal imperialism should stop you perpetuating it, either as a speaker or a listener. In a global world, we should appreciate the richness of the many ways that English can be spoken by second-language speakers. Adapting to your audience is always the first rule of all good communication. Listening with respect is the second. For your voice and speech, this means that clarity and establishing vocal rapport is your strongest priority.

Your understanding should also alert you to the fact that listeners may hold strong attitudes about the appropriateness of a particular voice. One of our colleagues, who works in a London consultancy, was recently asked to participate in a discussion on Scottish radio. The discussion was about the importance of speech presentation in the business world. Our colleague was immediately aware of the sensitivities of the situation, and she prepared herself mentally to present the most acceptable vocal image. She knew that she could easily sound like the 'posh Londoner' daring to give the Scots advice. She made sure that her accent was toned down and her style was not too 'pushy' in any way. When we listened to the interview, we could see how empathically she had given her advice, and how she had made sure that her vocal tones were free of the stronger elements of her educated English accent.

In deference to these attitudes, we always explore, with our broadcast journalism students, the realities of the expectations of accent in the media. In all English-speaking countries, vocal imperialism is evident from a brief scanning of the vocal images that dominate the media. For example, speakers with a strong southern accent do not appear on the national broadcasters such as CNN in the US. Similarly, the national broadcasters are unlikely to use forms of strong regional accents in the UK. Equally, it is not likely that a student with a flat and broad Australian accent or a nasal tone would be employed as a reporter by the Australian Broadcasting Corporation. These types of voice are unacceptable to particular audiences and would violate the expectations of listeners. All successful broadcasters have to make a decision to bow to the expectations of their listening audience.

There are some elements of accent which are worth changing if they do not sufficiently please the ears of our chosen listeners.

George Bernard Shaw was so convinced of this that he campaigned to have a standard form of English accepted in order to eradicate the class system in England. We are also reminded of a legendary example of the way your accent can cause you to be subjected to criticism. A well-known US anchor, Barbara Walters, could not escape her regional accent and was fondly satirised in a comedy sketch as Barbara Wa-Wa. A less capable presenter, having trouble with *l, r* and *w* sounds, may have been disadvantaged by their accent.

A very powerful example of vocal discrimination occurred during the political contest for leadership of Britain during 2001. British attitudes towards William Hague's voice were widely reported. As we mentioned in Chapter 7, Hague seemed to have image problems all round. However, it appears that his voice was one of the biggest downfalls in his bid to be Prime Minister, and he was often criticised for his pompous performances. One survey, by the Dairy Council, which was looking for a voice to star in their current milk campaign, revealed that the British public found Hague's voice to be 'high, childish and contrived'.[8] Not one person questioned for the survey had a good thing to say about Hague's voice, and the comments were caustic. This is a clear indication of how much people actually do hear and judge the image of a person from their voice. Many of us accept that the person within is represented by the vocal tones we hear, and we form our opinions accordingly.

A VOICE FOR THE TWENTY-FIRST CENTURY

It is important to realise that the beliefs and ideologies that surround us are subject to variation, and this can have an effect on the vocal tones we develop. The most obvious example of this is the reference we have already made to the changes wrought by feminism on women's vocal tones. However, there are other more subtle changes that are reflected in the voice, as the world of business experiences an ebb and flow of attitude. Patsy Rodenburg shared her experience of her consultancy work in large and significant organisations in her recent book, *Well-tuned Women*.[9] In one case, she was employed to take voice workshops with some young executives, the creative blood of the company, because they were alienating others by being arrogant and insensitive in voice and language. Although the company had always employed the brightest and most dynamic of graduates, they had begun to feel that a pompous vocal style was no longer appropriate. The company had identified a change in attitude towards workplace behaviour, and they were determined to keep ahead of the game.

Rodenburg notes a general trend towards changing needs in the workplace. She notes that women, who have, over the last decade, worked to have a more 'masculine approach' to voice, language and manner in order to find success in a male-dominated business environment, are now sometimes seeking help to rediscover their more sensitive style. She says that the men who sought her help in the seventies and eighties were often looking to find a more powerful style, while men in the nineties were being sent by their companies because their style could be seen as too bossy or too powerful.

This supports our contention that versatility is the key to vocal success, and being able to adapt to the situation and call upon the strengths of either our masculine or feminine energy, at the appropriate time, is the best solution. Above all, we need to be in touch with our voice and 'in the moment', if we are to achieve a flexible style. This means accepting the need to do some reflective voice work.

DON'T DESTROY YOUR IMAGE

We exercise the voice, in the main, to avoid the risk of vocal strain. Our health is more important than our image, and many speakers find they strain their voices and hurt their throats when they present. As you work through the exercises in this chapter, be body-conscious, be alert to those areas which need the most practice, and be aware of the dangers. Be sure to keep your throat relaxed and open when you vocalise. When people strain their voices, by putting pressure on the throat and allowing the vocal cords to bang together, they can develop nodules or corns which can damage vocal quality permanently. Be careful, because your vocal instrument is precious and you can, without caring for it, destroy it.

One common difficulty we have found, when working on the voice and physical presentation for clients, is that they often think their habitual way of speaking is nature's way and unchangeable, because they have become so used to it. Our broadcast journalism students are wide-eyed when they notice, on video, that their lower jaws are locked, as we have described to them, or that their throats are going into strain each time they breathe. Although you were born with a wonderfully free vocal instrument—you could, as a baby, scream for hours without going hoarse—the increased demands of life in modern society have resulted in increased and unnoticed physical tensions which inhibit your voice. If you can free these tensions and find the power of a natural and expressive voice that will carry your message with the most emphasis possible, then you will have the chance of direct contact with your listeners. After all, your strongest focus should always be on the intention of your message and a voice that supports that message with ease will be a great asset.

EXERCISE YOUR VOICE

Relax and breathe

The first important element for a good voice is a relaxed body. Breath is the life force of our voice and we can only breathe well with a relaxed torso. When our torso is tight and tense, the inter-costal muscles (the muscles between our ribs) cannot swing the ribcage up strongly and create the vacuum necessary to draw oxygen deeply into our lungs. Our lungs are pear-shaped and oxygen must be 'vacuumed' deeply into our lower chest to get the maximum supply of breath. If your intercostal muscles are strong and well developed, they will do the job, and do it well. Remember this message as you do the breathing exercise we are about to outline.

We once worked with a student, a young woman in her thirties, whose intercostal muscles were so weak and underdeveloped that they ached continually as she learned to draw breath into her lower chest. As she was breathing in such a shallow way, she had very little air to support her voice on the outgoing breath and, as a result, her vocal tone was commensurately thin and reedy. This is one of the more extreme stories of the many that any voice teacher could tell about bad breathing, and here is the moral of that tale. Never assume that because you are alive you know how to breathe. You may know how to breathe to physically survive, but perhaps not breathe well enough in front of listeners to stay vocally alive. Bad breathing is at the root of most vocal problems, for you must not only know how to breathe freely, but also how to support the voice on a strong outgoing stream of air.

Tension and tightness, which block and inhibit breathing, are endemic in modern western society, especially in modern urban society. Many of us lose touch with the vital breath force we need for strong physical effort. This is our commercial: oxygen is free, breathe deeply.

Begin these breathing exercises by doing the relaxation exercises described in Chapter 4.

Exercise

Now that you and your body are feeling relaxed, let's move onto breathing. Lie on the floor and raise your knees to allow your stomach and chest ease of movement. The muscle above your stomach, the diaphragm, needs to push down from its dome-shaped position and flatten out to allow your lungs room to expand downwards. The muscles between the ribs, the intercostal muscles, need to lift your ribcage upwards and outwards so that your lungs can expand from front to back and side to side. The muscles in your stomach need to relax and let this process happen—you need to relax and let your spare tyre show.

Now put your hands on the side of your ribcage and feel the movement. Take in a deep, free breath and make sure you do not tense the upper chest or gasp for oxygen in shallow breaths: the oxygen must rush into the lower chest and the movement in the upper chest should be minimal. We suggest that you should feel as if you are breathing in your stomach or your buttocks; although this is not physically possible, the image can help you to draw the breath deeply into the lower chest. We also suggest, if you find it hard to relax, that you yawn with a deep breath. It is important that you find the most relaxed and powerful way of breathing, and imprint it on your body-consciousness; it is important that you concentrate on what it feels like, and enjoy the rhythm and power of your breathing.

You could develop a program of full relaxation and breathing exercises that you can do for a few days before a presentation. The good speaker would have a daily program: you could also develop a program of quick exercises to do daily in your office. Here are some examples:

- If you put your head down on your arms on your office desk, you can concentrate on your breathing and see how much movement occurs at the back of the ribcage.
- You can also stand and bend from the waist, fold your arms across your chest to cuddle each shoulder and see if you have some movement in the back of the ribcage.
- If you can, exercise with a partner and check one another's breathing, or use a mirror to see if your upper chest is relaxed but your lower ribcage is freely moving.

We cannot overemphasise the importance of breathing deeply before you say your first words to listeners. One of our students recently suggested to us, 'Fear is really excitement without air.' This is one of the most concise ways to remind us of the great importance of powerful breathing, for life as well as for voice. Breath gives us confidence and can even replace fear with excitement when we have it working to our advantage.

Tone and pitch

Now you need to connect your breath to your voice without any blocks or tensions. Two aspects of voice which you will want to especially consider are tone and pitch. We have included exercises to work on both of these.

Tone

Good tone is an essential quality for a voice which holds the listener. It is the overriding sound that makes voice distinctive, and it comes from the sound that resounds in the hollow spaces of the

---

Exercise

While you are lying down, feeling relaxed and breathing freely, allow yourself a nice strong sigh on the outgoing breath. Make sure your sigh is relaxed (a relaxed sigh may not have a beautiful tone, but it should have a good deep sound which is carried freely on your breath stream). Connect a yawn with your sigh to relax your jaw. This relaxed sound is the natural sound you need to define your vocal image: this sigh is the sound you need to explore your voice and to get to know it more fully.

body—the chest, head and mouth. To illustrate the difference between pitch and tone, we use the analogy of violin and cello. Violins and cellos have different-sized hollow spaces: you can play a note of the same pitch on both instruments, for example middle C, and hear differences in tone between the two sounds. The cello sounds much deeper because of the largeness of its resonator and the violin much higher because of its smallness.

Our human vocal instrument has the three key resonators of chest, head and mouth. A good voice has a balance of the three.

1. The chest contributes to the depth of tone quality.
2. The head gives a pleasant high ringing quality to the tone (it is this quality that is missing if you have a cold or suffer from blocked sinuses).
3. The mouth, the most important resonator, shapes the vowel sounds clearly and communicates full vocal colour. It is particularly important to get your voice forward to the front of your mouth to give vocal vitality and to project to listeners: the hard bony surface of the palate at the front of the mouth is an excellent resonating wall. It is important that you never swallow your voice.

Here is an exercise to work on your tonal quality.

Exercise

Hum. You will feel your lips vibrating. If this vibration becomes stronger, then your voice is definitely in the front of your mouth. Now, imprint this feeling into your body-consciousness. It is also important that you relax your lower jaw to allow your mouth full resonance. The lower jaw is tension-prone and, if tense, it restricts the sound of your tone and communicates tightness in your face.

In your lying position, after listening to your voice in a strong sigh, move to listening to your voice in speech. Begin by counting aloud and concentrating on carrying your voice on your breath-stream. Counting does not have any particular sense requirements, so you can concentrate on strength and depth of tone. Do not hold your breath, but allow it, instead, to flow freely and carry a strong tone simultaneously.

The key is to listen to your voice, to get to know your voice, and to get to know it well.

Experiment with your different resonators by finding your deepest and lightest tones. Decide if you are neglecting any of these, and work to fully extend your tonal range (use the exercises we suggest at the end of this chapter). You can also extend your range by counting in a standing position and imagining the sound as colour, and then changing the tone to suit your image of that particular colour. Black could sound deep and strong, but pink could be light but warm—use your own images to find nuances of the voice. Or you can swing your arm and throw the number as if it was a handball against the nearest wall, aiming to extend the freedom and power of your voice. Always breathe fully before you exhale strongly and make sure that your throat is relaxed and open as you project the number fully on the voice.

You need to listen carefully, to feel for the freedom of your voice as you exercise. Listen for faults, obvious faults, like breathy tone: your breath may be flowing freely, but it may also be clouding your tone and reducing its strength (and unless you are aiming for a Marilyn Monroe effect, avoid noticeable breathiness). Listen for faults like not using enough breath: the tone of your voice will sound dry or harsh. Aim for a warm and comfortable tone where your breath and your sound flow strongly and freely. The key is to feel comfortable and relaxed. If you feel your throat getting tight or strangled, you are advised to stop your exercises immediately. If you become aware of constant problems when you exercise, you should consult a speech teacher or a speech pathologist.

Avoid nasal tone

Be alert to a nasal tone: when the sound travels up the back of the mouth into the nasal cavities, it is displeasing to the ear, it dominates tone, and subsumes most other vocal qualities.

Listen and make your muscles work in order to overcome any nasality. Stand in front of the mirror and say *mmmm* followed by *aaah*. Make sure that you cannot hear any nasal tone on the *aaah* sound and that you are moving the little flap, the uvula, at the back of your mouth up high on the *aaah* sound. Continue to listen to your speech and make sure that your vowel sounds are not nasal.

Pitch

When you make sound, the vocal cords vibrate. To achieve free vibration of the vocal cords, you need a relaxed throat. Tension in the throat can cause your vocal cords to tighten and force the pitch of your voice up. If your head is in alignment and the breathing is not creating a tension, which travels to the throat, you and your vocal cords should not have any problems. Your vocal cords initiate sound and control your pitch range through a loosening and tightening. A versatile pitch range is essential for a voice that gets attention and holds interest: we will return to this later in the chapter.

You will realise, at this point in the chapter, that we believe you need to feel relaxed and comfortable to make the best of your voice.

- Never wear a tight collar and tie to make a presentation.
- Realise that tight clothes will impede your breath and that very high heels can change your body alignment and make it difficult for you to breathe.
- Heavy-framed spectacles can inhibit your facial muscles and affect full resonance.

As you can see, the use of your voice is connected to your physical and fashionable appearance.

Words and clarity

After you have developed a vital and versatile vocal tone, think about word clarity. A mobile lower jaw is basic to achieving word clarity. Look at yourself on video or in the mirror and check that your lower jaw is not stuck, causing your mouth to open like a slit when you speak. Most of us allow tensions to lodge in our jaws and restrict the mouth, and if our mouths cannot open freely we cannot utter words with energy.

Yawning is a useful exercise, relaxing the jaw and freeing the mouth cavity. You can also rub the jaw hinges on either side of your mouth with the palms of your hands, or drop your jaw and consciously allow it to relax. For example, you should do this before you begin your reading exercises which we suggest at the end of the chapter. Check yourself as you practice, and make sure that your jaw has not returned to a tight position.

Just as the athlete trains to reach full physical fitness, to achieve word clarity you need the muscles in and around your mouth to be very agile. You need to exercise your lips and tongue, the most important of these muscles, to achieve this word clarity. It is most important that you have the ability and the agility to speak with pace and pronounce with ease. Why is it so important? As we have said, your listeners form an impression of your personality from listening to your speech. Your individual way of making vowel and consonant sounds with your mouth and lips contributes to the impression of your speech subconsciously noticed by your listeners. These aspects, among others, contribute to your vocal accent, character and colour. We are not suggesting that there is any such thing as the perfect accent, character or colour—individuality is of the utmost importance. We are suggesting that well-articulated words are expected of a good speaker, and they contribute to a sense of vitality. Try energetically and clearly speaking this sentence:

> The slightly intoxicated laughing lawyers were lost in the library, so they straggled up to the secretary to ask where were the contemporary contributions.

If you can speak it at a galloping pace, pronouncing all the syllables with ease, you may not need to practise further. Now try repeating the name Peggy Babcock over and over with clarity. If you can repeat that, you are definitely off the hook. If you cannot, spend some time keeping your tongue and lips moving to achieve energy and clarity by speaking quickly through the exercises at the end of the chapter. Remember that agility is harder when you are under the pressure of presenting to an audience and you are much more likely to fall over difficult words.

Using voice and speech to add meaning and variety

As you develop strong tone and clear speech, you become easier to listen to. Your next step is to smooth your phrasing; your next, to feel for the rhythms of language; and your last, to use oral grammar to interpret your thoughts for the listener. Through careful use of voice and speech, you can achieve focused meaning and add variety. For voice, consider pitch, tone and volume, and for speech, consider pace, pause and emphasis.

If you use oral grammar well, then voice changes and pauses can be the same sort of indicators as commas, colons and full stops. Therefore, your pauses will vary in length just as the comma, semi-colon and full stop vary in appearance. If you use tone, volume and pace well, you will reflect the changing moods of language; you will support meaning and add colour to your interaction.

Volume

Remember to vary the volume of your voice to aid the sense of your speech, but avoid fading at the end of the sentences. Fading volume at the end of a sentence implies a lack of confidence and conviction. Check yourself for this problem when you listen to the playback of your reading or speaking. If you use a change of volume (or stress) on important words to add emphasis, remember that this technique, although useful, can become monotonous.

Pitch

Pitch is one of the most important ingredients in your vocal kitbag. We change pitch by changing the tension in the vocal cords, just as someone does when they tune a violin. We can move pitch up or down. The stressed syllables of our speech carry the noticeable pitches. The pitch on a particular syllable is called an inflection and we speak of level, upward or downward inflections. Use the subtle technique of pitch changes to add emphasis and variety. Allow your pitch to range, and also use the device of upward or downward inflections to save your listeners from boring presentations. Use pitch also as a device to focus on the essential meaning of what you are communicating to your listeners.

Pitch patterns

If you looked at your voice patterns as a graph on a machine, you would see that they lift up and fall down in pitch. In fact, pitch follows a definite pattern, an intonation pattern, if it is used effectively to communicate with listeners. Inflection, the change of pitch on a stressed syllable, is used within the sentence to emphasise particular words and bring more focused meaning to the expression of your thoughts. A good English speaker should always begin a new thought or a new sentence with a lift of the pitch on the first stressed syllable—because English intonation patterns follow a descending order until the last stressed syllable of the sentence. If a speaker does not start high, the pitch range of a sentence will be narrowed and the intonation pattern can become monotonous and repetitious. You should, then, always give yourself time to take a good breath and lift your pitch to launch each fresh thought. Within each sentence you should keep the inflection on your emphasised words level or rising. A downward inflection implies that the sense is complete—it must only be used when the sentence is over. If you have not completed your idea, imply that you are to continue by using a definite upward inflection. In fact, all phrases within your sentence should be marked by upward inflections. When your idea, thought, or sentence is finally complete, the downward inflection must then be definite.

Your audio-cassette can become your closest friend as you learn to listen critically to your own voice and to hear your own patterns of intonation: it is vital to your education in oral punctuation and to your development in speech-literacy, which will strengthen your communication with listeners.

LISTENING FOR VOCAL VARIETY

In our exercises at the end of the chapter, we have included a final reading with a number of paragraphs. However, if you check, you will find that it is all one sentence. It is excellent practice for listening to upward inflection and for discovering and extending the variety of meaning you can introduce through this device. You can learn control over meaning, through control over your voice. This passage, by Lafcadio Hearn, was quoted by the famous Russian filmmaker Eisenstein because he loved the way it captures the interaction of sound and image.[10]

It is excellent as a reading for practising the interaction of all the vocal devices we have discussed. The opening paragraph will easily become monotonous if you do not find that variety for the upward inflection; you must seek and find the soft volume and light tone of 'the secret ghostly motions', then contrast these with loud volume, deep tone and the punchy consonants of the 'raging and racketing and rioting'. This is an ideal reading to find your voice. Ham it up for all you are worth, then listen to the playback with a critical ear. Is it an over-expressive voice or is it a voice with vitality and life? Be honest.

We advise that if you do not feel comfortable doing a particular reading, simply move to another one you are more comfortable with and return to the first later.

Remember, good speakers are not only technically able but also creatively able, and emotionally able. Not only is their speech clear and easily understood, but they enliven it with the power of vocal variety and direct meaning straight to the minds and hearts of listeners. We have included a voice and speech checklist at the end of the chapter to help you to examine your technical ability, and a section of that checklist to help you examine your style and attitude. Technical ability is not enough on its own. You need both style and attitude to succeed.

We recently encountered a student who was a particularly able broadcast reader technically, but something was causing his voice to sound 'stuffy'. Once he recognised this quality, he 'put a smile' in his voice and the attitude changed completely. Emotional quality communicates attitude beautifully to listeners; it is a great asset to speakers. It is one of the qualities which gave famous actor Richard Burton's voice its colour and power. President Bill Clinton also used this quality very effectively. As voice expert Patsy Rodenburg says, 'Vocal imagination, I think, getting in touch with the soul of whatever you are trying to say, is the first place to start working.'[11]

It is important that you work on your voice in your rehearsal sessions. Do your exercises and practise your readings each day until you feel comfortable with your oral grammar and your ability to interpret meaning for listeners. But do not work on your voice when the time comes to face listeners. It is time to focus on the content of your message and, more importantly, time to focus on communicating that message to your listeners.

Because you have worked on your speech presentation, you will find that your speech will not let you down. Your voice will respond to the call for meaning: the inflections practised and the tone, pace, pause and emphasis worked on will be there for you to support the meaning of this particular message. We can give a

100 per cent guarantee. We have worked on the voice for many years, and the many speakers we have worked with have responded to a program of exercise, reading and analysis. They have all produced a more varied and meaningful presentation when they returned to their original material. Audio-cassette and video-tape are the chief witnesses to the changes produced. Do not be afraid that this conscious effort will spoil your spontaneity. We have found, as English researcher and educator Christopher Turk has found, that 'the increased consciousness of what we are doing is usually not noticed by others, while the improved skills most certainly are'.[12]

INCLUDING YOUR VOICE IN YOUR KITBAG

You should follow a careful pattern for your voice exercises. After you have completed your relaxation and breathing exercises and followed with some intoning exercises—some sighing, humming and counting aloud—it is time to move on to exercises for clarity and inflection. After your program of background exercises, try some of the readings we have suggested and see if you can organise all the devices of a powerful, interesting and meaningful voice to work together. A kitbag without vital and meaning-making speech, without speech which can move your listeners to an emotional response when necessary, is a kitbag not worth carrying. You will be without some of the most important items on your list, if you do not find an expressive voice and vital speech to pack in a place of prominence where they can be found with ease.

TIPS

- Take care of your voice for the sake of your image as well as your health.
- Your voice should be versatile so that you can adapt to different situations and even different cultural demands.
- Relaxation and breathing are the bases on which a strongly expressive voice is built.
- An expressive voice can bring meaning and feeling through changes of volume, tone and pitch. Interesting speech relies on the use of changes in pace, pause, and emphasis.

- General voice and speech exercises will benefit your public presentation style, because you can re-pattern your speech habits into patterns which bring a sharper focus to the meanings of your message.
- Two further books which have not been mentioned during the chapter but which are very useful if you wish to improve your voice are:

  C. Berry, *Your Voice and How to Use it Successfully*, London, Harrap, 1975;

  M. McCallion, *The Voice Book*, London, Faber and Faber, 1988

Here are a set of practice exercises to help improve your presentation technique.

Exercise

Agility for word clarity

I had a hippopotamus

I had a hippopotamus; I kept him in a shed
And fed him upon vitamins and vegetable bread;
I made him my companion on many cheery walks
And had his portrait done by a celebrity in chalks.

His charming eccentricities were known on every side,
The creature's popularity was wonderfully wide:
He frolicked with the Rector in a dozen friendly tussles
Who could not but remark upon his hippopotamuscles.

If he should be afflicted by depression or the dumps,
By hippopotameasles or the hippopotamumps,
I never knew a particle of peace till it was plain
He was hippopotamasticating properly again.

I had a hippopotamus: I loved him as a friend;
But beautiful relationships are bound to have an end.
Time takes, alas, our joys from us and robs us of our blisses;
My hippopotamus turned out a hippopotamissis.

My housekeeper regarded him with jaundice in her eye;
She did not want a colony of hippopotami.
She borrowed a machine gun from her soldier nephew, Percy,
And showed my hippopotamus no hippopotamercy.

My house now lacks the glamour that the charming
   creature gave,
The garage where I kept him is as silent as the grave;
No longer he displays among the motor tyres and spanners
His hippopotamastery of hippopotamanners.

No longer now he gambols in the orchard in the Spring,
No longer do I lead him through the village on a string;
No longer in the morning does the neighbourhood rejoice
To his hippopotamusically-modulated voice.

I had a hippopotamus; but nothing upon earth
Is constant in its happiness or lasting in its mirth;
No joy that life can give me can be strong enough to smother
My sorrow for that might-have-been-a-hippopotamother.

Patrick Barrington. Reproduced by permission of *Punch*.

Emphasis

You need to emphasise the appropriate word in each sentence to construct the meanings we have suggested below that sentence. Remember that stress can become a monotonous means of emphasis. You need to develop inflection patterns which will carry your meaning to your listeners with interest.

1.   Mary's mother is living in Brisbane.
    a.   not Jane's mother
    b.   not her father
    c.   it is a certain fact
    d.   she is still alive
    e.   not outside the city
    f.   not in Sydney

2.   Simone said that her mother was thinking of buying a new car.
  a.   not Mary
  b.   she did say it
  c.   not my mother
  d.   not her aunt
  e.   not sure yet
  f.   not hiring
  g.   not a secondhand one
  h.   not a new house
3.   Can you come to the staff meeting on Wednesday?
  a.   would you be able?
  b.   not your partner
  c.   instead of writing your suggestions
  d.   not the general meeting
  e.   not the luncheon
  f.   not on Friday
4.   I have asked my secretary to come with us to the meeting.
  a.   nobody else asked her
  b.   I remembered to do it
  c.   but I don't know whether she can come
  d.   but I haven't asked your secretary
  e.   but not my manager
  f.   but she'll return independently
  g.   to travel in the car
  h.   not with the Joneses
  i.   not to the dinner
5.   We saw on the 6 o'clock television news that the fires were over.
  a.   did you not hear?
  b.   but we didn't hear the broadcast properly
  c.   not the 9 o'clock news
  d.   not the radio or other news
  e.   there may be other threats
  f.   so you must be wrongly informed
  g.   that they were completely finished

Change of emotional meaning

Give three different interpretations of each sentence. Each interpretation should have a different emotional sense. Notice the changes in rhythm, pitch, tone, and tone-colour and the pattern of the total speech tune.

1. Oh no, not really?
2. What have you done?
3. Don't go out tonight.
4. 1 can't believe you are doing this!
5. It was him, wasn't it?
6. She is a strange woman!
7. How far have we come?
8. You won't tell anyone, will you?
9. What an amazing story!
10. I won't let you do it. So don't try.
11. I thought I'd worked it out.
12. No, you can count me out.

If you feel bold after this exercise, remember that Stanislavsky (the famous Russian director) would ask his actors to say the simple phrase 'good night' in forty different ways. The story goes that Muscovites listening to this phrase on tape could correctly identify many of the contexts. Perhaps you could start with ten contexts and see how far you can go from there. *But,* we would not suggest this would be everyone's cup of tea.

Reading passage

Remember to ham up the reading passages and use them to fully develop all of your expressive vocal skills. In this passage, remember to keep your inflection rising until the end, as it is all one sentence. Use volume, tone, pace, pause, and emphasis to create the meaning and mood of the piece.

For me words have colour, form, character; they have faces, parts, manners, gesticulations; they have moods, humours, eccentricities; they have tints, tones, personalities:—
because people cannot see the colour of words, the tints of words, the secret ghostly motions of words:—
because they cannot hear the whispering of words, the rustling of the procession of letters, the dream flutes and dream

drums which are thinly and weirdly played by words:—

because they cannot perceive the pouting of words, the frowning of words and fuming of words, the weeping, the raging and racketing and rioting of words:—

because they are insensible to the phosphorescing of words, the fragrance of words, the noisesomeness of words, the tenderness or hardness, the dryness or juiciness of words,—the interchange of values in the gold, the silver, the brass, the copper of words:—

is that any reason why we should not try to make them hear, to make them see, to make them feel?

From *Letter to Basil Hall Chamberlain* by Lafcadio Hearn

Voice and speech observation sheet

Use this set of questions to reflect on the characteristics of your vocal style.

- *Speech*: Is your speech clear and well articulated?
- *Tone*: Is your tone rich or too light? Does your voice have changes of tone?
- *Pitch*: Do you use upward inflection when the sense is indefinite? Do you use downward inflection when sense is finished? Do you use inflection to aid meaning and emphasis? Is the intonation pattern interesting, or does the pattern become monotonous or repetitious? Does the pitch indicate the beginning of a new thought?
- *Volume*: Does volume have variety which aids the sense?
- *Pace:* Is the basic pace suitable? Do you use change of pace to aid the meaning?
- *Pause*: Is pause under control? Too long or too short? Is pause used as a device to aid meaning?
- *Emphasis*: Are the important words recognised by the interpreter? Are they suitably highlighted by the voice? Is there variety in the techniques used for emphasis?
- *Rhythm*: Does the speech have an easy rhythm? Are the rhythms of the language evident to the listener?
- *Attitude and style*: Do you manage to relay a sense of attitude and style in your use of voice and speech?

9

Speaking across cultures

The notion that English serves as a neutral lingua franca is a dangerous myth.[1]

Robert Phillipson

THE LANGUAGE CHALLENGE FOR THE PRESENTER

English is now regarded almost universally as the international language. That puts native speakers of English at a definite advantage when it comes to speaking to an audience. However, the increased movement of people from countries all over the world is bringing with it increasing demands for speakers to communicate using translators, or to communicate with audiences who are not confident with English.

This happens for a variety of reasons. The group you need to communicate with may have no English, their English may be very limited, the group may feel that it is a sign of respect for them as hosts that they receive the ideas in their own language, you may not be bilingual, or the topic and situation may be complex and important and the organisers feel that the costs of miscommunication are too high.

One story that demonstrates how serious such miscommunication can be concerns an interaction that occurred during the Cuban missile crisis in 1962. When President Kennedy met President Kruschev, a misunderstanding arose. During the negotiation, Kruschev used a common Russian saying that translates literally as

'I will be at your funeral'. The sense of it was 'I will live longer than you', and was intended to be understood metaphorically to mean 'communism will outlive capitalism'. However, it was translated for Kennedy as 'We will bury you'. At this point, Kennedy assumed that Kruschev was laying down the gauntlet, and so Kennedy stormed out of the meeting. CIA translators only later discovered the mistake.

This is a tale of mythic proportions, used by translators to remind themselves of their power, their responsibility and their important role in communication between cultures. It is also a lesson for all presenters.

Over the last two years, we have interviewed many translators and interpreters from different parts of the world, and we were struck by a recurring idea that they offered about what being a translator means. Many of them felt their job was to be a *bridge* or a *bridge-builder* between the English speaker and the audience.[2]

They pointed out that their job was to translate meaning, not exact words. In an interview with Spanish translators, for example, they saw their role as to mirror the communication of the speaker, with all its richness, including the hesitations, gestures, body movements, laughter and so on. In another interview with Japanese translators, they focused on managing to bridge the ambiguities of the Japanese language and the directness of English.

There is also considerable evidence to suggest that the role of translator or interpreter is even culturally specific. In places like the UK, Germany, North America, Scandinavia and Holland, interpreters aim to give an accurate, unbiased account of what was said in one language to those listening in another. The translator is supposed to be neutral, acting as a 'black box' in the service of language comprehension.

On the other hand, in many Asian contexts the role of the interpreter is quite different. Their role is to be an interpreter not just of language, but also of gesture, meaning and context. In the Japanese context, the role of the interpreter is to support the speaker, protect them from any rudeness, or even advise them on appropriate responses. In this role, it is clear just how important it is to work with a translator in a team approach.[3]

As an example of how this role works, we asked a Japanese translator to comment on a presentation given by one of us to a gathering of members of a chapter of a UNESCO citizens' group in Japan. The presentation was about differences between Australian and Japanese education. One point in the speech referred to the different forms of address used in the two countries between adults and students. To illustrate the point, a reference was made to the use of the Australian term 'mate'. Even though this term is often the subject of considerable humour for international audiences, as many Australians are greeted globally with 'g'day mate', the Japanese translator filled in the significance of the use of the term 'mate' for the Japanese audience. He said that filling in this context was an important contribution that he could make as a translator.

We are very aware, after watching, interviewing and being involved in giving presentations, using translation, that the speaker must take a number of very important steps to achieve good communication in this situation.

Now, let's imagine the mental preparation and self-talk of one English language speaker for a Japanese audience. He was preparing to give a presentation to a group of about thirty potential students for a university course on communication technology. Here's his reflection:

> Okay, let's see. I've got about twenty minutes, four courses, twenty possible units about emerging communication technology and design, some PowerPoints and some examples from current student designs.
>
> I guess most of them have some English as they intend coming to England to study, but it doesn't matter, because I've got a translator. I'll just read it out because they won't know these new technologies by name in English anyway, and the translator can explain. It won't matter that I am reading it— they'll be watching and listening to the translator!

This sort of preparation for a presentation with translation is a recipe for failure. Our speaker has already made his first mistakes.

RECIPE FOR MANAGING THE CHALLENGE OF LANGUAGE DIFFERENCES

In thinking about presentations where the decision is made to use a translator, or you are working with an audience with limited English, you need to consider the following issues:

- Be aware that your audience will most likely have some listeners who can understand you if you choose simple words, explain complex words, and avoid unnecessarily difficult words.

- Take the time to think about how to introduce technical vocabulary or ideas. Be imaginative with your approach. Remember that images, photographs, video or even graphic illustrations can be a bridge for communication.

- Think about how you can help your listeners by providing advanced organisers for them. Handouts, good, simple PowerPoints and visual images are especially important. Many second-language English speakers can understand a lot more in the written form than the spoken. This is the product of two processes. The education system in many countries values written language learning over spoken language acquisition. Seeing a foreign language can help listeners to identify the structure and context for what they are hearing. At an international conference that we recently attended, we presented a paper to many English as a second language speakers from all over the world. We worked with a Spanish translator who, we are told by a bilingual colleague, did a very good job. However, the feedback we received indicated that the colour images and simple clear PowerPoints aided our listeners most significantly, as the audience members struggled with their task.

- Especially remember the golden rule of good oral communication: help your audience to listen by using repetition and frequent summary.

- Make a special effort to appeal to the range of sensory perceptions of your listeners. Absorbing ideas can be enhanced if you appeal to as many of the senses as possible.

- Remember to speak slowly and clearly. One of us was strongly reminded of this at a meeting of foreign executive women in Japan. The common language of the group was English. However, there were many German, South American and Asian members, as well as the British and North American members. A charming, interesting North American expatriate journalist spoke about being a journalist in Japan. The English as a first language group thought it a wonderful presentation. The response of many second-language speakers was frustration and disappointment. They just couldn't keep up. So, don't exaggerate, but do enunciate clearly and aim to pace your presentation just a little below your normal speed. This will take discipline and constant vigilance, as we tend to forget our pace as we become absorbed in what we are saying.

- Allow some room for silence. Perhaps this can happen at the end of a main point or an important point. This gives the audience time to absorb your ideas, and a little respite and rest, before you launch into the next point.

RECIPE FOR SPEAKING WITH A TRANSLATOR OR INTERPRETER

If you are working with a translator:

- Discuss the topic, your goals, and your strategy with the translator, preferably a few days before the presentation. In our research with translators and in our experience in presentations using translators, we have found that translators for presentations believe that they can do the best job if they have a transcript a few days ahead. They believe they can do a better job for you if they have this time. They can check vocabulary, plan translations of ideas that do not easily make sense in a different language, and make their own personal presentation as smooth as possible. This benefits you as the speaker.
- Choose language to avoid metaphors that might be very culturally specific. For example, using image-based or culturally specific metaphors such as 'batting on a sticky wicket' or 'take the bull by the horns' can cause headaches for translators and missed opportunities for speakers.
- Limit your use of humour, irony and understatement when speaking to a group with English as a second language. Humour is language-dependent and requires a very quick sense of the meaning of words. It is also very culturally specific— while to those of Anglo background it may seem a very natural way to build rapport, it can be seen as unprofessional by some cultures, and is often lost on the audience. The British and Australian use of irony is often lost on many cultures, including US audiences, while German audiences find it unacceptable to use humour in a professional setting between strangers.[4] One of our interviewees shared a strategy he uses as a translator when a speaker tells a joke that is difficult to translate. He simply says, 'Now the speaker is telling a joke, but it's not very funny, so I won't bother to translate it.' At this, the audience laughs, the speaker gets their response, and the presentation can go on. Our advice on this: stay away from

humour for this type of presentation. Invest in other ways to interest your audience.

- Work at building rapport with your audience through non-verbal strategies such as eye-contact, facial expression and gesture. This is a very demanding requirement. When the speaker feels that the audience does not understand them, the tendency is to let the translator do the rapport building. This is a mistake! You must remember that much of what an audience achieves in communication with a speaker comes from the non-verbal aspects of the interaction. Despite your feelings about not being understood, persist with the positive engagement of your audience. Your relationship-building will pay dividends in the communication stakes.

To sum up on this: Speaking to an audience in a language that is not their first language, or through a translator, is one of your most challenging speaking opportunities. It requires all of the skills discussed in this book. You must fine-tune your communication so that it is clear, accessible and relevant. If you are using translation, you must develop a strong relationship with your translation partner so that they can bring the best of your ideas to the audience. Your own performance must then engage your audience and use non-verbal strategies to support and reinforce your ideas. As one of our interviewees said, both speaker and translator need to work at being the 'very best communicators they can be'!

PLACE THE TOOLS OF DIVERSITY IN YOUR KITBAG

Speaking across cultures is an increasing challenge for all of us. Societies like the UK, the US, Australia and New Zealand all have multicultural societies, and when we speak in classrooms, work-places and community groups, we must make sure that we cater for cultural differences. Sometimes this requires large adjustments in the way we present. However, sensitivity to our use of lang-uage, story choices, even the way we explain and criticise an idea, is important on all occasions. Pack this sensitivity and skill in your kitbag. It is becoming an increasingly critical tool for the twenty-first century.

TIPS

- Help your listeners by speaking slowly and clearly.
- Avoid complex ideas or culture-specific references.
- Use varied sensory stimuli to help listeners.
- Limit your use of humour, irony and understatement.
- If working with a translator, plan together.
- Maintain an engaged non-verbal style, even if you feel little response from the audience.

10

Using technology

The medium is the massage.[1]

As long ago as 1964, Marshall McLuhan was ringing alarm bells to waken society to the changing environment that was emerging as a result of the extraordinary developments that were occurring in technology.[2] He suggested that our way of understanding ourselves, as human beings, would be profoundly changed by these technologies. In many ways, his urging to reconceptualise how we might live and go about our business in what he called 'the global village' has had a profound effect on our attitudes to what is possible.

It is clear that many of the new technologies such as the computer, the Internet, the video camera, CD-ROMs and DVDs have already dramatically affected our communication activities. We can now talk to clients and colleagues in many parts of the world simply by turning on a computer, or by having a telephone or video conference. We can produce professional, polished graphics of current financial positions and photographs of potential sites for architectural development simply by pulling up a graphics package from our computer or by using a scanner or photocopier. We can film an example of the factory floor or training session to demonstrate exactly what we are talking about. As prosthetic extensions of human beings, technologies are changing the way we conceive of communication.

DANGERS

The danger in all of this is to allow these potentially helpful tools, the technologies available to us, to divert us from what we are trying to achieve—good communication. We must not allow the technology to drive our communication. It will undoubtedly support and probably even influence and shape some aspects of our communication. But an awareness of just how seductive these new technologies are should act as a brake to keep control of how we use them.

Some of the most difficult decisions many of our clients and students have to make, when preparing presentations, are choices about which of the myriad of visually exciting aids they should use. We recently saw a presentation by a senior executive who clearly could not make the choice, so he used them all. The result was to provide a collage of ideas and possibilities, but because of their visual diversity, the message was swamped by the visual stimulation.

A presenter for an engineering design competition that we recently judged made a similar mistake. He allowed the presentation to be driven by the technology rather than by the communication. As a result, most of the lights were switched off, the voice of the speaker wafted from somewhere up on the stage, and all personal sense of the speaker was lost amongst slides, sound and video. He missed his opportunity to develop his personal credibility with his audience, and he became more like a prosthetic for his technology rather than the other way round.

Despite these warnings, we are not suggesting that a technology-focused presentation does not have a place in your repertoire of effective communication strategies. On the contrary. There are occasions when these types of presentation will be the perfect choice. It is really a matter of determining the purpose and the objectives of your presentation. Generally, the personal credibility of the speaker is central to your persuasive intent. A 'faceless' idea may give listeners a sense of unease. However, schemes developed by groups of staff or by community groups, which might be best seen as jointly owned ideas, are good examples of presentations which, while being faceless, could still be very persuasive.

Figure 10.1 Some of the most difficult decisions that our clients have to make are choices about which of the myriad of visually exciting aids they should use

Cartoon: Fiona Mitchell

OPPORTUNITIES

One of the very interesting examples of effective communication choices that we have observed is a speech given by Rupert Murdoch, Chairman and Chief Executive of News Corporation, at the launching of his five-year plan for his corporation.[3] This speech was delivered live in London and transmitted via satellite to New York, Los Angeles and Sydney.

Murdoch exploited the capabilities of our new technologies extensively. He clearly understood, though, that while he had the expertise and resources of his innumerable media institutions at his disposal, the credibility of his organisation rested on him, not on a faceless institution. He responded to this knowledge by giving an imaginatively constructed and well-planned presentation. He was supported by a large video screen forming a backdrop (in fact, in Sydney his image was relayed to two full-size screens). The presentation outlined his plans for the next five years. The speech was introduced by a sophisticated, highly theatrical audio-visual presentation of the exciting possibilities for the future. One newspaper described the introduction as 'a Peter Pan eye flight over night-time London, with the narrator observing, "Big Ben, the Houses of Parliament . . . the birthplace of democracy".'[4]

This selection and arrangement of his communication, supported by technology and not driven by it, reflect the very arguments Murdoch wished to make about the role of technology in the future. The speech provides a useful model of how technology can contribute to effective communication. It is the focus of a case study in Chapter 13. We encourage you to think about such possibilities.

Your use of technologies can add enormously to the effectiveness of your presentation. In fact, a study by the Wharton Business School has demonstrated that the supporting technologies that you use have a direct influence on how your audience perceives you. If you tap these resources, you will be perceived as more professional than those who do not use such supporting aids. Complementing your speech with visual aids seems to be well worth the effort, according to this research. The Wharton Business School research claims that people remember

- 10 per cent of what they read
- 20 per cent of what they hear
- 30 per cent of what they see, and
- 70 per cent of what they see *and* hear.[5]

With this research in mind, we will provide you with a range of strategies to make the most of what you want to say. After all, technologies such as electronic presentations (that is, using a projected image from a computer, generated from a presentation software package such as Microsoft PowerPoint), videos, Internet website links, models and aural aids perform similar critical supportive functions to other non-verbal communication strategies such as voice and demeanour.

WHEN TO USE VISUAL SUPPORT

Here are some rules of thumb that will help you to decide if you need visual support.

You may have a set of figures or points that will support the argument you wish to make. Unfortunately, the human mind just can't store details the way a computer can. Graphs, lists and tables can help the listener to visualise the patterns without straining to remember the key arguments. Consider the pyramid representing Maslow's hierarchy of needs, which we used in Chapter 3. It allowed easy visual access to a list of ideas that are otherwise hard to retain.

You may wish to focus your audience on the key issues. You might create a theme or image that reflects your message, and this could be displayed at the beginning or end of a presentation, for example. We used simple diagrams to demonstrate the pitfalls of poor posture in Chapter 7. It really is quite difficult to describe some ideas, while an image can instantly draw attention to the key aspects of a concept.

You may find an illustration that adds humour or which simplifies a complex idea. The cartoon in this chapter humorously suggests how difficult it is for users to get technology right.

You may wish to bring the outside world into your audience's view. Photographs or soundtracks from real places and events such as those described in the case study at the end of this chapter turn difficult arguments into compulsory viewing.

Many examples throughout this book demonstrate the awareness that good speakers have of the potential value of such aids.

CHOOSING YOUR MEDIUM

You have so many different types of audio and visual supports to choose from with the improved and portable technologies available: desktop presentation software and output devices; transparencies; videos; whiteboards; Internet linkups; models; audio-tapes.

Desktop presentation software

One of the most impressive developments in computer technology is the introduction of software packages that help you to create an integrated presentation package designed and developed at your desk. This will help you to create a professional look for your visual aids.

One package that we find particularly user-friendly and yet capable of impressing even the most sophisticated of listeners is Microsoft PowerPoint. This package is designed to give you the opportunity to create thematised text, colour graphics, matching diagrams and graphs, and clip art in a unified style, using a feature called 'Design Template'.

Such software allows you a great deal of flexibility, because you can alter screens or change the sequence to suit a particular audience. It also adds a touch of professionalism because all your text and images can be set on a template, using colour and/or images that unify the presentation.

PowerPoint can assist the speaker to integrate support material into a presentation, if used wisely. For example, you can add sound, video, digitised photographs, and hyperlinks to the Internet, to create a seamless professional presentation.

In fact, with this software you can even set up a slide show that can be timed to match your oral message, or set to run continuously if you are doing a product demonstration. There is a drawback, however, for those who allow their belief in the power of their message and their own credibility to be outweighed by their awe of technology. Expecting the timing of an oral presentation to be precisely matched by the slides may inhibit your communication orientation (see Chapter 1) and turn the presentation into a mechanical exercise. More importantly, unforeseen circumstances can spell disaster if you and your presentation become unsynchronised! Be determined to keep your sights on the communication of the message as the driving force of the presentation.

One of the powerful aspects of PowerPoint is the ability to 'animate' the information on the screen, point by point. This gives the speaker the ability to speak to each point in turn, and the ability *not* to forecast what is about to be discussed. The previous point can be made to disappear or lessen in importance (by changing colour), so there is no confusion about which point the speaker is currently discussing.

This animation technique can bring graphics to life, building a graphic image gradually, so that the speaker maintains narrative control of the information.

All of these facilities have their dangers, and careful practice is required to familiarise novice users. A colleague related this story of the dangers awaiting unsuspecting or uninitiated users. He had the opportunity to listen to a presentation on the 'Marketing of the Year 2000 Sydney Olympics' and, coincidentally, to see a desktop presentation package in action.

> I arrived at the presentation anticipating learning about the Olympics. My attention was immediately diverted to the visual support instead. The software package used by the presenter certainly offered a range of interesting features to present information to students in a professional, low-budget format, but what I experienced was a product of the capacity of technology to drive a presentation. The presenter used a range of transition effects and clip that explored *all* the features of the package she was using. Instead of the information on the Olympics becoming the focus for the audience, the capacity of the technology became the main feature. After the presentation, the only aspects I recalled were those features of the technology that I could use to enhance my presentations. However, the presentation was not on technology but on the Olympics.

In addition, one feature of these packages which can be misused is an automatic organiser facility. In the case of PowerPoint, it is called 'Auto Content Wizard'. It is designed to help you to create a structure for your presentation by giving a range of speech outlines to get you started with a presentation. There are a number of pro-forma templates such as *progress reporting* and *developing a proposal.*

While this feature has the potential to support your planning, it is crucial that you do not allow it to substitute for your detailed attention to the specifics of your situation, your listeners and your purpose. It may inhibit your own creativity by allowing you to use someone else's solution to your problem. Our observations support our advice that allowing technology to drive your presentation is rather like getting on a train and hoping that the driver will know where you want to go.

One final point about using PowerPoint. Our students and our clients are continuously telling us of their PowerPoint 'paralysis'. This particular illness is the product of PowerPoint overload and leads to intellectual atrophy! Some of our students report that the rhythm of a PowerPoint presentation is more soothing than a good meditation CD. This anecdotal evidence is backed up by an international presentation skills consultant from Rogen International. He suggests that 'another' PowerPoint show can go down like 'flat champagne' for an audience who may feel that they have endured one multicoloured bar chart too many![6]

Output devices

Until recently, using desktop presentations was limited by the high set-up cost for organisations to fit a space to project the images, or the inconvenience of carrying a heavy data projector (called an LCD projector—liquid crystal display) to the presentation site. Recent developments in technology have solved many of these issues. The capacity to project computer software using small lightweight LCD data projectors has made desktop presentation relatively cheap and portable. The device, about the size of a traditional 35mm slide projector, or even smaller, connects to your computer. The projector sits easily beside your computer, on a table or stand, and projects the image onto the screen. With most of these devices, the room lights do not have to be greatly dimmed, as the light output is sufficient to project strong colours and clear text. There are several brands on the market to fit a wide variety of budgets and purposes.

Videos/DVDs/Internet video

Technological advances of breathtaking speed have provided many new opportunities to enliven your presentations. One of the most radical has been through the use of images either from videotape, still digitised images, DVD discs or Internet sites. These images can be projected via data projectors onto large screens, or via traditional TV monitors in the case of videos and DVDs. It is now possible to videotape and play back scenes and interactions, so that, say, an audience who has never been to New York can experience the grandeur of your Head Office. Student presentations can also be made more exciting by links to websites to demonstrate a company advertising campaign or branding strategy. Visual images offer you the capacity to inform or motivate an audience in a way previously unavailable.

Transparencies

One of the most common visual aids used by speakers since the 1990s has been the overhead transparency. These days, it is almost expected that a well-prepared speaker will turn up with a Power-Point show. Sometimes, however, it is just not practical to do this. You may be presenting in a situation where no data projector or laptop is available, or it may simply be inconvenient to have to organise the equipment. A set of transparencies may be adequate to talk your audience through your ideas. However, just as with a desktop package, transparencies have their dangers. While transparencies can support your presentation, they can detract if there are too many of them or if the visual aids distract from the focus of the message.

The use of overhead transparencies offers you flexibility because you can change the order or drop one out at will during the presentation, confident that you can keep your presentation on track, because the outline is there for you and the audience to see. Transparencies also offer you the opportunity to use high-impact colourful charts and text, because colour printers are readily available.

Slides

If you do not have a computer/data projector at your disposal, high quality images can be presented using 35mm slides. The medium can provide subtlety of colour along with the impact of strong and dramatic tones. It also provides excellent resolution with sharp clean lines for charts.

Slides have a number of advantages over transparencies. They can be used in very large venues without loss of quality, and can be operated by handheld remote control. This allows a speaker to move around and, with careful use, the slides can be orchestrated as part of the overall performance of a presentation. For example, one clever presenter whom we observed prepared some extra slides detailing costs of his project. During question time, he simply called the slide up to support his answers to questions. This 'magic act' certainly impressed his listeners.

There are some drawbacks. Slide projectors can be touchy, and so you need to check that the projector is ready to go when you arrive at the venue.

One drawback of a slide projector is that you have to lower the light in a room for a slide show, and this can turn you, as a presenter, into a distant voice without the immediacy of your personal presence. This makes it difficult for you to assess the impact of your ideas on your listener.

Traditionally, good-quality slides were fairly expensive to produce and needed professional production using specialist recorders. However, new developments in digital cameras make it easy to link images directly to your computer. This development, with its 'snap image' high-level clarity, provides the opportunity for you to create your own slide show from your own desk.

Document cameras

Document cameras can also be used to project an image, via a TV monitor or LCD data projector. You can show three-dimensional objects, as small as postage stamps, as well as pages from books and brochures, for example.

Models

While sophisticated technologies have tended to replace models as visual aids, sometimes there is no substitute. We were particularly struck by the effective use that an engineering graduate made of a piece of pipe from a chemical plant. The company was looking to decrease downtime for its machinery during repairs by using inserts made of materials that would withstand the abrasive quality of strong chemicals. By demonstrating the progressive damage over time using several of these pipes, he had the engineers in the room on the edge of their seats working hard with him to find a smart design solution. The presence of the problem intensified the reality of the difficulty for the listeners.

However, models do not always support presentations. In fact, if the model is not easy to use for demonstration or clear enough and big enough for ease of viewing, it can take focus away from the message of the presenter. Another graduate engineer's attempt to demonstrate how stresses in buildings are manifested during earthquakes showed only that it is hard to handle wire and blocks of wood while simulating an earth tremor. In this instance, the message about safety of construction was replaced by an unintended message about complex models.

Audio-tapes/CDs

Audio-tapes and CDs can provide a touch of magic to a motivational presentation. Voice-overs and music can add to your message by providing variety and support to your own voice. For example, a piece of music might start or finish a presentation to give focus to your ideas. One example of the effective use of music comes from final-year graduates in our organisational communication program; they concluded a presentation on a training initiative for a not-for-profit organisation for the deaf by picking the theme song 'Speaking Hands and Hearing Eyes'.[7] This music reinforced their idea, and motivated the listener to further value sign language.

Always be careful to keep any audio support short. An audience can quickly lose interest without visual images.

HOW TO USE VISUAL AND AUDIO SUPPORT

1. Select carefully to support the message. Do not allow the aid to divert from the speaker, unless you intend to provide a 'faceless' presentation.
2. Become familiar with the facilities in a venue—especially important for new speakers in a new venue. Not knowing how to dim the lights and turn on the facility immediately reduces your credibility with an audience.
3. Use an audio or visual aid only at the precise moment when you want your audience to focus on it. Turn off the projector or screen when you are not using it, so that neither the image nor the sound of the machine distracts from you as speaker. One of the most powerful aspects of PowerPoint is the ability to 'black out' or 'white out' the screen. This gives the speaker the chance to draw the audience's attention back to the speaker at will.
4. Keep any support material as simple and uncluttered as possible. If you are using video material, select enough to give the context of the idea you want to focus on, but keep it short so that your audience does not stray from your main idea.

5. When referring to any support material, give sufficient clues to the audience to help them through the detail. Always discuss the screen, video, or aspects of the graph or image; don't just show it and hope the listener will fill in the details.

6. All handling of aids must be manageable in the venue you are to speak in. This requires your careful research of the facilities and arrangements for all technologies well before the day of presentation.

7. It is better to choose a few powerful aids than aim for too many which will take your energy and focus away from your message. Of course, in these days of multimedia software, you are able to run a highly complex presentation with the click of the mouse.

8. Be aware of unexpected sounds in the PowerPoint presentation. Practice with the sound turned on, to avoid surprises such as 'screeching brakes'.

9. Always have a contingency plan in case of technology failure. In our experience, the new technologies can be unreliable. The challenge for you, as a good presenter, is to keep command of the situation and to remember that your message is the driving force of the presentation, not the technology. You can manage without it!

There are also useful general guidelines for developing visual aids that are appealing for any of the media discussed above.

DEVELOPING TEXT CHARTS AND GRAPHS

1. Keep your aid truly visual. Do not allow it to become full of narrative text.

2. Pay attention to consistency of fonts and layout, with an uncluttered look to make it easy for your audience.

3. Support your ideas with graphs and images. Keep these as simple and striking as you can.

4. Use colour carefully. If you are creating a straightforward chart, you can use only about three colours, one for background, one for headings and highlighting, and one for the text itself. If you are creating graphs, use no more than five colours. If you need more than this, it is probably too complicated and you are giving too much information in one visual image. For transparencies, use light colours on a dark

background. For 35mm slides and LCD projectors, a dark background with light text is most effective.

5.   Be consistent with colours. It will give your presentation a unified and professional appearance.
6.   Exploit the capacity of PowerPoint to animate graphical information by building data piece by piece.

Deciding how and when to use technology can be a challenging task. Here are two case studies that demonstrate the power of careful, creative, and effective use of technology for presentations.

Case study

The 'big event' often uses technology to enhance the speaking situation and to arouse the emotions of the audience. In the twenty-first century, the lone speaker in front of a large crowd is a rare occurrence. The events surrounding the Sydney 2000 Olympics have extended the use of technology in Australian presentations. Because Olympic events always tug on the heartstrings, they are a perfect occasion to bring together the music, images and sound effects that will stir an audience to support their country and its star athletes.

This is what you live for: Themeing Paralympics 2000

A Paralympic Team 2000 dinner, held a few months before the Sydney 2000 Olympics, was the occasion to celebrate the success of the state athletes who had been named, earlier that day, as members of the Sydney 2000 Australian Paralympic team. The audio-visual production and delivery for the event was organised professionally by The Presentation People.[8] They proudly showcased their unique Immersion Themeing, one of their virtual themeing products. The event took place in the ballroom of one of the city's grandest hotels and was host to five hundred people. Three walls of the ballroom carried large screens, with the largest in the centre being a dominating 8 metres by 6 metres in size. As the speakers also appeared on these screens when addressing the audience, they became larger than life and always the centre of attention in their bid to hold their audience. This is one of the strong ways in which the technology can support the live speaker and assist them in keeping audience attention.

The atmosphere of this dinner was, therefore, dominated by the power of the audio-visual presence. When people were taking their seats, the large visual of the flaming torch, which is always atop the stadium during the Olympics and finally lit at the opening ceremony, appeared on all screens. This made the audience feel as if they were actually at the Olympics and the excitement had begun. The immersion themeing presentation lasted only three minutes, but it burst upon the room like a powerful sudden explosion, with the sound quality loud and stentorian.

As the presentation began, we saw images, on the large screens, of future Paralympic champions battling against the odds: the behind-the-scenes preparation of a blind runner's early race meet and an intellectually disabled shotputter training on the family farm. All the while, the stirring music's lyrics encouraged them to reach higher for their dream. Then the training images gave way to that magic moment when the dream was realised. They were walking and wheelchairing in their uniforms into the Olympic stadium at the opening of a Paralympic Games. Suddenly, as we were viewing these many champions, the walls of the room were covered in projected crowd scenes from floor to ceiling, and the sounds of a tumultuous crowd, aroused to fever pitch, surrounded us. This was the surprise element of the presentation. The three vast cream-curtained walls had become alive, in every space outside the three screens, to represent the multitudes of people who would be at the Games to support the athletes. The noise of this cheering imaginary crowd was deafening; the excitement was contagious. The pride in the team and the anticipated emotion of their future success filled the room.

The second audio-visual, towards the end of the night, used the split screen technique and could therefore show multiple images of athletes striving for gold. Images of the beauty of Sydney Harbour and the Harbour Bridge as well as the nationalism of Australian supporters with faces painted with the Australian flag, and other such rousing scenes, propelled us mentally forward to the actual Games. This presentation was more traditional and showed us Phil Brady, the Australian singer, with guitar in the environs of Sydney, and introduced the official song for the 2000 Australian Paralympians, 'Rise to the Moment!' The words 'this is what you live for' and 'this is what you came for' surrounded the audience as they looked at athletes competing and receiving medals for their efforts. The audio-visual presentations contributed enormously to the emotional ambience of a special event.

In an interview we conducted about the reasoning behind the development of strategies for the event, the paralympian who helped plan the presentation suggested that the organisers were looking for images and sounds that would stimulate the sensory perceptions of the audience.[9] He wanted to take the audience through the experiences that a Paralympian competitor faces. We were to experience the struggle, the hopes and the aspirations, from the early training meetings, through state and national triumphs, until the success of being chosen is finally achieved. That success was what this night was all about. The other intention was to capture the excitement and unique feel of the Sydney Games. As he said, 'many people have not seen wheelchair basketball or wheelchair tennis' and the images would transport the viewer into the reality of the Games and what they would be like. The chosen music and other sound effects would add to this atmosphere. At another part of the evening, when an auction for fundraising for the Games was taking place, he chose sound effects which would take audience members out of their seats at the dinner tables and place them in the atmosphere of the conviviality of the Sydney Games—sound effects such as a plane taking off, to involve people with the excitement of travel, or waves crashing on the shore, a very Australian sound, to remind us that this was 'our' Paralympic Games. All of the sounds and the vision had been chosen to arouse memories and sensations, and carry our minds through to other times and places; times and places which were a part of Paralympic struggle and Paralympic glory.

It is important to remark, however, that many members of the audience may have been equally moved by the 'live' presentations they experienced. There was the speech of the Paralympic swimmer, as he recited a simple poem he had written for the occasion and shared his enthusiasm for life and sport with his audience.[10] The ambience of the evening was established early by a group of four local schoolboys playing their guitars and singing the national anthem. One of the members of the audience at our table, who is a business development executive at the local large convention centre and attends many such events, spoke of the moving experience of hearing a choir singing the national anthem along with a large visual presentation. These are indicators that it is important to keep the balance of the living person as well as the technology to fully involve the audience.

The evening was also balanced by an enormously humorous speech by a man who was introduced as Mr Phillip Psaltis, the Executive Director for the Olympic Games in Athens 2004. This speaker seemed very credible, and was an unusually entertaining speaker for an Olympic official, with a great knowledge of his Australian audience. As the audience laughed and laughed at the many jokes he was making, often at the expense of Olympic officialdom and his Australian audience, some audience members must have become suspicious. He also used the visual backup in the room to perfection. As he spoke, we saw many images, including those of his cycling champion father, the Australian pie he had come to look forward to eating in our country, the pope, Mussolini, and even the mafia, as he spoke of Greece's battle with Italy to win the Olympics. He hastened to add that his Greek aunt could get us into the closing ceremony of the Games if we were prepared to wear a platypus (a native animal) suit and be on the bottom of a human pyramid. The images were all perfectly timed to accompany his speech. The audience, who had mainly collapsed into laughter at the end of his forty-minute presentation, were then induced to stand and dance around their tables to the music of *Zorba the Greek.*

This mixture of living and audio-visual presentations highlighted the strengths of each. It is much more difficult for an audio-visual to hold the audience for the length of time, and get them involved in the same way that the 'Greek official' from the speaking consultancy Corporate Impostors was able to do with his humorous presentation using visual backup. It is true that an audio-visual presentation can carry us into the heart of a world that only the best speaker could help us to fully visualise through descriptive language, but it cannot entirely recreate the personal touch of a powerful living speaker.

Case study

Making Brisbane the livability capital of Australia

Another presentation has also demonstrated to us that 'going all the way' with technology can sometimes be the best solution.[11] The presentation was a launch by a community group who wished to persuade their local and state governing body that it was important to reconsider their plans for developing Brisbane. The proposal was presented to the Urban Renewal Task Force, a group of mainly traffic engineers and town planners.

The community group determined that their purpose was to interrupt the process of planning that had so far been dominated by the technical concerns of many road planners. Therefore, it needed to be a highly persuasive and motivational presentation that would capture both the minds and hearts of the listeners. As technical professionals, the listeners already had a great deal of knowledge, and even, from their perspective, superior knowledge of the solutions available for traffic and town planning problems. For a community group to shift such legitimate and highly respected knowledge, it needed to come up with some very convincing arguments.

There were also some other constraints that they needed to address. Firstly, as a group, they tended to understand problems of traffic planning in terms not just of traffic flow, but of how planning works to make cities good places to live in. Therefore, they viewed the problem of Brisbane's livability as a global problem, not just a local one. They wanted to demonstrate to traffic experts that Brisbane could find a solution, and that this solution might show the way for many cities throughout the world.

Secondly, they needed to address the credibility problem that faces all non-experts who are trying to gain a hearing. Their solutions had been developed out of a community consultation process. This was achieved under the guidance of a Steering Committee led by an experienced community leader who had successfully led a campaign in his own area to stop a major road through the suburbs. A self-taught and battle-hardened spokesperson for new ways to approach modern city living, he knew that he could not provide the credibility required for this professionally trained audience.[12]

Finally, as in so many situations where important and effective communication must be achieved, time and money were limited. The time-frame for the development of the presentation was only five weeks, and this in itself put considerable restrictions on what was possible. And, of course, the whole launch had to be funded by this community group.

Coming up with 'the big idea' to make people sit up and take notice was the major challenge, according to the organisers. The idea emerged when the group started to tie their problem to their listeners' experience. The city had, in the previous few years, achieved a major success with its recycling and waste disposal program. The whole city had become involved in changing habits and recycling, not just dumping. This city-wide experience led to the creation of a simple but powerful message, which could be tied to the more difficult problem of traffic planning.

Creating a visual image of a recycling bin half-filled with cars (see Figure 10.2), the theme became 'Reduce: Recycle'.

Having established 'the big idea', the challenge was to motivate the audience. What was now needed was a sense of drama and a sense of professionalism to match the importance of the shift in thinking that the community group wanted to induce in their expert audience.

The group believed that the audience would expect a presentation by their high-profile leader, one of the type that they had seen many times before. Therefore, it was important to remove the face of the community leader, to professionalise and depersonalise the launch. The solution they came up with was a multimedia presentation with voice-over.

From the moment of their arrival at the launch, the audience was treated to a sense of drama. They arrived at the door to be given an A3 size booklet that was colourful and filled with flow charts and diagrams that would be used in the presentation. This larger than normal 'landscape' booklet hinted at the size of the vision the group had developed. The audience, once inside, was greeted by two large screens and a sense of the professionalism they might see at a launch for new technology by a company like IBM or Macintosh. The group admitted to taking care of every detail because, 'Every single aspect is part of the message'.

The presentation was a 25-minute slide show using colour photographs, graphs and diagrams to propose an innovative and yet feasible direction for a new livable Brisbane. By structuring the presentation around two scenarios, Brisbane 1995 and Brisbane 2006, the slide show set up a vision for the future.

Slides of the ugliness and inconvenience of the poorly planned cities most of us live in were juxtaposed against slides of some success stories such as Curitiba in South America and Portland in the United States. The use of photographs, which provided hard evidence of the strategies presently being used in other places in the world, led towards an outline of what an ideal Brisbane could look like in the year 2006.

Figure 10.2   This image, redrawn from a still of the video 'Making Brisbane the livability capital of Australia', linked past successes with future visions

Source: Reproduced by permission of David Engwicht and The Bowen Hills Business and Residents Association.

Graphs provided the audience with accessible images of the statistical evidence to support the claims for the need for a change in direction from major freeway construction to alternative arrangements such as light rail, bikeways and local, community-focused arrangements for living and working in close proximity.

Another technology which supported this visually commanding presentation was the use of voice-over by a trained actor who projected warmth and credibility. This strategy completed the package for the presentation from a committed but amateur group who wanted to have experts sit up and take notice.

By recognising the power of the medium in such a presentation, the community group was able to communicate with the professionals on their own terms. The presentation provided substantial and detailed evidence of the failings of the present approach as well as examples, backed by statistics and photographs, of success stories. Change was needed. In this instance, the technologies used were a powerful tool in the hands of the group to present themselves in a highly professional and persuasive way.

The presentation did interrupt the process of planning in Brisbane. A combination of great ideas, the power of language, and the tools of modern technology can create a formidable force to achieve your persuasive purpose.

MORE TOOLS FOR THE KITBAG

There are many advantages in using the variety of technologies available to us in the twenty-first century. Maintaining knowledge of what's available and how to use it well will be an ongoing task. It is another important tool for you to keep in your kitbag of resources. As a good presenter, you should remain open to the possibilities of new technologies while keeping a critical eye on what will help you to communicate your message and what may hinder you.

TIPS

- Select your visual aids carefully to support your ideas, not distract them.
- Too many visual aids can tire your audience.

- Provide visual variety to stimulate your listeners' interest. A mix of text, graphics and images can do this.
- Keep your visual aids truly visual, and avoid using too much text.
- Help your listeners to work through the detail of your visual aid. Discuss the transparency, slide or graphics, don't just assume your listeners will make the interpretations that you want.
- Choose visual aids which are practical and easy to use. Models and demonstrations which are complex can be more trouble than they are worth.
- Keep alert to developments in technologies. These can help you turn an average presentation into an impressive performance.
- Use technology to support the ideas that will help you to achieve your purpose. Don't let the technology drive your presentation.

11

Selling your ideas: Proposing and pitching

I'll introduce you to the magic that happens in big pitches, when the whole is bigger than the sum of the parts, when 'something clicks' and a dull pitch becomes very special.[1]

'And the winner is . . . Sydney!' With these words, Juan Antonio Samaranch announced the reward of winning one of the world's most lucrative pitches for business. Sydney had won the honour of staging the 2000 Olympic Games. This was a very public pitch that was televised and beamed around the world for all to see. The Olympic pitch, occurring every four years, is the archetype for business pitches but, in fact, there are many important pitches taking place every hour in all parts of the world. These are presentations that are designed to persuade the audience to a definite course of action in accepting the services of the presenting team and their organisation.

Selling your ideas, your goods or your services is one of the most challenging and potentially creative communication situations you may ever be in. As a way of communicating the power and complexity of selling, we will tell you a story about one of the most creative and persuasive of sales.

The management of British Rail, after a considerable amount of criticism and customer dissatisfaction, approached a large public relations firm in London to handle a publicity campaign to get them 'back on track'. An appointment was made for them to meet with the public relations team at the firm's offices.

On arrival, the British Rail group went immediately to reception. As they approached the desk, they were surprised to hear a beautifully groomed but poorly spoken assistant on the phone talking loudly about her escapades of the previous evening. She ignored their presence and went on enjoying her socialising. Finally, she put down the phone, and in a rather uninterested way, directed them to the principals of the firm for their scheduled appointment. They were, in fact, directed to the wrong room, and after some confusion, finally found the right conference room.

By now they were feeling somewhat concerned, but this turned to anxiety when one of the principals rushed in, apologised for being late, and said there would be a short hold-up before the meeting could start.

At the same time, a badly dressed tea lady entered the room, picked up some rather cheap and cracked china and offered tea. The British Rail executives were shaken.

The public relations team then swiftly entered the room, stood smiling but confident, and opened the presentation of their campaign proposal by saying, 'You now know how it feels to be a customer of British Rail.'[2]

Needless to say, they won the £3 million contract.

At Portobello Road in London, you can observe some of the experts in the art of pitching as the crowds gather to hear them sell their wares. Whether you are a professional in an advertising agency, law firm, accounting firm, construction company or another kind of business, you may have to sell your products every day in the twenty-first-century marketplace. This may seem a long distance from the spiel and high energy of Portobello Road, but those salesman may be able to offer very sound advice, as there are many cases where pitches are notoriously poorly planned and under-prepared. The expert pitch requires a strategic plan and a creative ability to carry it off.

You may think that you will never be called upon to present a really high-powered presentation, but remember that whenever you set out to influence others, such as when you are on a committee, or even presenting a seminar or research proposal, you should apply the same principles. There may also be many times when you have to develop a formal proposal to suggest ways to change your workplace or policies.

Remember that the strategies suggested in this chapter can be of use to you in many situations where you want to influence others to accept your ideas.

Now we are going to tell *you* how you can start winning contracts and influencing others to adopt your ideas.

We propose that there are four important strategies you should consider:

1. Develop a strategic approach to help you prepare.
2. Show your audience the benefits of your plan.
3. Attend to the concerns of your audiences and develop counter-arguments for those concerns.
4. Demonstrate the soundness of your arguments and the credibility of your position.[3]

DEVELOP A STRATEGIC APPROACH TO HELP YOU PREPARE

Your main purpose may be to be chosen for the work on offer or to have your audience accept your proposal for change. However, that is far too general a purpose to carry you into a focused pitch or proposal. The real purpose is strongly linked to what the granting company or audience would give as its main reasons for choosing you or your ideas over other contenders.

Check your most important messages, or those of each member of the team, and keep the focus on these throughout. Remember that you only cloud your main points by too much extraneous detail. Choose the number of things you are going to be able to say, keeping to the rule of spending three or four minutes to build each point thoroughly. You need to extend the statement 'we want to be chosen because . . .' or 'this is the best plan because . . .'. Keep sight of the practical side of what you have to offer, and you could also be balancing the economic advantage of the path you are choosing. You may even wish to offer alternative solutions, to give the audience a choice of budget options or outcomes. Focus on your purpose early, although the purpose should be open to modification in the planning stage. This will help to keep your planning relevant.

We have talked about group presentations in Chapter 4, and you will remember the importance of choosing and balancing the capabilities of your team. These points need to be reviewed when you are beginning planning. Do not forget to appoint a team leader, if there is not a natural leader in the hierarchy of your organisation or student group who should fill the role. Remember that the bonds you show as you interact, listen, and refer to one another during the presentation are representative of the extent to which you will be seen as a cohesive cooperative team.

Your professionalism and attention to detail during the pitch will be taken to reflect your abilities, as a company or group, to continue these strengths in the service you give. One of the client's strongest concerns is often the fact that, while the pitch may be presented by senior members of the company, more junior staff will actually carry out the work. You need to face this objection and counteract it with clear proof of the leadership and service that the presenting team is ready to contribute.

Undoubtedly it is important, also, that you try to get your team into a good position on the pitch list on presentation day. Pitches can be won from any position, but first or last are the most memorable spots, as the research into primacy and recency has shown. However, you would probably not choose to go at the end of a long day with many pitches ahead of you, unless you are sure you can bring a strong element of surprise and interest. You would certainly avoid a repetition of any obvious elements if placed in this position, as they have probably already been reiterated too many times.

When you are in the planning stages, you need to follow the advice that we have given you earlier in the book, to collect all data that may be useful, and to brainstorm and keep your options open.

An important part of the process of data-gathering and synthesis is to learn the rules of the game that the audience you are addressing likes to play. This includes the sort of language they understand and appreciate, the image they feel most comfortable with and, indeed, all the aspects that could be called their cultural norms.

It is important to structure clearly, with a focus on the speaking situation. One of the most dangerous pitfalls for proposal and pitch presenters occurs when they also present a long and complex written submission. We recently worked with a management group from the construction industry. The presenters wanted to fill their half-hour of presentation with all of the important details from their lengthy written submission. When experts in a field know a lot about a topic and have spent a great deal of time on the details, they have the tendency to want to share it all. It was important for the management group to realise that speaking is a completely different medium. Consequently, our clients had to start all over again from a different perspective.

They had to ask themselves clear questions, such as the following:

- What is the most important thing we want to say?
- How should we phrase that 'most important thing'?
- Could that become a theme for our presentation?
- Which elements of our written submission should be kept in a spoken situation?
- How could we best structure our presentation to be coherent and focused and present the big picture, but not leave out the concrete evidence?
- How can we best present our own experience to support our claims?

Written submissions are often very complex and detailed—but not even the best listeners can retain very much detail. Our clients needed to let go of this detail and hope that their earlier written document, and any follow-up material, would do this task for them. Remember not to distract the listeners with written material when you are speaking. This should always come as a follow-up to your powerfully interactive presentation.

There are some circumstances where you may want your audience to take careful notes as you progress through a point-form discussion. In these instances, the PowerPoint handout may be used as a support, and could help your listeners to consider the detail after the event. The handout might also act as a prompt to memory, and help to distinguish your proposal from others, if it is competing with several on the same day.

Our management group needed to find interesting anecdotes and stories that would represent their experience and capabilities, and which would, at the same time, help to show their humanity and approachability to the people they hoped to work with. These are usually not the stories you include in a formal written document, and so it is a very different kind of preparation.

For example, when one construction manager told his personal story of saving several thousands of dollars on a large hospital complex simply by being 'on the ball', he showed the importance and usefulness of having his pitch team oversee the project. He explained that there can be oversights when builders execute the design from a complex set of plans. This is, he argued, where construction management is so important. He showed that his team would attend to many details, such as making sure that ordinary power points were not installed by mistake where points capable of handling extra electrical capacity for special hospital machinery, such as x-ray machines and generators, were required. With these anecdotes he built up the confidence of his audience in his ability to carry out the task. This sort of information and credibility-building is easy to include in a spoken presentation, but is not appropriate in a written submission.

One of the participants commented at the end of the session that this structuring in a focused way was the most important thing we had talked about, from his point of view. He commented that he believed that structuring should be a strength for people in his profession, as they dealt with systems all the time. However, it is difficult to rethink in terms of the strengths of structuring for the spoken word, and find a different approach, in professions where the written submission has been very dominant. It is important to spend time on the overall structure, and on each individual's structure also.

As a preparation strategy, to help you approach your task, we recommend that you take speech consultant Neil Flett's suggestion. In his excellent book *Pitch Doctor*, Flett suggests setting up a 'war room'[4] where you can keep all your cuttings, visuals and plans together, and have a spot that is seen as the strategy area. Charts on the wall or your whiteboard that reflect your planning stages can help you to quickly pick up the threads as each meeting progresses. Even for student presentations, the idea of a war room has its merits.

SHOW THE BENEFITS OF YOUR PLAN

This strategy has the explicit purpose of focusing your listeners on how your idea, product or service can benefit them.

Usually, as the owners or providers of a service, we have a particular commitment to that service. We feel it has particular qualities that make it a good service. However, this strategy demands that you take your concerns away from what you believe are the best qualities of your service, and research the benefits your clients will experience if they use your service. It demands that you consider the organisational objectives of your client to find ways to describe how your service matches the uses to which your client will put it.

Our Chapter 2 emphasises the importance of getting to know your listeners, but this is even more important, on a personal level, when preparing for a business pitch. You will need to spend as much time as possible getting to know the decision-makers who will accept or decline your offer. Neil Flett suggests that you use every excuse possible to spend more time getting to talk to and formally interview your audience members before the event. He suggests that this is not *an* important part of pitching business—it is *the* important part.[5]

You need to imagine what your competitors might offer, and work out how to counter that by being better or different in your approach. You need to put yourself 'inside the head' of your potential client.

Imagine that you have a courier service which, if used five times a week, is cheaper than competing services. However, you have a potential client who is likely to use a courier service only during intensive periods, say three times a week. So you research the client and find that what they need is a speedy and reliable courier for those three jobs a week. Your service has the benefit of a two-hour turnaround time, which you guarantee. You have a match.

The important thing is to show your clients how the service particularly benefits them.

ATTEND TO YOUR CLIENTS' CONCERNS

Whenever clients anticipate problems or expect expensive solutions, their listening becomes clouded by those negatives. This third strategy has the explicit purpose of focusing you on creating a positive image of your idea, product or service.

One way to get the attention of your audience is through the use of a creative opening. Remember the suggestions we have given in Chapter 5 about introductions and conclusions. The example of the British Rail team gives you a prototype for the very daring creative opening. The pitch that won the Olympics for Australia opened with the room in darkness and the *crack* of a starter's pistol to jolt the audience. This was followed by video footage of previous and more recent Olympic Games in which Australia has always competed. The video finally moved to the music of Australia's favourite song, 'Waltzing Matilda', to create an emotive nationalistic opening for this bid.

It is important to realise that you need to take some *pathos* out of your kitbag when you are making a pitch. Realise also that, in a group presentation, each speaker should find a mini creative opening to keep the interest strong throughout the presentation.

You should describe the strengths and successes of your idea and use concrete examples. In addition, analyse the situation to anticipate any negative images your clients might hold of your company or service. By anticipating their concerns, you can build counter-arguments into your proposal or pitch.

Imagine that you are proposing an innovative way to calm traffic in the streets of your area, and you anticipate some community concern over access to the local shopping centre. You treat it as a minor inconvenience and describe a detour that would require only a small change in routine in return for a large change in the environment. You successfully counter with the positive image of reduced traffic and noise and put the problem quickly into perspective.

DEMONSTRATE SOUNDNESS AND CREDIBILITY

This strategy requires you to use the full range of persuasive tools available to you, to call up all three rhetorical proofs *ethos*, *pathos* and *logos* (Chapter 3). There are many ways in which the use of these can be helpful. It may seem obvious that you will need to establish your credibility and present your evidence, but realise that many decision-makers are really responding to their 'gut feeling' about your company or argument. So, do not be afraid to explore any emotional appeals you can incorporate.

It is often possible to include an emotional appeal through a reference to the prestige of the client company, for example, and how you can contribute to building that further. Neil Flett suggests that you should also remember to put the client logo in the prominent position on your visuals and place your own at the bottom.[6] This shows a strong respect for the client's interests first, and this is surely what you want to convey, to win their trust as well as their judgement. This type of strategy could be equally applied as an appeal to the authority of your supervisors or lecturers in a proposal for a structural change or a research project.

You should also demonstrate that your proposal fulfils the criteria that have been set for you. When you claim to have a solution to a problem, you need to provide a detailed and careful account of how your idea, product or service will benefit your audience. You need to talk through your line of reasoning and detail the assumptions that you have made about their needs, and how your service or idea would fill those needs.

In recent years, for example, there has been considerable concern about recycling rubbish. Local governments have been looking for systems and services which might solve this problem. But persuading city councils to use separate bins for recycling rubbish would require proof that people would actually bother to separate their rubbish. Your proposal, then, would require not just an outline of how a recycling system would work, but evidence that the system would be used by ordinary citizens. You could use a survey that demonstrated that people would use the system as it was designed, and results of a pilot study of one typical suburb for this purpose. If this one typical suburb took to recycling, and public opinion was in favour of the strategy, it would be reasonable to assume that recycling would work throughout the city.

This takes care of *logos*, the logic of your proposal, but what of *ethos*, what of your credibility? *Ethos* could be mobilised by clearly outlining to local government the origins of the claim made in the survey. You could do this by providing a background of the researchers who conducted the study, and by showing your expertise in the field through offering examples of other cities which are using recycling systems. This will make your idea seem credible: people here are willing to use it, and it will work. You would effectively demonstrate that you are worth listening to and that your ideas are worth believing in.

You have now used two out of the three rhetorical proofs, but what of *pathos?* Don't underestimate its role in this proposal. Remember that, as we all suspect at certain times, most important decisions are made on the basis of emotional, not rational, commitment. Recent awareness of the importance of the environment to our very survival has changed the way we think and feel about using and abusing natural resources. Along with the proof about the practicality of a waste disposal system to recycle rubbish, you should call on emotional commitment to the environment and the question of its and our own survival. Equally, remind local government of the positive attitudes to the strategy that ratepayers had in your study: appeal to the vote-catching aspects of the system.

A mix of all of these proofs is useful. But a good communicator is careful to balance that mix. What separates the good communicator from the mediocre one is an awareness that, even in the most technical of presentations, listeners are human and will be swayed not only by facts, by the *logos*, of the proposal or pitch, but by the speaker's credibility, the speaker's *ethos*, and by appeals to emotion, by *pathos*; what sets a good communicator apart is a demonstrated skill in harnessing listeners' imaginations and in helping them to see the potential of the speaker's offerings.

DETERMINING THE KEY ASPECTS OF PROPOSALS

Whenever you have to present a proposal, you have to determine:

1. an outline of the problem that you are dealing with
2. the objectives you are setting out to achieve
3. the product or service that you propose as a response to this problem
4. the plan of action or schedule for its implementation
5. the cost of this proposal.

Depending on the particular proposal and the context in which you are presenting, some aspects will have a higher priority than others. A technical proposal to the research division of your organisation probably requires considerable details of the product and its design and implementation, whereas a proposal to your marketing staff probably requires less attention to technical aspects and more to useability and adaptability. In addition, comparisons with competing products on the market would become the key to securing support for it within your organisation.

Case study: The proposal

Keeping all of the issues we have raised in mind, consider this case study of a proposal which we believe was an impressive persuasive effort to gain financial support for a venture project developed by a young engineering graduate.[7] He presented his proposal to a group of investors; his sole purpose was to get them to commit their money to his project. He needed to persuade them not only that his idea was a feasible one from a technical point of view, but also that it was marketable. The investors would have a lot to lose if his idea was not saleable.

As you are examining his proposal, pay some attention to how he has structured the proposal. He has used a modified form of the motivated sequence, a pattern of arranging material that we covered in Chapter 5. He uses an attention and needs step and a satisfaction and action step, but omits the visualisation step. The motivated sequence is a useful structuring device to use for business proposals.

An outline of the problem: An introduction

The engineer started his speech with a description of the end product of the venture project he wanted them to support: a new portable electro-cardiograph device.

He immediately established credibility for his idea by stating that heart specialists at the Princess Alexandra Hospital (a local well-respected hospital) had given him his idea. This statement served three purposes: first, it identified his device as a legitimate medical need; second, it intimated that he had contacts with high-status medical staff; and third, it indicated that such a device is desired and supported by the marketplace. He then explained that present systems cannot serve the same function.

> A cardiograph itself is used when a patient exhibits symptoms such as dizziness, chest pain or heart palpitations. This is where we currently face problems. If the symptoms are only sporadic, recurring say, once a week, obviously it is very impractical, inconvenient, and expensive to keep the patients in hospital for a long period of time. This is where the cardiologist could use a portable electro-cardiograph.

Notice his use of the list of three words to draw attention to the problems of the present system—'impractical, inconvenient, and expensive'. The use of rhythm adds impact to this statement of fact.

He then proceeds to ask three rhetorical questions: 'What's so special about this product?', 'What makes it so interesting?' and finally, 'Why build another one?'

Rhetorical questions encourage listeners to engage with arguments. Clearly, our engineer is throwing up challenges to his investors. He is opening himself up to their questions and telling them that he has good answers for them. All this adds to his credibility. He is telling them that he has no hidden agenda: he has a good useful product and he is going to prove it. He answers his third question like this:

There are many electro-cardiograph devices available on the market. So why design another one? Why build another one? Well, there's room for improvement. There are problems with the existing devices, and most of these problems revolve around the way that these devices actually store the information.

One of the most common methods with the device itself is to connect it to the patient, turn it on and from that point onwards all ECG activity is stored. What happens here is that the memory becomes full very, very quickly. To get around this problem, manufacturers will reduce the sampling rate to a lower-quality sample rate so that the memory lasts longer. Of course, you end up with a lower-quality recording in the long run.

Another problem with this method is that the cardiologist is then faced with an enormous amount of data to have to sort through to try to find this one event occurring. A method that is available and tries to overcome this problem is to purchase a patient trigger device where the patient feels the symptom and triggers the device to start it recording from that point onwards for a set period. This, too, has a fundamental problem. By the time the patient actually feels the symptom and presses the device to start it recording, the event has usually passed. The information captured is of very little use.

This is where my design comes in and solves all of these problems.

He completes an important part of the overall presentation by explaining the problem that exists, the objectives in designing a device to solve the problem, and the features of the device that he has designed.

The objectives to be achieved

In clear, technical but accessible language, he outlines the four objectives he has set for his design. It needs to be

- patient-triggered
- portable
- able to store information, and
- able to capture 20 seconds each side of a palpitation—as cardiologists consider this appropriate.

The product which will solve the problem

He then outlines some of the features that are required to achieve this.

So, let's look at some of the features. Obviously, if the device is to be worn for a long period of time it needs to be as unobtrusive as possible, so it needs to be pocket-size and lightweight. It is battery-powered and I'm currently running it on two AA 1.5 volt batteries and this gives a battery life of around eight days. It needs to be easy to operate and reliable.

Two other external features are necessary. What it needs is a signal to display the status of the device to the patients themselves, so that they always know what's happening. It also needs a method of communicating the data back to a personal computer for analysis and display. With this feature, I've built in some options. Either you can use an RS232 communications link which gives you high speed, but there's a bulky socket involved, or you can use an infra LED link. This has no socket but a slow communication rate.

Notice his careful structuring of the key features for his listening investors. The language is sufficiently accessible to make sense to the non-technical investors, but sufficiently specific to demonstrate his credibility.

He has also carefully ordered particular aspects of the presentation to suit these particular listeners. He outlines, first, those features that might be considered within the range of knowledge expected by the investors. He then signals that he will outline technical features. He moves out of the more limited range of investor knowledge to establish his technical credibility. He has accounted for the fact that some investors may have the depth of knowledge to judge him on his technical skills; less technically knowledgeable investors will feel more confident if they have some understanding of what he is attempting to achieve in a technical sense. So, from this perspective, it is imperative that he give adequate detail to impress, while keeping control of the complexity of the explanation. He then outlines those technical features, detailing the device's micro-computer, its sampling rate, its memory loop that allows for recording both before and after an incident, its storage capabilities and its four-channel system.

At this point, it is useful for any speaker, and important for any listening audience, to take stock of what has been said. A great deal of new and important information has been presented by the speaker and heard by the listeners. This speaker assists his listeners by putting it into context: he provides an internal summary of the issues, and then an internal preview of the practical implications of getting the device to the marketplace.

So, I've covered why the device is needed, what the device does, how it will function, and also its capacity. All that is really left for me now is to give you an idea of how far along the road this project actually is.

The plan of action

For anyone building a prototype, this can be a difficult stage. Even good ideas seem to meet opposition in their implementation phase. Trying to finance a new product is equally tough. That is why it is so important that our engineer structure this part of his presentation carefully to persuade his potential investors that he really can deliver on his promise.

Here is his attempt to achieve this goal. Perhaps the best test of its success is to ask yourself if you would invest. We believe he was convincing. He picks up his prototype and displays it.

> Here I have a fully functional prototype which I've implemented using these two boxes. The first box is the analogue stage and it has been implemented using miniaturised components. The components are actually tucked up in a corner here, and most of the box is taken up by the input and connection hardware.
>
> The second box is the digital stage. It has not as yet been implemented using miniaturised components. We see it here in full-size components and there's an enormous size difference. As I said, the device is fully functional and all that really remains is the miniaturisation—I see this as unproblematic. It is merely a formality to take that step. Preliminary experiments show that I should be able to get the device down to something roughly half the size of my wallet.

Notice his careful word choice to demonstrate that the project is achievable, technically—'the device is fully functional'—and his use of a concrete example—'roughly half the size of my wallet'.

The cost of the proposal

His handling of the cost issue is also exemplary.

> So, let's consider marketing this device. If I were to go out today and purchase a single-channel version that uses memory inefficiently and only samples at a rate of 60 hertz, it would cost around $2500. I could buy a multi-channel version. It is certainly very hard to find one on the present market because they are so memory-inefficient. I did find one, and it costs $48 000.
>
> My device has a component cost of around $200. I plan to market and retail the device in a single-channel version for $1000 and the multi-channel version for $1500. And this, as far as I can see, will open up the market.

> Instead of just selling to cardiologists and specialists in the field, we can now sell to general practitioners. I know many people myself who've gone to their GP and said, 'I have a heart flutter that comes and goes, what is it?' The GP usually responds with, 'There's nothing I can do.' Now they can use this device.

He makes a clear cost comparison followed by a personalised account of the marketability of the product. These strategies support his well-argued position. Flourishing a wallet is useful visual support to emphasise the useable size of his prototype.

His focus on logical argument is complemented by emotional appeals. His notion of 'opening up the market' calls up important financial concerns but focuses on possibilities. Equally, to locate a particular market for his device is powerful in the argument about financing the venture. This concrete example of the use that GPs would make of the innovation heightens his investors' sense of the possibilities for such a device and, simultaneously, subtly draws on altruistic motives to gain support.

A conclusion

In a range of carefully structured illustrations of the benefits and practicalities of his device, our engineer has gathered support for the logic of his argument, the credibility of his work, and the possibilities for marketing his new design. He needs now to conclude strongly, to overview dynamically, and to speak engagingly. We think he does so. What do you think?

> So, in summary, let's have a look at what I can offer you. I've constructed a device that is based on an analogue stage and a digital stage. The main function of the device is to store and capture ECG recordings either side of the trigger point, and what this does is to give us the ability to send a patient home. We have a cost-effective solution now, and instead of keeping patients in an expensive hospital bed for long periods, we can now send them home and be confident in the fact that if an event occurs, we will capture it. What I have done here is to produce a useful, viable, and very marketable product.

Case study: The business pitch

This case describes a three-part encounter to work with two lawyers and their research officer in perfecting a powerful pitch. On our first encounter with the team, we worked out the strategy and plan for the pitch.

A large finance organisation asked each of five contenders for their business to present their ideas in a one-hour segment. One hour is quite a long time for a pitch and can become a trap if the pitch presenters try to hold the interest of the audience in a one-way monologue for that length of time. We discussed the possibility of any interactivity between team and audience. As it turned out, this was a perfect pitch in which to include an interactive segment.

Building a relationship with the client

The pitch team was made up of two presenters. They were a male senior partner of the firm and a woman lawyer associate, each with different backgrounds and experience to balance what they could contribute to the corporate mission that the client had in mind. They were both extremely strong presenters. The associate had just joined the practice. She had previously worked as a lawyer in industry and, in this past position, had been a client of her new workplace. In convincing a large finance organisation that they understood the company's problems, these lawyers could hardly offer more proof than the involvement of someone who had recently left a position on the client's side of the table.

The pitch presenters were vying for a job that included a considerable amount of facilitation with the staff of the employing corporation. It was decided that the pitch team would spend fifteen to twenty minutes of their time in a 'demonstration facilitation' with the senior corporate team who would be judging the pitch. This was the first breakthrough in our plan for an exciting and more risk-taking pitch than the other companies would be likely to present. We then planned a foolproof approach to the facilitation by focusing it down to a specific area of inquiry, and making it one in which the presenters could easily revert to giving information if the audience members were quiet and not outgoing on the day.

They chose to look at the 'barriers' that members of the audience could foresee would have to be overcome if the new process was to have a highly successful outcome for the company. The pitch team's research had already uncovered barriers which companies in general were concerned about, and they could use these to stimulate the audience if response was at all slow. Copies of this corporate list would be held up at the end of the facilitation and left for the client to peruse at their leisure. In this case, the pitch presenters were invited to a 'scoping' meeting with the client in advance of the pitch, and it was decided to make sure that the client representative was happy with the facilitation idea. The finance company encouraged the innovative approach, and the green signal was given for the plan to proceed.

Structuring the presentation

In our second meeting, we outlined a full structure for the pitch. They had a clear plan with three points to be outlined before they moved into their facilitation phase. We planned a segment of about twenty minutes to cover these aspects. They had simple and strong points under three headings: 'Meeting your needs', 'Adding value' and 'Partnering with you'. They used clear uncluttered PowerPoint slides to emphasise the points within these headings. They then divided these aspects so that each of them would speak to their particular strengths. At the end of their forty minutes of presentation and facilitation, there would be a short segment on the budget, which was to be followed by a strong summarising conclusion, and they would be sure to complete the presentation within the hour.

Their budget section was also carefully thought through, so that the client had a choice of three alternatives. They outlined the services the client would receive for what they described as their standard budget offer. They were aware that they needed to put forward a competitive budget here, as the accounting firms who were their competition might have some advantages in the budget area. They then offered two more costly options, which would include further specialist activities that could enhance the project. They emphasised that the basic important activities would occur whichever option was chosen. This gave the client plenty of opportunity for movement if the budget became a 'sticking point' for them.

No handouts would be given during the pitch to distract the audience from the content. However, it would be accompanied by a professionally presented booklet that would contain copies of the PowerPoints and other important information that the client might wish to look back on after the team had left.

Choosing the right words

Next, we thought about the possibility of a theme statement that would unite their thoughts and 'punch home' their message. They had already developed that theme within the ideas they were presenting, and we drew it out into the important positions at the beginning and end of the presentation, with possible reference to it at other times. The theme would be that their contribution to the finance group would be one that would make that company 'even more exceptional'.

We spoke of the importance of developing concrete examples and using vibrant language to enhance the messages of the pitch. As the team knew that the other competitors were all accounting firms, they realised it was necessary to counter any thoughts that they might approach the project with stereotypical, scholarly law jargon. They used down-to-earth descriptions such as 'one-stop shop' in their PowerPoint headings. The woman lawyer, having just left her position as a client representative, could ask the rhetorical question: 'How many of you have received advice from a lawyer and didn't understand a word of the 90-page document, or found the answer on page 86?' The audience would likely respond with recognition and this would break the ice, and thrust home the point of the practical solutions the team would bring to the task. They purposely used very down-to-earth language throughout the presentation to reflect their commitment to clear communication with the client.

The outcome

As consultants who are often called in to contend with presenters who struggle to be charismatic, focused, articulate and confident, it is exciting to see a final rehearsal of a pitch such as this one. The presenters used powerful eye-contact and interesting language, from the colloquial to the more learned. They used excellent concrete examples of what they could offer, supported by meaningful anecdotes of their own experiences. The structure of their pitch was a clear and spare skeleton, and they added plenty of substance to fill out its shape. They showed an understanding of, and involvement with, their audience. All of these things contributed to a memorable pitch—the presenters brought a great deal of skill and creative ideas of their own, but they were also able to take any suggestions we made and bring them to life in a powerful way. Of course they won the business! The client showed absolute faith in choosing their most costly option!

POWERFUL PROPOSALS AND PITCHES—ANOTHER ITEM FOR YOUR KITBAG

These case studies of a proposal and a pitch cannot be used as templates for every proposal and pitch you will ever need to give. However, what they illustrate are important strategies that can make your presentations persuasive and engaging. Good communicators know that translating complex technical or financial or theoretical ideas into understandable, interesting and meaningful communication requires imagination, energy and commitment. Our earlier chapters on knowing your listeners, structuring your presentation and choosing effective language, both verbal and non-verbal, complement this chapter.

Presenting a proposal or pitch can be a satisfying and challenging experience: it is one of the great speaking opportunities. But a flat, jargon-filled and pedestrian approach can prevent you from achieving good results, cost you promotional opportunities or cost your organisation marketing opportunities, whereas an exciting, engaging and persuasive presentation can reward you. It can enhance your credibility, help you to build good relationships and, ultimately, win you contracts. It is worth spending the time and creative energy to do it, and do it well.

TIPS

- Plan a proposal or pitch carefully, using the four guidelines:
  - Develop a strategic approach to help you prepare
  - Show your clients the benefits of your proposal
  - Attend to the concerns of your clients and develop counterarguments for those concerns
  - Demonstrate the soundness of your arguments and the credibility of your position.
- Outline carefully the specific purpose of your pitch or proposal.
- For a team pitch, appoint a leader.
- Exploit the talents of individual team members.
- Structure your pitch to balance the capabilities of your team.
- Consider using the motivated sequence as a possible structure for your pitch or proposal.
- Build a strong case for your idea.
- Present it with confidence and flair—using our suggestions on language (both verbal and non-verbal).
- Always prepare answers to the hard questions about your proposal, including any information that you did not have time to build into your presentation.

12

Handling the media

*Are we the captives of television, as some have claimed,
or its masters . . .*[1]

If the fear of public speaking is so great, what can we say when
it comes to speaking to the mass media? This possibility may daunt
you even more. After all, you will be questioned by a stranger
whom you may not entirely trust. You may be speaking to an in-
animate object such as a camera or a microphone, or the telephone,
and you can never be sure how many anonymous people will
actually be listening to you.

Remember, however, that speaking to the mass media can be
worth a great deal in public relations to your organisation if you
handle it well. Realise, also, that you can prepare yourself for the
eventuality of a media interview by working on the advice given
throughout this book, which is applicable to all speaking situations. Also, especially as media grabs are quite short, you can
prepare yourself, in broad terms, for the main points you wish to
make. Last, but not least, a report of 'no comment' can be enormously damaging, so it is not one we would advise. Gird your
loins and think about getting your important message to, hope-
fully, an interested interviewer, and through them to your public.

KNOW THE AUDIENCE

We return again to our first principle for speaking to people. Know
your audience. Each media outlet has a different section of the

marketplace as its listening audience. You need to have a general understanding of this in order to pitch your interview to suit the particular listening audience. For example, the British, American and Australian public broadcasting corporations have a different tone and different viewing/listening audience from the commercial broadcasting stations. Accordingly, you will usually find that inter-viewers from the public broadcasters are prepared to probe and move into areas that can be shared by the more knowledgeable audiences they have access to. However, a national broadcasting station which is oriented to a young audience may explore things differently from the way the same issues would be approached for the major network audience.

You cannot lump all of the commercial stations into one neat package either. The news-gatherers vary considerably from station to station in their depth of outlook towards stories, and the amount of sensationalism they are after. This is probably affected by station policy, but is also influenced by the current head of news or the particular current affairs program in question. If you are in a position where you may be interviewed, or just wish to be a capable communicator ever ready, you should compare and contrast and keep notes on the various programs. If you have a good public relations section attached to your company, they should do this for you, and you should consult them to stay up to date. You may unexpectedly receive that call for an interview. This is particularly important if you are in the position where you may get a confrontational interview. You need to be briefed straight away on the style of the interviewer and the type of audience to expect.

PREPARE

Whatever media outlet you are dealing with, it is important to realise that you must keep your statements simple and under-standable. Your listeners will not be experts. They are likely to be listening and watching you while they are doing something else, and so you must keep the language and the concepts clear and free of jargon. The best way to do this is to prepare carefully. Jot down your map of ideas and prioritise the ideas you most want to express. Speak these through, aloud, and either jot down some phrases or put some ideas on audio-cassette. Work through some scenarios and prepare for the interview to head in several possible directions. As a beginning to your preparation, make sure that you know the 'Five Ws and How' (Who, What, Where, When, Why and How). Make sure you prepare the most catchy phrases or quotes to bring concrete examples and interest to your media persona. Do not, as we have heard in examples when training, use over-formal and rather dry expressions such as 'fiscal policy consolidation'. You will most likely daze rather than dazzle your audiences this way.

When you are preparing, you may find that some ideas are too complex to express simply and concisely. If this is the case, you must abandon them, as they are not suitable for this medium. If you are a scientist or an academic who is used to lecturing, you may find this a particular trap, as you have to curb your desire to talk about complex matters or to over-explain. We recently worked with an academic who was responsible for a 500-page government report. You will realise that it is very difficult to synthesise such a large amount of information, and to decide which points to use in interviews. In a situation like this, the current interest surrounding your topic should be carefully researched, so that you are alert to those issues currently being explored by the media outlets. You need to be able to provide a couple of quick sentences to answer the obvious questions, such as: 'Why was the report commissioned?' and 'What did it find?'

If you are about to embark on a convivial interview, the good producer or interviewer will tell you the way they intend the interview to go. This is your opportunity to interview the producer or interviewer and get all of your background information. It is essential to know the name of the interviewer, so that you can address them in conversational terms.

Remember that, if you are being interviewed, it is because you know your topic and have something worthwhile to say about it. After all, an interview is a form of conversation. It is important to treat it as an informal chat and allow your personality and knowledge to flow.

To prepare for the media, keep the following ideas in mind.

- Know your audience and prepare with them in mind.
- Prepare your key points.
- Decide on what should be avoided as unsuitable for the medium.

- Prepare answers for the most difficult devil's advocate questions.
- Find good examples, anecdotes and colourful language to carry your message.

MATCHING YOUR MESSAGE TO THE MEDIUM

Print

If you are doing an interview for print, you should relax and give yourself time to think. Choose your words carefully, as there are no time constraints and you may sometimes be quoted verbatim. Always summarise and check that the interviewer has understood your difficult points, to avoid misquotation. Most of the time you will have to accept that reporters do not have time to allow you to check their story. Never say anything you are not prepared to see in print or as a headline in the paper. Remember that editors are looking for catchy headlines, and this can be outside the reporter's control. Here is a case in point.

One of us was caught in what turned into something of a media frenzy, following some research into the non-verbal languages of two political leaders during a national election. If world news is at a low ebb, your story will suddenly become of more importance to the news-gatherers. The reporter traced me to a hotel where I had just arrived for a conference beginning the next day. A hasty but extensive interview was conducted to record the research for public consumption. Unfortunately, at the end of the interview, in response to considerable interest in the topic from the reporter, I commented that every minor detail could affect non-verbal communication when a face is in close-up on camera, even a leader's eyebrows.

I felt a little embarrassed the next day, when a large headline referred to one leader's eyebrows giving the other leader the 'flick'. The editor was looking for the catchy headline and had certainly drawn attention with this unusual statement. Fortunately for me, the reporter had written an excellent and well-balanced piece with just the small mention of eyebrows in a suitable context. Anyone who read the article would have still seen me as a credible source, but the headline certainly reminded me of my own maxim to take care in providing quotations for print articles.

Radio

Your voice will be the most important element if you are doing a radio interview. If it is an early-morning call, do a few exercises to warm your voice before you start to speak. You must be sure not to allow nerves to dull your vocal quality. Remember to smile, unless it is inappropriate, as you start to speak, to give life to your vocal tone. Breathe deeply instead of resorting to sound if you feel a bout of umms coming on. This advice is particularly important for radio interviews.

Try to paint pictures for the audience, so that they can respond with their mind's eye, since there is no visual backup on radio for an audience which is now used to television.

If you are at home doing the interview, choose a quiet room so that family members or your friendly dog cannot suddenly distract you. Also, make sure you are in a comfortable chair and your notes are close by, in case you need to quickly check a detail. For the most part, you are best to put your notes away and concentrate on the conversation. You will be fine as long as you have done your preparation and focused yourself on your main points before you start. Do try to work in the juicy anecdotes, which you have prepared, to make your points.

If you are doing a morning current affairs program, you may have to prepare very short grabs and make your points concisely. Remember that graphic language will help you to strike a chord with the listener. You need a punchy and definite style. On the other hand, an afternoon chat show may run an interview for quite a few minutes, and you will be encouraged to converse more extensively and to use multiple examples. You need to know exactly what is needed and prepare accordingly. If you do not know the program well enough, then ask the producer the answers to these sorts of questions to fill you in on what style they are looking for, when they make contact. The interviews on non-verbal communication, in the election that we discussed earlier, included: early-morning public broadcast radio in the national capital probing the political angle, late-morning commercial chat programs, which ranged from the serious approach to general tips for the listeners on non-verbal messages; and afternoon talk programs which were longer and more relaxed, and wanted to probe my ideas about the non-verbals of many public figures. It is important to know what will be expected, and then to respond to the style of the interviewer; to go with the flow.

Television

Here your appearance is very important. Before an interview, consider the points we made about non-verbal communication in Chapter 6, because the camera in close-up will pick up every mannerism and sign of tension. It is particularly important for credibility that you appear relaxed and breathe freely, or the camera will notice it. The key is to come across to the audience as a pleasant and approachable person but, of course, not smiling if it is inappropriate. The audience will 'read' your facial expression and form their opinions from this. You should be seen to be a responsive person, a warm and caring individual, as well as an efficient one. Unfortunately, tension can be mistaken for guilt if you are facing a hard-biting interview.

You need to keep direct eye-contact, with your head in alignment, not drooped to one side or the other, and facial expression relaxed and alive. If you are sitting, be sure that you sit in a straight position in the chair. If you are wearing a suit, then sit carefully on your coat so that the collar does not creep up at the back and look untidy. Of course, do not fiddle with anything or wring your hands or move constantly. Remember to keep your hand gestures away from your face if you are in close-up, as it looks most odd to suddenly see a hand fly past your face as if from nowhere. Especially avoid crossing and recrossing your legs, or swinging your feet, which will distract from the stillness that is needed on camera; this can cause you to look unsettled.

Just as on radio, you need to be careful to avoid such mannerisms as a 'tch' sound, or 'ummm' or 'er', which distract from your image of calm and clear thinking. Prolonged ummms can be irritating to the listener. It is best to go for clear pauses and a strong pace when you are speaking. Be careful not to bite your lip or show facial mannerisms, and be aware of facial expression when you are listening, as the camera can always move to show your response.

We feel that our clients always find speaking to the media easier if they have a 'live' interviewer present. In this case, you should speak to the interviewer, as it looks unnatural if you speak to the camera. Sometimes you will do an interview that is on-line from a different location, or a camera crew will have been sent to relay your image, and you will find yourself speaking to a camera lens with only a monitor in the studio or earpiece in your ear. If this happens, remember to talk to that lens as if it were the interviewer in person. You must explain to the lens, smile at the lens, look thoughtfully at it, or whatever response is required.

Unless it is a casual daytime chat program, you will not be given the opportunity to make long, well-developed replies to questions. This is the world of the 'thirty-second grab', as it is so often called, and you need to be prepared for that. For a recent television news interview, I had only a short time to talk to the presenter before a deadline, but he was very professional and said clearly, 'I expect the story to run for two minutes and would like three grabs.' He also suggested the major thrust he would be looking for. This gave me a clear sense of his purpose to match with mine. Make sure you seek the answers to these questions concerning length if you get a less experienced presenter who does not brief you clearly.

For one of the long in-depth interviews, we were able to supply audio-visual material which supported the story. Remember that a good alternative, if journalists are unable to visit the site, is for you to provide photographs yourself. In fact, any visuals you can bring to the situation could help your message. If you have artist's impressions or product samples, or even videotape that will help your story, then take them with you to the television station.

What to wear

Let your appearance reflect your position and the reason for the interview. If you are a business person representing your company, then a suit and tie for men and appropriate business attire for women, as outlined in Chapter 7, is necessary. If, however, you are being interviewed at home at the weekend, smart casual dress is acceptable and looks more suitable. As women have a larger range of choice, they may carefully consider whether the interview requires a sombre or light approach, and dress accordingly. One politician suffered a media beating when she chose to wear less than sophisticated business dress for an interview conducted in her home. The lesson is that, while women may have a great range of colours and styles to choose from, they may be safer to underline their business image, both in the office and in the home.

Whatever you choose, here are some tips that are important.

- Avoid white shirts and choose cream, beige or blue instead. It is best to avoid strong contrast, and a light-coloured suit is better than a very dark one.
- Avoid fine stripes or checks as they can cause a blurred effect.
- Red is not a good colour as it can 'bleed'.
- Women need to be careful of the jewellery they wear. Shiny jewellery can catch the light and dangly earrings can be very distracting.
- Pastel colours are usually best.
- It is better for women to wear a blouse, or something with front buttoning, so that there is a spot for the microphone to be attached. It is too noticeable to attach it to a round high neckline.

One of the colleagues we work with on media training programs is a former television producer, and he recommends, for a non-studio interview where no make-up will be available, that men rinse a cloth in after-shave lotion and wipe it over the face. He says that 'this has a cooling effect, but also removes shine caused by grease on the skin'.[2] You may know that, some years ago, during the Kennedy–Nixon campaign in the US, the Kennedy camp were very aware that Nixon was prone to sweat and felt that his wiping of his brow under hot studio lights would rebound to the favour of Kennedy. The importance of not sweating in a stress interview is still in the foreground with the media minders. It was also reported that an interview with Australia's General Peter Cosgrove during the East Timor crisis is 'now a standard part of media training for personnel at key US defence training establishments'. When US Deputy Secretary of State Rich Armitage was asked why this was so, his answer came swiftly: 'He doesn't sweat. Pretty important, that.'[3]

In a similar vein, the commendations of Colin Powell as cool under pressure, when he handles the media with great patience, would seem also to come from the strength of his military training. In the midst of the 11 September terrorist crisis in America in 2001 it was said that 'there's a notable lack of hysteria around Powell'.[4] It seems that he also is a soldier who 'doesn't sweat' psychologically, as he faces the most difficult or even the most unfortunate questions.

THE CATCHY MEDIA GRAB

If you are doing a relaxed, informative interview, it is important to prepare an interesting slant on the story, or some phrases or anecdotes which will capture audience attention. For example, one of us prepared the image, borrowed from the management expert Rosabeth Moss Kanter, that a large organisation is somewhat like 'an elephant on a tightrope' as it faces the difficulties of change in a modern world. This was used in an interview to extend people's knowledge of a new course in Organisational Communication. It is important to capture the audience's imagination with images and stories. These can range from very colloquial language, such as President George W. Bush saying, of the terrorists responsible for the 11 September attack on the World Trade Center, 'we will smoke them out of their holes',[5] to the grander, carefully prepared grab from his State of the Union 'war' speech of the same month, which spoke of murderous ideologies ending up 'in history's unmarked grave of discarded lies'.[6] Of course, we all know that politicians have specially trained minders to help think up these clever statements—but I am sure you can come up with a few of your own, if you give yourself some concentrated preparation time. One politician was heard to quip cleverly, 'There is just a fraction too much fiction in this debate about the factions.' I am sure you do not believe that this was an off-the-cuff remark. Of course, it was a carefully prepared attention-getter.

There are often minor aspects of a topic which will capture the attention of an interviewer and an audience. The Gulf War in 1991, an outcome of invasion by Iraq of the small nation of Kuwait and the swift reprisals of the west, led by the US, was one of the shortest wars in history, but media coverage was perhaps the most intense of any war in memory. Because so much coverage was given, particularly of American air attacks and the bombing of Baghdad, and the possible effects on civilians, there was a great deal of interest in the rhetoric of this war. We were involved in interviews seeking to analyse how the western powers talked about the war. We drew the audience's attention to small but interesting details such as the way George Bush Snr (the then US President) had chosen to pronounce the name 'Saddam' (Hussein, the Iraqi leader) in a harsh manner, without the second long syllable, so that it sounded close to western words like *Satan*, *sadist* and *Sodom*. This captured audience attention and offered a new slant on the intensive coverage of the war.

STRESS INTERVIEWS (WHEN THE MEDIA CONFRONTS YOU)

The most difficult media interview is one where you are not given time beforehand and suddenly find you have to face a stress interview. This may arise from unwanted publicity or some crisis facing your organisation. Professor Elizabeth More, in her research into Australian organisations, shows that many of them are ill prepared for the eventuality of crisis.[7] As late as 1994, of 101 companies surveyed by More, only 35 had crisis management plans and only three-quarters of these had specific plans on how news of the disaster was to be communicated to the public. Another more recent international study suggests that this situation hasn't improved very much in the last decade. Other researchers have suggested that communication is a central function of crisis management that is often overlooked.[8] If you think that you will never find yourself in this position as the spokesperson for your organisation, you need to realise that bad decisions are not the only cause of crises. As Mitroff suggests, 'Once organisations come to grips with the normality of crises, and realise that good decisions can cause crises, their response to them will improve dramatically.' He reminds us that 'organisations need to break out of the mind-set that crises are not "normal" events'.[9]

Good communication planning will recognise three types of information that you need to convey at different stages of the crisis. These are:

- *instructing information*: this tells people affected by the crisis how they should physically react to the crisis;
- *adjusting information*: this helps people psychologically cope with the magnitude of the crisis situation;
- *internalising information*: this allows people to formulate an image about your organisation.[10]

We have held special media training courses for people who are in the sort of business that may face sudden interviews in the field, such as large chemical companies and others that work in danger situations. If there is any chance of this eventuality, you are foolish if you do not make sure that your organisation gives you clear directions and provides training. At the least, give yourself some practice on the possible scenarios that worry you most. It is important that you know the right answers and all of the details.

If it is a large company you are speaking for, you need to know the processes which are in place to prevent industrial pollution or serious accidents, or whatever else you may face. The public relations officers in your company should be charged with keeping information up to date and keeping you briefed. If you have practised some possible scenarios, and the best answers to these, or at least run them through in your imagination, you will find that you can usually transfer the understanding of credible answers from one situation to another. You must think through the devil's advocate responses you could get from an interviewer.

We suggest that you need always to be honest, as the damage to your company is so much greater if you are not, and the camera is very adept at revealing any kind of deception. On the other hand, do not allow the journalist to fudge you with negatives. Know the positives of your company's performance or practices and keep these up front. If you can't answer, then say calmly that the question is outside your expertise and you are happy to provide an answer after an opportunity for checking with those who know more on the subject. Research shows that certain responses will be most damning for your company. Try to avoid responding by 'an embarrassesed silence, downplaying, denial, stereotype responses, inadequate information, concealment and deceit',[11] and deal with the issue of responsibility with courage and sincerity.

On the other hand, reject calmly and clearly any negative labels that may be thrown at you. It is very easy for journalists to set the scene by negative labelling. For example, one televised public forum, which covered protests against the building of an ugly flyover freeway in an inner city area, was dubbed 'People Against Progress'. Notice the way the anti-globalisation protesters are often labelled as 'mainly political activists and other disaffected groups in the community'.

Remember that it suits the journalists to set up conflict, as it enhances ratings, but you have the right to define yourself in your own terms. If you are introduced, for example, as the head of a militant union, you need to deny the label with effective statistics relating your union's record before you begin to answer. Simply say: 'Before I answer your first question, I would like to take issue with the description you have used . . .'

While it is important to be assertive, you must also avoid appearing defensive. An angry reply can infer guilt and rebound against your image or that of your company. Hollywood actor Nicole Kidman provided an excellent example of remaining assertive in refusing to speak about her marriage break-up with Tom Cruise, while at the same time managing to appear open and non-defensive. She was interviewed in various parts of the world on the opening of the film *Moulin Rouge* that she had just completed. While asserting that she would never speak openly about the failure of her marriage, she was still able to answer a question about the effect of the close film relationship she shared with husband Tom in *Eyes Wide Shut*. Carefully considering the question, she answered that she believed it had strengthened their bond, not damaged it. Her admission that she had lived the worst five months in her thirty-three years came from the heart.

Honesty and integrity about your personal life can enhance your credibility by allowing the audience to get to know you. United States politicians are past masters of this art of vulnerability. For example, in a bid to overcome his stiff image, US Presidential candidate Al Gore was introduced to the American public by a video photo album of family snapshots, narrated by his wife Tipper, with these words: 'Come along for just a little while and see the man I love in a way you may not have seen him before.'[12]

You should also be careful not to be trapped by descriptions or questions. One politician's handling of just such a situation is instructive. After having worked hard to achieve the implementation of a policy of quotas for women electoral candidates for her party, she was asked, in an interview, what she thought of the latest poll that revealed that people were against quotas for women. Being an experienced warrior in this arena, she asked the obvious question about details of the poll: what questions had the public been asked? When the reporter revealed that they were: 'Do you want more women in Parliament?' followed by 'Do you want them selected on merit or by quota?', it became obvious that the poll had been built on a false opposition between merit and quotas, and any thinking person would have to reject these results. It was then easy for her to make her own important point about the false representations which are often made on this issue.[13] An important rule here is: keep calm, and do not be afraid to do your own probing if necessary.

Listen carefully to any paraphrasing of your words. If the meaning is distorted slightly, you may be agreeing with something you did not say. Always remain assertive, and state your position strongly if you feel there is a subtle difference in word choice. If you are asked more than one question at a time, then say something like: 'You have asked me several questions there, so I will first of all address . . .' or 'Which question would you like me to answer first?'

If the journalist interrupts and it is important for you to finish your statement, then do so before you answer the interruption. Treat the situation as an assertive conversation where you have equal rights. Make sure that, after you have answered any direct question, you take the opportunity to add one of your own key points. If you have to admit something which is not positive about your company, try to use the 'yes, but' or 'yes, and' approach, following up your admission with a positive idea to balance the picture.

If you have reason to call a press conference, it is best to schedule it for early in the day. This allows you to maximise your coverage with the local media. Start the conference by outlining how you will proceed. It is a good idea to read a statement, to let the journalists know the key points, and then open to questions from the floor. You can always be available for individual questions after, so it is a good idea to keep a time limit on the question session. Prepare carefully, as we have suggested, for interviews, and keep calm in the face of difficult questions.

Case studies

Exxon, Tylenol and the world at 'war'

If we look at some recent case studies, we can see that it is dangerous to avoid the media, and it can cause untold damage.[14]

When the multinational oil company Exxon had a devastating oil spill in Alaska in 1989, it failed to handle the crisis in a way which would minimise damage to its image. One study suggested that the *Exxon Valdez* incident remains one of the most remembered corporate crises.[15] Why is this so? After all, there were many worse oil spills prior to this time that we do not even remember. The perception that the public remembers from media coverage on the Exxon spill is one of ineptness and lack of cooperation. It is the perception and not the facts that finally matter, when dealing with the media. Executives failed to appear immediately and accept responsibility publicly. They needed to admit liability and take the honest approach as quickly as possible. The Exxon CEO was characterised as:

opposed to serving as a spokesperson, or even publicly showing interest, because he remained in New York until two days after the spill. When he finally entered the scene, he presented himself as rigid and aggressive, not bowing to the groups that opposed him or to the media. His inflexibility may have cost him opportunities to seek positive relationships with the various publics.[16]

The company made other mistakes in handling the media. For example, it focused on the facts concerning the clean-up and let the impressions about long-term effects on the region form on their own. It located the crisis centre in Port of Valdez. The distance from the main media centres and head office of the company caused communication breakdowns. Exxon's full-page apology advertisements were badly timed and full of conflicting messages. The actual apology statement did not appear until the last paragraph of the advertisement.[17] Therefore, the company was not able to counter the powerfully moving images of sea life dying in oil-affected waters. The billions of dollars which were awarded in punitive damages against Exxon were surely increased because the company did not appear to show an immediate and honest response to the disaster. The importance of having an effective pro-active communication policy for handling the media was brought home to all corporations by this unfortunate example.

The CEO of Exxon has been unfavourably compared with the CEO of Johnson and Johnson who had handled the Tylenol crisis a few years earlier. When the drug company was faced with a scare that its tablets were being tampered with, its executives made full statements immediately to the media, keeping them posted on all of the details. The chairman formed a seven-member strategy group and made sure that every employee was informed and involved during the crisis. Although the factual evidence indicated that it was tampering, and not production, that had caused the problem, the company immediately removed all bottles from the shelves and assumed full responsibility. Johnson and Johnson was happy to show the media their production process, and kept them posted on all of the actions it was taking to overcome any possibility of further tampering. Despite the impact of deaths in Chicago from cyanide poisoning associated with the Tylenol capsules, the company, because of its instant and open response, weathered the storm. Most customers returned to buying the product after the scare because, evidently, they were impressed by the credibility that the company established through expert use of the media in a time of crisis.[18] The handling of this difficult situation has, indeed, provided a model for dealing with potential image problems.

World Trade Center crisis

When the world faced the major terrorist crisis of 11 September 2001, the American leadership was put under severe pressure. As America faltered under the weight of the collapse of the two 110-storey office blocks in New York that were the symbols of capitalism worldwide, President George W. Bush was being rushed around the country for security reasons. Later, commentators would complain that this was an unseemly display, that his speech at the end of the day was tepid and that he did not show the statesmanlike control of a Churchill or a Kennedy. There is no doubt that he could not have faced a greater test so early in his presidency. However, this once again confirms that leaders are expected to hold their ground against all odds, to demonstrate their strength and to get to the media very quickly with the appropriate words. In this case, it was the Mayor of New York, Rudolph Giuliani, who was seen as the hero and who received the accolades for this type of leadership. He was on the scene quickly and spoke calmly of the strength and greater bonds that Americans would show because of this terrible day. His impressive performance during this crisis has subsequently earned him the nickname 'Rudi the Rock' and the admiration of New Yorkers.

Many in the world spoke of the importance of a rhetoric that would heal the wounds of a possibly divided nation and divided world. As many voiced the fear that Muslims could now become demonised in the west, it was ex-President Clinton who referred to New York as the proof that the peoples of the world should stay united. He spoke of the fact that New York itself was a living example of forty or fifty different ethnic groups of every different religion, including Arabs and Muslims, who were saying 'we hate this, we deplore this, this is not who we are'.[19] These early days were days in which crisis management through the media was sorely tested.

To be fair, President George W. Bush's State of the Union address on 20 September, ten days after the crisis began, was received with great popular response by the American people and many other supporters worldwide. It seems that the speechwriters were now striking the right chord to appeal to the majority of fearful listeners, and Bush had the non-verbal power to carry the message with a confidence that helped many to believe in his leadership. Some compared this power to that of Churchill in rallying Great Britain during World War II. But for those in the community who wanted to be doves and not hawks, one of the most memorable phrases of the previous century remained as an echo to their ears; they preferred to remember 'make love, not war'.

There is no doubt that media silence or lack of preparedness is a dangerous path to take. Like Johnson and Johnson, you need to make sure that all information is supplied quickly and candidly to the media. If they have to find things out for themselves, your side of the story cannot be controlled. Use your kitbag and be a good spokesperson for your organisation, especially in times of crisis.

THE KITBAG GETS HEAVIER

Although you may feel that packing this resource is an onerous task, you probably realise that the benefits or liabilities associated with it make it an essential effort. In the twenty-first century, companies need spokespersons with more than people skills. Media skills become essential if you want to be pro-active in the marketplace. We return full circle to Aristotle's advice—you will need all of the *ethos, logos* and *pathos* that you can muster, to reach out through the lens or the microphone to the wider public.

TIPS

- Know your audience. Keep your media research up to date.
- Prepare key points and work from these.
- Prepare by thinking of concrete examples and clear phrasing and quotes which will carry your information strongly to your listening public.
- Prepare your facts and figures, and find creative and colourful language to emphasise your message.
- Remember to make your points concisely at all times.
- For television, you need to plan carefully what you will be wearing.
- Avoid mannerisms and be sure that your non-verbal communication suggests your strength.
- If you may have to face the media in a time of crisis, prepare answers to all possible scenarios in advance so that you can present the best and most honest image of your company to the public.
- Stay calm and take the time to express yourself clearly in a print interview.
- In fact, in all situations to do with the media, it is essential to *stay calm.*

Developing leadership through speaking

The difference between mere management and leadership is communication. And that art of communication is the language of leadership.[1]

Leadership is required of us in many different situations. An integral part of your ability to lead will arise from your speaking opportunities. This final chapter provides a number of case studies which we consider to be exemplary attempts to lead through speaking.

THE INGREDIENTS

Having read this book, you are aware that a number of ingredients are necessary to become a successful leader through your presentations. The content and style, including the language, structure and creativity of your chosen public pieces, are vital. Your personal presentation through the language of posture, facial expression, gesture and voice will greatly influence your audience. In a media age, we recognise that image has become more prominent than ever in shaping audience response. In fact, research supports the claim that these non-verbal elements are the greatest influence on the way your audience will respond, at an emotional level, to your presentations.

It is also important to realise that these ingredients come together and form a *gestalt* or combination of meanings which can be more powerful than the sum of the individual parts of the message. In addition, it is useful to know that while some aspects of your personal style may detract from your presentation, these can be strongly counteracted by those that enhance the overall effect. It is always a good idea to analyse and know your strengths and use these to the fullest advantage. Analysis and understanding of others and how they develop opinion leadership can also help to shed light on your own style. For this reason, we feel it is worthwhile to devote a chapter in this book to some examples of how presentations can provide powerful leadership.

POLITICAL LEADERSHIP

Politicians, especially, have to show their abilities to lead through their presentations to the public. Some of the powerful leaders who are remembered for these abilities in a pre-television age are Abraham Lincoln, Winston Churchill and, of course, on the European stage, Adolf Hitler.

It is interesting to note that Abraham Lincoln did not have the deep and powerful voice he is always portrayed as having. In fact, he had what has been termed a tenor voice. This lighter quality of voice is often considered a setback for a leader. Gary Wills, an American academic, has suggested that a baritone voice was considered to be more 'manly and heroic' at that time.[2] However, Lincoln, as a very tall and imposing man, exploited his size along with his ability with words to counteract and disguise his lesser ability in vocal power. In fact, as we know, he changed the course of history with the 272-word Gettysburg Address. He transformed failure into triumph, and revolutionised the cause and course of the American Civil War far beyond expectations. As recently as 1992, Wills published his 300-page book to analyse the power of those famous 272 words spoken so long ago.

Of course, the power of Lincoln's voice would have been more noticeable in a media age. Recently, one of us was asked by a radio interviewer whether Abraham Lincoln's craggy face would be in trouble in a modern election. It was a response to an assertion about the importance of charisma for leaders in the television age, backed by Canadian research that showed that voters chose attractive candidates two and a half times more often than unattractive ones. This question was difficult to answer. There is no doubt, however, that the televisual charm, coupled with the strong communication ability of say, Bill Clinton, would be tough competition for Abe's lighter voice and craggy face.

The powerful voice of Winston Churchill also deserves comment. Of course, the predominance of radio as a medium, at the time of his leadership, meant that the voice was of paramount importance. We were surprised to learn recently that a famous English actor claims to have often done radio speeches in his Winston Churchill voice, and no one knew the difference. What was required from this actor was a voice that had a resounding and rich tone. However, when Churchill's voice is analysed, it is surprisingly inflexible in pitch range, and almost drones, completely relying on the power of that tone.

Churchill's power with language is also legendary, and he is renowned for the effort he put into his speeches. He admitted, for example, to spending many hours trying to find a word which adequately described the Soviet suppression of human rights and the dramatic and immovable division facing Europe when the Eastern Bloc was turning to communism in the 1940s. He reported that the idea of the 'Iron Curtain' came to him when he was on a train and noticed the curtain dividing his sleeping compartment from the rest of the stateroom. He used this idea in a speech the following day: 'From Stettin in the Baltic to Trieste in the Adriatic, an iron curtain has descended across the continent.' This choice has certainly taken its place in history.[3]

Adolf Hitler was, according to all accounts, an inspirational speaker for those who attended the vast rallies which he addressed. He used a great range of voice and gesture as well as employing all of the devices of language and repetition. However, when you watch the effect on film, it now seems a melodramatic style to those of us who are used to the 'realism' of our times and the smaller, more natural performances that are required for media persuasion. It is, all the same, always worthwhile to unlock the secrets of the great persuaders.

You may wish to read some of the speeches by famous American politicians such as Martin Luther King Junior (civil rights activist of the 1960s) and John Fitzgerald Kennedy (former US President), both particularly remembered for their speaking prowess, to enrich the power of your own rhetorical skill. They are useful models to help you to extend the range of strategies you have at your disposal.

These speeches reveal the strength of persuasive language which uses a range of rhetorical devices and careful structuring. They were also delivered with powerful conviction and energy, both physically and vocally. It is interesting to note that these speeches were the end product of a culture that has always encouraged the study of rhetoric for all students attending US universities throughout this period. This tradition has created an emphasis on the power of rhetoric and possibly explains why the British managers, that we referred to in the Introduction to this book, rated their US counterparts as superior presenters.

You may also recall the interesting story about former British Prime Minister Margaret Thatcher's attention to her image. Her advertising agency aimed carefully to capture the ideal of the Iron Lady. That she was a woman added to the complexity of creating this image, if only because we are inexperienced in responding to a woman in such a prominent and powerful position. All politicians, in the age of the media, ignore their image at their peril.

Now let us look at the case studies of some political leaders from our own time and environment.

Case study

Bill Clinton

When Bill Clinton was elected for his second term as US President, it was abundantly clear that his claim as one of the great leaders of the twentieth century was secure. We have spoken in this book of the many attributes he has as an orator and master of non-verbal communication. However, it is interesting to look at a further aspect of his leadership and his ability to maintain his power. Despite a severe crisis which almost saw him impeached as President after revelations about his sexual behaviour, Clinton managed to remain as a popular President, and continues as a force in post-Presidential politics.

One of the secrets of his continued success was the extreme versatility he showed as a communicator. In a most unexpected and unusual move, he consented to confront the worst-case scenario which was facing him as a near-end-of-term and disgraced President, and debunk his opposition through humour. If people were suggesting that he was now a 'lame duck President', he would show what a lame duck President should do with his days in a video. The video, which was released by the White House, showing Clinton watching the washing machine as it washed the clothes, riding his bike down the hallways as if he had nothing else to do, and making his wife's lunch, amongst other mundane tasks, fully revealing the absurdity of seeing Bill Clinton in this light. This was another public relations coup for his image, as it showed a man who could stand back from taking himself too seriously, and who could display a genuine sense of humour and some humility in relation to his predicament.

Now Bill Clinton can travel the world as the most highly paid orator of the twenty-first century. The leaders of industry are prepared to pay large sums of money to hear him speak and share his wisdom. With a US$10 million down-payment for his autobiography, he remains a leader of great interest to the world's readers. As one public relations man quipped, 'Clinton is a rock star. There has been no president like him in the last hundred years. He's the best orator in the world at the moment.'[4] He is certainly a living example of the power of oratory as the continued key to great leadership.

Case study

Junichiro Koizumi: Prime Minister of Japan

Japan, like the UK, the US and Australia, has recently recognised the value of a strong image for its leaders. Japan found a new, popular Prime Minister in Junichiro Koizumi. His style is in strong contrast to the last, quiet, error-prone Prime Minister Mori.

During 2000 and early 2001, the image of Prime Minister Mori was very closely scrutinised, with his many gaffes, including describing Japan as a 'divine' nation, being enough to cause not just international criticism, but also strong reactions within Japan itself.

Local wisdom in Japan is that the bureaucracy controls government, not the Prime Minister. Politicians, traditionally, have metaphorically ridden an *omikoshi* (or portable shrine), so the logic goes that the lighter it is, the better.

Prime Minister Mori exuded an aura of reliability and, at close quarters, he appeared kind and generous. He was reported to be good at politics at a local and regional level. However, he was reluctant to take initiative, was clearly uncomfortable and stony faced with the media, and clumsy and nervous with his international counterparts, with stories of his ineptitude and gaffes with the English language, when meeting Bill Clinton, widely reported.

In April 2001, Junichiro Koizumi stepped into the limelight, starring in a new role for Japanese politics. His image as lion-maned, spritely, and a passionate orator, is balanced by his determination to direct the shrine, not

Figure 13.1   A new image for Japan: Junichiro Koizumi shows flair

be carried in it. He has carefully chosen and repeated slogans such as 'structural reform without sacred cows' to demonstrate that he is leading a change that many Japanese know is needed, although they fear it will be difficult, and have little faith it can be achieved.

He has also demonstrated his strength and determination as a leader who will do what he thinks is appropriate, despite criticism from many sources, including the Opposition, by making a very public visit to a shrine for war heroes (variously cast by critics as war criminals) during Obon in August, a special time of remembrance for the dead in Japan.

Koizumi has acquired almost superstar status, appealing to a broad age group, by letting it be known that he loves karaoke, opera, Elvis Presley and heavy metal music. His party, the Liberal Democratic Party, has carefully orchestrated this new image by selling picture posters, caricature mobile phone straps, and 'special favourite Elvis Presley CD compilation', selected by Koizumi.

On the international scene, he has further strengthened his image and challenged stereotypes of the Japanese through his relaxed style, use of humour, his non-verbal expressiveness, such as thigh-slapping and smiling, and his dexterity with English, moving easily and smoothly from Japanese to English, depending on the formality or informality of the remark. He also challenges the stereotypes of formality, by looking comfortable whether shaking hands with senior politicians or media corps, as a recent visit to Australia demonstrated.

Currently, in its difficult economic downturn, the Japanese people have indicated that they want three things of a Prime Minister.

1. They must show a vision for reconstructing Japan, with an up-front attitude, acknowledging the difficulties and persuading the general public that it will be necessary to endure those difficulties to reach the desired goals.
2. They must show they have the power to suppress the power struggles of opposing factions and rivalries.
3. They must have presence on the international stage, and have the necessary negotiating skills to build up cooperative relationships.

Koizumi demonstrates the multi-faceted appeal of a leader who recognises that leadership entails managing an image that captures the imagination, builds rapport and simultaneously commands respect. He seems to be ably responding to these demands.[5]

Case study

Paul Keating: 1993 policy launch

Paul Keating, Prime Minister of Australia from 1991 to 1996, was a very colourful politician. His ability to coin 'the memorable phrase', although some may consider those phrases often tawdry, added to his high profile and his opportunity to be successful. He constantly lived up to the description of 'energetic and pugilistic with a biting tongue'.[6] He was so fast on his feet that he could usually turn an attack on himself into an attack on the Opposition.

One of the best examples of a superior presentation on the Australian political scene was the Labor Party policy launch which helped to take the party to an 'unwinnable' victory in the 1993 election. Let us take a look at some of the persuasive strategies which were used to move the audience and, through the camera, the Australian viewing public.[7]

The carefully prepared script had a strong opening: 'When you wake up on March 14 there will still be unemployment, still be problems to solve.' From this simple, but effective, beginning Keating began to offer his solutions. They centred around the wages Accord, cooperation, keeping Medicare, equity in access to education, keeping the social security net and, most of all, no goods and services tax. The crowd applauded strongly at appropriate times, and Keating backed them up with strong 'Aussie' statements like 'too right, too right', with definite emphasis. There was mention of the opponents bringing 'discord' instead of Accord; of the Opposition speaking of Australia's failures and not successes.

He also suggested that the Opposition lacked the patriotism of the Australian Labor Party and its 'belief' in the people. Keating said that Australia was now *more* than a quarry and a farm, and subtly left the inference that previous Liberal governments had left it in that state. He repeated the words 'under Labor', as he emphasised with pride the successes of his government compared with what the Liberal Party offered. There was a simpler presentation of figures than in the Liberal campaign, and a clear outline of advantages against disadvantages. He used emotive language, 'It would be a tragedy, I think it would be a tragedy', as he expressed his despair at possible changes.

The theme of cooperation ran throughout the speech. Simple references like 'The lesson I learned growing up in Bankstown . . . in hard times you stick together' served the purpose of emphasising Keating as a man of the people and a battler against the recession, and also acted as a call to the party faithful not to abandon him.

All the camera shots showed interested and eager fans. When Keating spoke of the policies for women and the family, we saw his own wife and perfectly attired children sitting in the front row.

When speaking of Medicare, Keating quickly picked up the word 'Shame' from an audience member and, with every appearance of total spontaneity, sincerely remonstrated, 'Shame, it is a shame!' These sorts of statements gave a strong appearance of spontaneity to the *pathos* injected into the speech. They added to Keating's credibility as a caring politician. There was also *pathos* mingled with *logos* as he presented his arguments. One of the strongest antithetical images of the speech was a statement about a Liberal Party policy to give youth employment opportunities. Keating taunted with: 'Three dollars an hour for Australia's youth and three dollars a minute for Australia's doctors.' This encapsulated the bourgeois allegiances of the Liberal Party, and implied that they were the unfair 'punishers and straighteners' of one of his earlier accusations.

The speech built to a strong conclusion, emphasising its theme of 'the bonds between us'. He spoke of 'our pride and why we love Australia'. He emphasised that we 'must make sure that the ties that bind us are never ever broken'. The inference was that only the Labor Party could offer this, and that the Liberals would destroy mateship and everything truly Australian. The audience applauded strongly.

Keating had looked up throughout the speech with great emotion. With a crescendo he finished emotionally, 'That's Labor! That's Labor! It's always Labor!' as his children ran on stage to hug their father and the whole family posed for the finale. The party faithful began to chant 'We want Paul', and the fervour of grassroots political theatre was captured for the viewer.

The words 'Advancing Australia: Building on Strength' appeared on our screen. The policy launch had gone as well as could be expected. This is an example of superior speechwriting. The speech, written by Keating in conjunction with his speechwriter Don Watson, showed the attention to detail that is needed for every aspect of the communication to carry the strongest support for the messages intended. Of course, in the final analysis, it had, at its centre, a capable political performer.[8]

In fact, Tony Blair very publicly took advice from the Keating Labor Party team on how to manage his upcoming election bid, which resulted in Blair's success in becoming the British Prime Minister in 1997.

BUSINESS LEADERSHIP

Here are case studies of two very different high-performing business persuaders.

Case study

Rupert Murdoch: Five-year plan

In Chapter 10, which looked at the importance of using technology to enhance your communication, we gave an overview of what we believe to be a very interesting and effective speech by Rupert Murdoch, media tycoon and one of the most important financial driving forces behind the explosion of access to global communication.[9] This speech was delivered to his corporation in 1993, and was designed to lay out, before both his own staff and the world (via later dispersion to print and other media outlets), his vision for the future of global communication. Many of these plans have now come to fruition.

The speech was undoubtedly carefully and expensively constructed for its audience. While most of us do not have the resources of speech-writers and filmmakers, or access to a setting such as the one Murdoch used, the speech serves as an example of the possibilities for persuasion offered by intelligent and careful use of a range of rhetorical strategies.

The setting for the speech was London's historic Banqueting Hall in Whitehall, replete with large dining tables, silverware, dinner-suited executives and elaborate traditional architecture. Invited guests included well-known and successful public figures such as British Prime Minister John Major, Sir Norman Fowler, Lord Rees-Mogg and Maurice Saatchi. Murdoch was positioned at a podium high enough above the heads of the 500 guests to look as if he was delivering a command. Around him, the largesse of the surroundings suggested the success and profitability of News Corporation. He was linked via satellite to guests at a cocktail reception in New York, a luncheon in Los Angeles and a breakfast in Sydney.

The presentation opened with a short video on the history of democracy and its link to the future of the technological revolution. At its conclusion, after his introduction by Sir David Frost, star of British television, Murdoch took the podium. His speech, after the initial formalities, opened with the following:

> If you look up you will see some fine paintings by Rubens. I am particularly fond of Hercules crushing Envy—from which we have suffered much—and Minerva crushing Ignorance, from which we have suffered more. I also see Plenty, which we hope will soon be with us, and Wise Government, which must at some time happen.
>
> We are on the edge of a new technological revolution. It is confusing, frightening, and breathtakingly exciting.

What a strategically incisive opening this is. Murdoch simultaneously captured the attention of the audience and established his credibility through exploiting the connotations of the stability and quality of the educated man's appreciation of art and, *ipso facto*, his inherently strong moral fabric. This gave confidence to the audience. Murdoch reassured his audience of his imaginative response to the technological revolution by using all of its capabilities.

Murdoch also understood the importance of presenting to an informed audience. He proceeded to acknowledge the dangers of such a revolution, suggesting that the motorcar brought an increase both in personal mobility and in pollution, while nuclear power gave us access both to limitless energy and to limitless capacity for destruction. Having established his even-handedness in his assessment of the new technologies, his final example, of 'the possibilities of totalitarian control by Big Brother laid out by George Orwell in his frightening *1984*', was turned around as he asserted that a decade after 1984 the fears have been proved to be unfounded. In fact: 'Advances in telecommunications have proved an unambiguous threat to totalitarian regimes everywhere.'

These opening strategies are rhetorically powerful ways to prepare the audience to place their trust in Murdoch's later claims about his vision of the future, one in which there will be increased freedom and choice for all humanity.

He uses some striking images throughout the speech to support these claims. For example, he exploits and develops the image of the 'superhighway' with which we are so bombarded these days.

> The new superhighways of communication will lead where consumers
> decide they want the technology to take them, not where laboratory scien-
> tists, no matter how brilliant, want them to go.

He continues by extending the metaphor to suggest that many industries and many companies may share this journey.

Another strategy that plays an important role in this presentation is Murdoch's identification with visionaries such as Astronomer Royal Richard Woolley and futurologist and writer Arthur C. Clarke, an elderly intellectual with whom most of the audience would undoubtedly be familiar. He quotes from both during the speech. Through this strategy, Murdoch strengthens the audience's belief in his own credibility to have the stature to create such a future, and enhances their willingness to take this journey into the unknown with him.

This framing of the Murdoch vision as a historic achievement combines the setting, the actors on stage and the technology to draw a commitment from the audience to his vision.

You are probably reminded of the parallel with Paul Keating's use of his family and the banner saying 'Advancing Australia: Building on Strength' to complete the persuasion in his presentation.

Speeches such as these, which are designed to lead, need to stir the imagination of the would-be followers. Creative use of a combination of language and other symbols and careful structuring of the message achieve effective leadership for these speakers.

Case study

Carly Fiorina: CEO of the Hewlett Packard–Compaq merger

In July 1999, Hewlett Packard, the world's second biggest computer maker, appointed a woman as its new CEO and President. In 2001, she has done what she then promised: she has reinvented the firm in three years. Fiorina has pulled off the acquisition of Compaq, to create a US$87 billion dollar technology giant. The appointment of Carleton (known as Carly) Fiorina to such a prominent position in male-dominated Silicon Valley attracted world attention. Fiorina had been named by *Fortune* magazine as the most powerful woman in American business and dubbed a 'supersaleswoman'. She immediately set out to transform Hewlett Packard's slipping profits and worldwide image. While she hasn't yet managed to stop the slipping profits, she has transformed the image. She applied her 'supersaleswoman' abilities to the many speeches she made as an ambassador, worldwide, for Hewlett Packard. A visit to the Hewlett Packard website reveals the richness of her speeches <www.hp.com/hpinfo/execteam/speeches/fiorina/ceo>. Every month she seems to be speaking in a different country: America, France, Germany, Taiwan, India, to name a few. What are the secrets of her great abilities as a communicator?

It is interesting to see that her speeches range from the more person-ally revealing, such as her Commencement Address at her alma mater, the Massachusetts Institute of Technology, to the highly specialised leadership representations of the age of technology. This ability to range so widely, and still so warmly, to an audience is a great strength. Let us briefly note some of the strategies she uses to bring her speeches to life.

In her Commencement Address, Fiorina shows that she is willing to really listen to her audience. Indeed, before the address she asked the audience to email her about what they wanted to hear from her. She decided that they wanted to hear about her life experience, and she is prepared to unabashedly speak about her own 'journey' through life. Like all good speakers, she is fond of metaphor, and the image of the journey, with which we can all identify, is one she often uses. She gives advice, based on her own experience, in a down-to-earth way:

> All you really have to do is engage your heart, your gut, and your mind
> in every decision you make, engage your whole self and the journey will
> reveal itself with the passage of time.

The Commencement speech sets out her own life story from the age of four, and outlines, openly, the lessons that she learned from difficult

Figure 13.2   Dubbed a supersaleswoman—Carly Fiorina of Hewlett Packard–Compaq

decisions, such as the one to abandon Law School despite the disappointment to her law professor father. She does not flinch from emotional appeals to listen to the heart as well as the head in life's journey. Her speech is one that motivates and uplifts the graduating class and their families, and exhorts them to have the courage to believe in their abilities, by identifying the success of her journey with their approaching future careers.

She speaks of leadership as being about 'empowering others to reach their full potential'. She is eloquent on this point of leadership being about people and the importance of 'challenging minds and capturing hearts'. This is a theme that runs through all of her speeches. It is an aspect that captures the audience, because she has the credibility of her position to support these statements, and they are an appeal to the dignity that many people yearn for in a highly technological world.

Carly Fiorina motivates others because she is not afraid to appeal to their humanity. However, a quick scan of her business speeches shows that she is also eloquent in expressing her optimism and her belief in the possibilities of a new world order of technology. She coins terms that speak to the audience concisely but imaginatively, to foreshadow a better world. She speaks of the 'digital renaissance', for example. She shows that she is a learned business woman, one in fact armed not only with an MBA from the University of Maryland and a Masters degree in Science from the Massachusetts Institute of Technology, but also with a degree in Medieval History from Stanford University, and she constantly scans the big picture of society in a technological age.

Her speeches are always carefully structured, and she outlines, clearly, the journey ahead for the audience. For example, in her speech to the Japanese Chamber of Commerce and Industry, she outlines these themes:

- the new business and technology landscape
- the transformation of organisations
- the transformation of industries and markets
- the transformation of countries and economies, and
- the transformation of leadership.

She shows her singular preparation for this particular audience by likening the Renaissance period in the west to the Meiji period in Japanese history. Erudite, yet never speaking down to her audience, she also carefully explains her ideas and is easily understood by her educated audience. For example, having mentioned the advent of the printing press in the first renaissance, she describes the digital renaissance as 'an era when a new technology is again [1] liberating the imagination, [2] removing barriers and [3] connecting us all'.

She constantly uses language in a way that uplifts her listeners and evokes a positive response from her audience.

The careful overall structure of her speeches is also mirrored in the careful structure of her sentences. The three-part list is always effective in evoking audience response.[10] You will notice the use of the three attributes of the digital renaissance in the example quoted above, with our addition of bracketed numbers to highlight this for you. Perhaps you also remember her reference to the mind, heart and gut in the Commencement Address.

If you look closely at her speeches on the Hewlett Packard website, you will see many examples of this strategy.

Towards the end of her Chamber of Commerce speech, she says: 'The greatest strategy in the world, the greatest financial planning, the greatest turnaround in the world is going to be only temporary if it is not grounded in people.' Here you can see the clever building of impact through three important elements. This strategy emphasises her point, and then returns to her key message about leadership and people. This last message—about the importance of people—is what listeners want to be assured of.

Carly Fiorina's power and success in the business world is undoubtedly drawn, in part, from her great skill as a communicator to, and motivator of, audiences worldwide. Of course, in times of change any CEO is on a precarious journey and communication is only one of the tools that equips her for success. If Fiorina cannot continue to use her superior communication ability to lead the opinions of all of her stakeholders, she may indeed be in danger of losing her position as CEO and the final success of a difficult merger deal.

COMMUNITY LEADERSHIP

Community leadership is a difficult and sometimes frustrating experience. It has particular problems. There are often tensions and conflicts as the members of the group are personally involved and affected by the success or otherwise of such leadership. Often leaders can suddenly find themselves targets of charges that they have stopped representing the very supporters that they started out with or, as moods shift in a community, the initially apathetic can become involved, and vice versa.

Case study

A recent experience at a local school council reminded us, once again, of how important it is to be flexible, and to use careful planning for presentations. Sometimes, as you have read in many of the cases outlined, a balanced mixture of *ethos, pathos* and *logos* is crucial to the success of a presentation. However, when emotion is running high, counter-strategies are needed to shift the energy of the listeners to rational decision-making. One example of community leadership that we observed provided some clues on how to handle such situations.

The speaker, a traffic consultant, but also a parent in the school, had been called on by the president of the school council to assess the viability of a public carpark on the school grounds. The need to make a decision had been precipitated by an offer of $100 000 from the government to build a carpark in the grounds.

The school was in a growing but relatively isolated and mountainous part of a major city; little or no forward planning had been done to handle the growth of traffic in the area. However, the community was committed to the relatively undisturbed, green environment, and saw development of any kind as a threat to the reasonably elite space they occupied within the city. Consequently, the issue of a carpark became caught up in a sense of threat to the very identity and continuation of the community as they knew it. The 'outsider' status of the speaker, as a resident in a neighbouring community, compounded the problem. Countering the level of emotion became the most important rhetorical function of the speech.

The speaker introduced himself as a traffic consultant who had conducted a study of the needs of the community, in relation to school and local traffic. This established his credibility to speak, but was risky because it elicited strong emotional responses from less 'expert' but potentially more at-risk members of the audience. In addition, because of the context in which the presentation was given, there were added difficulties. As a community meeting, its atmosphere was traditionally less formal, with interjections and debate as regular features.

The speech used a topical order to address the problem. It outlined the details of a study conducted on traffic use in the area, including concrete details of how the measurements were done, the high levels of speed of some cars passing through, and projected growth for the area. The speaker provided new information that even local residents, some of them involved in professional activities similar to those of the speaker, could not have known. This appeal of *logos* diverted and reduced some of the air of emotion that charged the room.

The speaker then moved to the second topic, the alternative sites for a carpark in the school grounds. The structure that responded best for this topic was a spatial arrangement. By outlining the four options for a carpark, carefully and methodically describing the advantages and disadvantages of each, the speaker projected the objectivity of the expert.

When members of the meeting attempted to interrupt, to engage in debate, and to generally stir the meeting to precipitate rejection of the plans out of hand, the speaker firmly but quietly directed the meeting back to the project of considering all four options. Each site discussion was supported by a visual aid to focus the listeners' attention and remove any possible confusion.

In a short, clear statement, the speaker concluded,

> The results of my study are unambiguous. Growth of traffic in the area poses a threat to the safety of our children. Increased use by cars using our local road for speedy access to the city and growing student numbers are combining to cause us concern.
>
> However, the proposal for a carpark in the school grounds cannot change the situation. It will degrade our grounds without solving our parking and safety problems.
>
> I recommend that we reject the carpark proposal.

The mood of the meeting shifted considerably from the initial resistance to his 'expert talk'. Rather than deliver his own assessment of the best alternative option, he stopped speaking at this point and returned to his chair as a member of the meeting. This gave the other members of the meeting time to contribute, to take ownership of this information, and then to move to an alternative solution. This came quickly and met with little debate and considerable support, when the speaker, now seated in the meeting as a parent, proposed alternative use of the money to provide traffic-calming strategies consistent with the growth needs of the area. The atmosphere moved from a heated, determined refusal to change the status quo to a relatively calm, collaborative, problem-solving one.

Handling community leadership so effectively required the careful strategic construction of the message and the deliberate re-orientation of community feeling.

Clarity of purpose is the driving force of effective persuasion. In this case, the language of leadership was indeed a gentle art.

UNPACKING YOUR KITBAG—A FINAL INVENTORY

In this chapter, we have shown you how to pack your kitbag in such a way that you can take any journey you need to take as a public speaker. We have offered a final inventory of techniques and styles to suit many occasions by drawing on the expertise of speakers who put so many of the skills and understandings that we value into practice.

Throughout this book we have offered you much advice. However, we all know that advice is only as useful as your willingness to use it. Our kitbag should have all the resources you need. We have included many examples and exercises to get you started on the road to success as a speaker. We hope that, through the journey you have taken with us, you now know just what you need to pack for the many journeys you will take in the future. Happy travelling!

Appendix

AUSTRALIA: VENICE OF THE SOUTHERN HEMISPHERE

This speech is a slightly abridged version of that presented by Rupert Murdoch at the Asia-Pacific Business Congress in October 1992. His leadership in the development of new technology diffusion makes him one of the most important and powerful entrepreneurs of the decade.

The eighteenth-century Irish bishop and philosopher George Berkeley, reflecting on the successive rise to power of Babylon, Greece, and Rome, wrote, and I quote: 'Westward the course of empire takes its way'.

Anyway, it seems Bishop Berkeley's 250-year-old prophecy is still operating. The course of empire is still moving westward. The centre of global gravity appears to be making a further shift—into the Pacific. Which is not to say, incidentally, that I think the United States is going to be left behind. In fact, I think exactly the opposite. And this is without knowing the presidential election result.

The sheer size, scope and complexity of the American phenomenon means that it can never be written off. As ex-Prime Minister Nakasone said in the *Economist* magazine a few years ago: 'The 20th century was the American century, the 21st will be the American century.' Several powers industrialised—following Britain's lead—and together they shared Western Europe's moment of greatness. In this next century, the fastest-growing of the several powers sharing America's moment of greatness seem likely to be around the Pacific rim.

This is a region whose share of the world trade was about 13 per cent in 1980, and is projected to reach some 33 per cent in the year 2000. It's a region that already contains eight of Australia's eleven top export markets; whose total trade with Australia is greater than that of the European Community.

Recently, Milton Friedman, the Nobel prize-winning economist, said: 'The combination of political and technological change (that we have recently witnessed) . . . constitutes a real revolution in possible co-operation between capital-rich countries and labour-rich countries.'

And he made this prediction: 'It could give us the equivalent of another industrial revolution.'

'Another industrial revolution'—that's why I say that in the Asia-Pacific region we are looking at something that affects the future of humanity itself. Because in all of human history, there's never been anything like the industrial revolution in terms of the way it transformed the lives of ordinary people.

After the industrial revolution, people lived lives that were radically improved in terms of economic goods, that were recognisably human. We sometimes overlook this fact because we hear so much about the transitional disruption that was involved. But Karl Marx, for example, was in no doubt that the industrial revolution was a breakthrough for humanity.

Well, now we have the chance to make another breakthrough—to extend to the whole of humanity the benefits that we enjoy in the developed world. And what's powering this breakthrough, in very large measure, according to Milton Friedman, is that we are now able to tap the potential of new areas, and that pre-eminently means the Asia-Pacific region.

But there is a problem. The problem is Government.

Friedman expressed it as follows: 'What bothers me is this: not only the US but other countries seem to be missing this enormous opportunity. The capital-rich countries are going in a protectionist direction, building walls around their blocs. Fortress Europe. The US with Canada and Mexico.'

Obviously, this is a problem we are all too familiar with in Australia.

But let me give another example. Obviously, the untapped potential of the East Germans is a tremendous asset to the world economy. But it has almost been turned into a debit, because of the way the West German Government chose to handle it. The hasty unification of the currencies, the extension of West German regulations and benefits, distorted and in fact virtually destroyed the system of price signals that would otherwise have guided East Germany efficiently into its appropriate place in the free world.

So let me summarise my thoughts on the significance of the Asia-Pacific region. The emergence is a cause for great hope but not for complacency. It's a great boon for mankind. But it's not beyond the wit of mankind to mess it up.

Now where does this leave Australia? We can state it simply by adapting a famous phrase. What has happened is that technology has abolished the tyranny of distance.

We have to get used to a new reality: Australia is now well-located.

It's well-located with regard to the Asia-Pacific region, firstly, as a matter of geographical reality. We are, after all, only 8 hours from Hong Kong. California is 12 hours. Europe is 24 hours. But the technology that is truly reducing the importance of geographical reality, however, is electronic. If you have a computer and a telephone, you can dispatch vast volumes of information to the other side of the globe just with a keystroke, and at insignificant cost.

Whole new industries are developing around this fact. And they are developing in some remarkable places. For example, every time I fly from Los Angeles to the Rockies, I cross the Utah desert. I can look down on a little town in which there now lives one of the hottest software operations in America. For those of you who follow these things, it's the home of the WordPerfect word-processing program.

It's the equivalent of finding a major industry in Alice Springs. And—and this is the point—there's absolutely no reason why that company couldn't be in Alice Springs. Australians could have written that software. They could be sending it all over the world. In the future, I believe they will.

And this ties right back to Australia's role in the Asia-Pacific region. The prosperity of this region is not a question of tapping great new reserves of national resources, or even unskilled labour. It's not like the opening-up of Africa in the nineteenth century. What counts in this region is skills.

Australia is lucky in that its natural resources complement this great regional surge in economic activity. It means that Australian prosperity has strong underpinnings. But ultimately, to participate fully in the Asia-Pacific boom, Australia has to get right beyond natural resources altogether.

I don't mean by that to repeat the conventional wisdom that Australia has to go from extraction to processing from primary industries to secondary industries. That kind of thinking still reflects a natural resources fixation, the fallacy that only tangible products are real. I mean exactly what I said: Australia has to get beyond natural resources altogether—into the tertiary sector, the knowledge industries.

Prosperity in this hemisphere is going to be a great arch of skills, vaulting from Australia to the emerging economies of the north. Australia will participate to the extent that it develops its skills.

In the case of the computer industry, for example, it is a mistake to focus on trying to stimulate hardware manufacturing here by keeping imports out. That reflects the natural resource fixation again.

Instead, Australia should allow as many imports as it can afford, to drive down the cost of computer power and encourage the computer hackers—because it's from this hacking subculture that software products emerge. And that's an industry with vastly more potential than bolting any number of widgets onto circuit boards—and an industry in which Australia is at no competitive disadvantage.

Finally, there is a third sense in which Australia is well-located. And that is in a political, cultural and historic sense.

Australia is the representative in this hemisphere of the larger English-speaking world. It is and should be much more so, the point of intersection, the nexus, between that world and the emerging economies of east Asia.

The fact that Australia is part of the English-speaking world is a crucial asset. English is the international language of trade and technology. For this reason, as well as because of recent history, English is going to be the *lingua franca* of the Asia-Pacific region. That's a critical advantage for Australians doing business there.

And it's potentially a great source of invisible earnings for Australia. For example, Australian schools and universities are becoming national profit-centres. They are finding a rich market among the citizens of the Asia-Pacific region who want their children to learn English and the ways of the English-speaking world. And, I don't have to remind you, invisible earnings of that sort are just as real as the manufacture and export of physical goods.

More generally, however, there's the issue of what we might call historical location.

The Asia-Pacific region is entering the world economy because it is passing through the peculiar process sociologists call modernisation. Its societies are being forced to become more open and decentralised, less hierarchical and authoritarian.

And this is not just because of the moral force of the democratic idea, although we saw in China that this cannot be indefinitely denied. It's because openness and lack of hierarchy are functional necessities if any society is to absorb and adapt, let alone advance, technological change.

Well, the English-speaking world wrote the book on modernisation. In fact, nowadays modernisation to a very large extent really just amounts to Americanisation. And this is something that Australia understands and has shown itself able to handle easily.

Australia has achieved that very rare prize: freedom combined with political order. And I think this is too easily taken for granted. I'm not sure we've achieved it in Los Angeles.

For that reason, in the Asia-Pacific region Australia has a historic role: to serve both as a model and as a guide. To the extent that Australia can influence the emerging powers of Asia to follow the example of the English-speaking world, all of humanity will be in its debt.

So, summarising my view on Australia: The tyranny of distance has been abolished.

Australia is no longer on the periphery. It is now strategically located. It has the potential to become a great cultural and commercial entrepot.

Australia could be the Venice of the Southern Hemisphere— profiting from the Asia-Pacific boom as Venice profited from trade following along the ancient silk road into the Mediterranean.

Of course, we'll have to do without the canals. But Sydney Harbour is good enough.

I say Australia could be the Venice of the Southern Hemisphere because, as I mentioned earlier, it is certainly not beyond the wit of mankind to mess this opportunity up.

Obviously, Australia must avoid West Germany's mistake. Australians must learn to read the signals of the market if they are to identify and exploit all the possibilities that are open to them. Anything that interferes with those signals—tariffs, regulations, controls, discriminatory taxation—is going to damage Australia, in profound ways that cannot even be fully predicted.

Fundamentally, Australia has to shift from a defensive to an offensive approach.

There's a precise analogy to sailing a yacht—you can sail along slowly, being content with slow but sure progress. Or you can spread your sails and catch the winds, it takes intelligence and quick reflexes. But it's faster. And more fun.

On top of which, there's this further point: when the wind blows strongly enough, it will capsize you anyway—even if your sails are furled. And some of Australia's protected and obsolete industries are already shipping water.

I saw this process at work in British newspapers, for example. Unions, managements and government effectively collaborated in an attempt to contain and control change. And it was strangling the industry. Since we opened it up, by moving our printing operations to Wapping and finally introducing the so-called new technology, there's been a silver age in British journalism with more newspapers and better jobs for everyone.

I say this is obvious, but let me make a personal confession here. I would not have said this 30 years ago. At that time, I assumed with a lot of other people—and I'm thinking particularly of my old friend Jack McEwen—that government could and should intervene—that market forces can be contained and controlled. I absolutely understand the sentiments of those who still want to do things in that satisfyingly direct fashion.

But I've learned the hard way. In my own business that it just doesn't work. We don't have the predictive powers it would require, and there's the question of moral hazard—our efforts too easily become corrupt and self-serving.

And that's even though television continues to erode total readership. Because television is a classic example of a wind of change that's blowing up anyway, that cannot ultimately be contained or controlled by regulation, that will one day capsize all media businesses that try to ignore it—or be immensely beneficial to the companies and countries that catch it in their sails.

So, in conclusion, the Asia-Pacific region offers the potential for a new upsurge of global economic growth.

Australia has the opportunity to become the Venice of the Southern Hemisphere. But it must learn to read the signals of the market—and not to repress them.

And then, we may well see Bishop Berkeley's prophecy finally completed, with the world reaching new heights as it comes full circle, and Australia—and Sydney—playing an important part.

Our thanks to the Asian Business Review *for their kind permission to reproduce this speech from the November 1992 issue.*

A REEL DOCTOR'S ADVICE TO SOME REAL DOCTORS

This speech by Alan Alda was presented to the 210th graduating class of New York's Columbia College of Physicians and Surgeons in May 1979. One of America's best-known actors, Alda played a medical doctor in the television series M*A*S*H. *Public opinion polls have shown him to be one of America's most respected public figures.*

Ever since it was announced that a nondoctor, in fact an actor, had been invited to give the commencement address at one of the most prestigious medical schools in the country, people have been wondering—why get someone who only pretends to be a doctor when you could get a real one?

Some people have suggested that this school had done everything it could to show you how to be doctors and in a moment of desperation had brought in someone who could show you how to act like one.

It's certainly true that I'm not a doctor. I have a long list of nonqualifications. In the first place I'm not a great fan of blood. I don't mind people having it, I just don't enjoy seeing them wear it. I have yet to see a real operation because the mere smell of a hospital reminds me of a previous appointment. And my knowledge of anatomy resides in the clear understanding that the hip bone is connected to the leg bone.

I am not a doctor. But you have asked me, and all in all, I think you made a wonderful choice.

I say that because I probably first came to the attention of this graduating class through a character on television that I've played and helped write for the past seven years—a surgeon called Hawkeye Pierce. He's a remarkable person, this Hawkeye, and if you have chosen somehow to associate his character with your own graduation from medical school, then I find that very heartening. Because I think it means that you are reaching out toward a very human kind of doctoring—and a very real kind of doctor.

We didn't make him up. He really lived as several doctors who struggled to preserve life 25 years ago during the Korean War. In fact, it's because he's based on real doctors that there is something especially engaging about him.

He has a sense of humour, and yet he's serious. He's impertinent, and yet he has feeling. He's human enough to make mistakes, and yet he hates death enough to push himself past his own limits to save lives. In many ways he's the doctor patients want to have and doctors want to be.

But he's not an idealisation. Finding himself in a war, he's sometimes angry, sometimes cynical, sometimes a little nuts. He's not a magician who can come up with an instant cure for a rare disease without sweating and ruining his make-up. He knows he might fail. Not a god, he walks gingerly on the edge of disaster— alive to his own mortality.

If this image of that very human, very caring doctor is attractive to you—if it's ever touched you for a moment as something to reach for in your own life—then I'm here to cheer you on. Do it. Go for it. Be skilled, be learned, be aware of the dignity of your calling—but please, don't ever lose sight of your own simple humanity.

Unfortunately, that may not be so easy. You're entering a special place in our society. People will be awed by your expertise. You'll be placed in a position of privilege. You'll live well. People will defer to you, call you by your title—and it may be hard to remember that the word 'doctor' is not actually your first name.

I know what this is like to some extent because in some ways you and I are alike. We both study the human being. And we both try to offer relief—you through medicine, I through laughter; we both try to reduce suffering. We've both learned difficult disciplines that have taken years to master, and we've both dedicated ourselves to years of hard work. And we both charge a lot.

We live in a society that has decided to reward my profession and yours, when we succeed in them, very highly. It can sometimes be easy to forget that the cab driver also works 14 or 15 hours a day and is also drained of energy when he's through. It's easy to think that because our society grants us privilege we're entitled to it.

Privilege feels good, but it can be intoxicating. As good doctors, I hope you'll be able to keep yourselves free of toxins. It's no wonder, though, that people will hold you in awe. I know I do. You've spent years in a gruelling effort to know the structure and process of human life. I can't imagine a more difficult task. It has required the understanding of complexities within complexities, and there has been more pressure placed on you in four years than most people would be willing to take in a lifetime. I stand here in utter amazement at what you've accomplished. And I congratulate you.

I only ask one thing of you: possess your skills, but don't be possessed by them. Certainly your training has encouraged you to see the human side of your work, and you've examined the doctor–patient relationship. But still, the enormity of your task has required you to focus to such an extent on technique and data that you may not have had time enough to face your feelings along the way.

You've had to toughen yourself to death. From your first autopsy, when you may have been sick, or cried, or just been numb, you've had to inure yourself to death in order to be useful to the living. But I hope in the process you haven't done too good a job of burying that part of you that hurts and is afraid.

I know what it's like to be absorbed in technique. When I write for *M*A*S*H* I'm always writing about people in crisis with what I hope is compassion and feeling. And yet one day I found myself talking to someone who was in a real crisis and real pain—and I remember thinking, 'This would make a great story.'

Both of these things—becoming set apart and becoming your skill—can make it tough to be a compassionate person. All right, that's my diagnosis of the problem. Here's my prescription.

I'd like to suggest to you, just in case you haven't done it lately, that this would be a very good time to give some thought to exactly what your values are, and then to figure out how you're going to live by them. Knowing what you care about and then devoting yourself to it is just about the only way you can pick your way through the minefield of existence and come out in one piece.

It can be a startling experience when you try to rank your values, though. Just ask yourself what's the most important thing in the world to you. Your work? Your family? Your money? Your country? Getting to heaven? Sex? Alcohol? What? (I don't need a show of hands on this!)

Then, when you get the answer to that, ask yourself how much time you actually spend on your number-one value—and how much time you spend on what you thought was number five, or number ten. What in fact is the thing you value most?

It may not be easy to decide. We live in a time that seems to be split about its values. In fact it seems to be schizophrenic.

For instance, if you pick up a magazine like *Psychology Today*, you're liable to see an article like 'White Collar Crime: It's More Widespread Than You Think'. Then in the back of the magazine they'll print an advertisement that says, 'We'll write your doctoral thesis for 25 bucks.' You see how values are eroding? I mean a doctoral thesis ought to go for at least a C-note.

The question is, where are their values? What do they value? Unfortunately, the people we look to for leadership seem to be providing it by negative example.

All across the country this month commencement speakers are saying to graduating classes, 'We look to you for tomorrow's leaders.' That's because today's leaders are all in jail.

Maybe we can afford to let politicians operate in a moral vacuum, but we can't afford to let doctors operate under those conditions.

You know how we're feeling these days, as the power and fuel monopoly has its way with us. Well, you people graduating today are entering a very select group. You have a monopoly on medical care. Please be careful not to abuse this power that you have over the rest of us.

You need to know what you care about most and what you care about least. And you need to know now. You will be making life-and-death decisions, and you will often be making them under stress and with great speed. The time to make your tender choices is not in the heat of the moment.

When you're making your list, let me urge you to put people first. And I include in that not just people, but that which exists between people.

I suggest to you that what makes people know they're alive— and in some cases keeps them alive—is not merely the interaction of the parts of their bodies, but the interaction of their selves with other selves. Not just people, but what goes on between people.

Let me challenge you. With all your study, you can name all the bones in my body. You can read my X-rays like a telegram. But can you read my involuntary muscles? Can you see the fear and uncertainty in my face?

If I tell you where it hurts, can you hear in my voice where I ache? I show you my body, but I bring you my person. Can you see me through your reading glasses?

Will you tell me what you're doing, and in words I can under-stand? Will you tell me when you don't know what to do? Can you face your own fear, your own uncertainty? When in doubt, can you call in help?

These are things to consider even if you don't deal directly with patients. If you're in research, administration, if you write— no matter what you do—eventually there is always going to be a patient at the other end of your decisions.

Now, of course, everyone is for this in principle. Who's against people? But it gets harder when you get specific. Will you be the kind of doctor who cares more about the case than the person? ('Nurse, call the gastric ulcer and have him come in at three.' 'How's the fractured femur in Room 208?') You'll know you're in trouble if you find yourself wishing they would mail you their liver in a plain brown envelope.

Where does money come on your list? Will it be the sole standard against which you reckon your success? How much will it guide you in relating to your patients? Do patients in a clinic need less of your attention than private patients? Are they, for instance, less in need of having things explained to them?

Where will your family come on your list? How many days and nights, weeks and months, will you separate yourself from them, buried in your work, before your realise that you've removed yourself from an important part of your life?

And if you're a male doctor, how will you relate to women? Women as patients, as nurses, as fellow doctors—and later as students. Will you be able to respect your patient's right to know and make decisions about her own body? Will you see nurses as colleagues—or as handmaidens? And if the day comes when you are teaching, what can young women medical students expect from you?

Questionnaires filled out by women at 41 medical schools around the country have revealed a distressing pattern. The women were often either ignored in class or simply not taken seriously as students. They were told that they were only there to find a husband and that they were taking the places of men who would then have to go out and become chiropractors. (Logic is not the strong point of sexism.)

They were often told that women just didn't belong in medicine. And at times they were told this by the very professors who were grading them. They would be shown slides of *Playboy* nudes during anatomy lectures—to the accompaniment of catcalls and wisecracks from male students. And in place of discussions about their work, they would often hear a discussion of their appearance. These are reports from 41 different medical schools.

I'm dwelling on this because it seems to me that the male–female relationship is still the most personal and intense test of humane behaviour. It is a crucible for decency.

I hope you men will work to grant the same dignity to your female colleagues that you yourselves enjoy. And if you're a female doctor, I hope you'll be aware that you didn't get where you are all by yourself. You've had to work hard, of course. But you're sitting where you are right now in part because way back in 1848, in Seneca Falls, women you never knew began insisting you had a right to sit there. Just as they helped a generation they would never see, I urge you to work for the day when your daughters, and their daughters will be called not 'A woman doctor', or 'My doctor, who's a woman', but simply 'My doctor'.

It may seem strange to rank the things you care about. But when you think about it, there isn't an area of your work that won't be affected by what you decide to place a high value on and what you decide doesn't count. Decide now.

Well, that's my prescription. I've given you kind of a big pill to swallow, but I think it'll make you feel better. And if not—well, I'm only human.

I congratulate you, and please let me thank you for taking on the enormous responsibility that you have—and for having the strength to have made it to this day. I don't know how you've managed to learn it all.

But there is one more thing you can learn about the body that only a nondoctor would tell you—and I hope you'll always remember this: The head bone is connected to the heart bone—and don't let them come apart.

Our thanks to the Columbia College of Physicians and Surgeons for their kind permission to reproduce this speech which first appeared in P&S Journal, *vol. XXIV, no. 2, Summer 1979.*

DO WOMEN STILL NEED A LEG UP?

This speech was presented by Patsy McCarthy, Senior Lecturer, Queensland University of Technology, at a Labor Party fundraising event in 1994, as part of a debate about the use of a quota system to ensure representation for women for pre-selection for

*Parliament. Patsy McCarthy is well known as a performer and
speech consultant in Queensland. This is a transcript of the spoken
presentation.*

Bertrand Russell said, 'There was, I think, never any reason to
believe in any innate superiority of the male except his superior
muscle.'

Now, I think he was talking about muscle—strength. However,
it seems that the absence of one particular muscle has kept
women in what Linda Grant has called the phallic jurisdiction for
more than the last 2000 years. Therefore, the members of this team
will argue that 'No, women do not need a leg up but men need a
hand down.'

Oh now I can hear you thinking that this is just semantics—
the clever twisting of words. Well I'm here to prove to you that the
clever twisting of words creates reality and that that reality is what
we are talking about here this evening.

Now, of course, talking of the clever twisting of words: in
order to get some words for the debate here this evening, I turned
to my trusty dictionary of quotations and I found that under *W*,
under women, there are 154 quotations, 146 of which are written
by men. Rather interesting, isn't it? It shows a great interest in
women considering there are only 18 quotations here which men
have written about themselves. Quite a difference!

However, if you read the quotations I'm sure you would not
be heartened by most of what was said.

Well, let's just go back to the beginning. Between the 3rd and
4th century B.C. Menander was saying things like: 'There are many
wild beasts on land and in the sea, but the beastliest of all is woman.'
Well, I don't think they've given us a very good start, do you?

And when we go back to that time and we think about the
images of women that these men penned, what are the images
that come to your mind? Perhaps the most evil seductress of all
time, the destroyer of a nation—Helen of Troy? Or, the worst of
mothers, the woman who could murder her own children—
Medea? What about the sirens? They sang men to their doom. Or,
most of all, that Gorgon, Medusa, with the snakes coming out of
her head? Perhaps the snakes were really in our bed.

I gather you think that it must have improved through time.
Well, let's go forward, shall we, and come to maybe the eighteenth
century and pick a quote from there. Benjamin Franklin says:

'Women die as poets sung,/his heart's the last part moves, her last the tongue.' Well, don't worry, Oscar Wilde tried to fix it up 150 years later and he said: 'Women are a decorative sex, they never have anything to say but they say it charmingly.' So it seems we can't win!

I guess that Freud would say that at the base of all this there must be some fear. Why else so much attack in these 146 groups of words? I don't know. What would men fear? That we might stop breeding them? That we might stop needing them? I don't think so. That we might start *leading* them? 'Ay there's the rub.'

Now, what was said one hundred years ago when women tried to get the vote? These are the sorts of rational responses that men gave: 'It would threaten the sanctity of marriage.' 'It would threaten the stability of the family.' One even said that giving women the vote was 'flying in the face of God's will', and of course, that famous Australian quotation that we would 'bear feeble and rickety children'.

So, obviously there has been a war of words and images. Even if women had not had the responsibility of bearing and, for the most part, caring for the human race, this war of words would be quite a heavy weight to work against. Now, if this was the patriarchy 'we had to have', I would like to think that it would soon come to an end.

And we on this team would say, we do not want you to go away from here with the image that women are corsetted and trussed up and in tight skirts, and therefore have to rely on a groom to give them *a leg up*, and a touch up if he feels like it (and especially if he is in the mould of some members of the NSW Parliament). But we would like to feel that patriarchal men would like to come off their high horse, come down beside us, and let us through.

Further reading

Throughout this book we have provided references to books which have influenced our thinking. Here are some useful guides for further reading.

Atkinson, M. *Our masters' voices: The language and body language of politics,* Methuen, London, 1984.

Beamer L. & Varner, I. *Intercultural communication in the global workplace,* McGraw-Hill, New York, 2001.

Berry, C. *Your voice and how to use it successfully,* Harrap, London, 1975.

Bradley, B. *Fundamentals of speech communication: The credibility of ideas,* 6th edn, William C. Brown, Dubuque, 1991.

Brydon, S., & Scott, M. *Between one and many: The art and science of public speaking,* Mayfield Publishing Company, California, 1994.

Burgoon, J., Bullet, D., & Woodall, W. *Nonverbal communication: The unspoken dialogue,* New York, Harper and Row, 1989.

Conradi, M. & Hall, R. *That presentation sensation,* Prentice Hall, London, 2001.

Denning, S. *The springboard: How storytelling ignites action in knowledge-era organizations,* Butterworth–Heinemann, Boston, 2001.

Flett, N. *Pitch Doctor,* Prentice Hall, Sydney, 1996.

Gilgrist, D., with Davies, R. *Winning presentations,* Gower Publishing Ltd, Hampshire, England, 1996.

Hatcher, C. & McCarthy, P. *Speaking strategically: Planning an effective speech,* QUT, Brisbane and Allen & Unwin, Sydney, 2000.

Humes, J. *The language of leadership,* The Business Library, USA, 1991.

Larkin, T. J. & S. *Communicating change,* McGraw-Hill, New York, 1994.

Linklater, K. *Freeing the natural voice,* Drama Book Specialists, New York, 1976.

Lucas, S. *The art of public speaking,* 5th edn, Harper and Row, New York, 1995.

Mackay, H. *Why don't people listen?* Pan Macmillan, Sydney, 1994.

Rodenburg, P. *The right to speak,* Metheun Drama, London, 1992.

——*Powerspeak: Women and their voices in the workplace* in Armstrong, F. & Pearson, J. *Well-tuned women,* Piatkus, London, 2001.

Stuart, C. *Effective speaking: The essential guide to making the most of your communication skills,* Pan Books, London, 1988.

——*Speak for yourself,* Piatkus, London, 2001.

Thompson, P. *Persuading Aristotle,* Sydney, Allen & Unwin, 1998.

Turk, C. *Effective speaking,* London, Methuen, 1985.

Notes

INTRODUCTION

1. This quote is well known to many of us and we believe it to be anonymous.
2. J. Tapper, 'Preparing university students for the communicative attributes and skills required by employers', *Australian Journal of Communication*, vol. 27, no. 2, 2000, pp. 111–30.
3. We were reminded of this in a recent conversation with Ellen Fanning, a QUT graduate who is a presenter for both television and radio.
4. This survey was conducted for Christina Stuart, managing director of Speak First, a speaking consultancy in London, in 2001.
5. J. Humes, *The language of leadership*, The Business Library, USA, 1991, p. 114.

CHAPTER 1 GETTING DOWN TO BUSINESS

1. A. Harrington, *Life in the crystal palace*, publisher unknown, 1959.
2. Quoted in H. Simons, *Persuasion*, McGraw-Hill Inc., New York, 1986, p. 104.
3. M. Motley & J. Molloy, 'An efficacy test of a new therapy ("communication-orientation motivation") for public speaking anxiety', *Journal of Applied Communication Research*, vol. 22, 1994, pp. 48–58.
4. Ibid.

5. M. Motley, 'Public speaking anxiety qua performance anxiety: A revised model and an alternative therapy', *Journal of Social Behavior and Personality*, vol. 5, 1990, p. 90.

6. This term was coined by Dorothy Leeds in her excellent book *Powerspeak*, Piatkus, London, 1988. We highly recommend this book to increase your knowledge of public presentations.

7. E. Herman & N. Chomsky, *Manufacturing consent: The political economy of the mass media*, Pantheon Books, New York, 1988.

8. Herbert Simons uses the word 'co-active' for this approach to persuasion in his excellent book, *Persuasion*, op. cit.

9. Quoted in K. Legge, 'Listen up', *The Weekend Australian Magazine*, 1–2 October 1994, p. 18.

10. Quoted in J. Cornwell, 'Just who do we think we are?', *The Weekend Australian: Review*, 21–22 August 1993, p. 4.

CHAPTER 2 GETTING TO KNOW YOUR LISTENERS

1. Oliver Wendell Holmes, 'The Poet at the Breakfast Table', *Oxford Dictionary of Quotations*, Oxford University Press, Oxford, 1979, p. 253.

2. Significant research has been conducted by C. Burton and reported in *The enterprising nation*, a report commissioned by Industry Task Force on Leadership and Management Skills, 1994; and D. Sheppard, 'Women managers' perceptions of gender and organisational life', in *Gendering organisational life*, eds A. Mills & P. Tancred, Sage, Newbury Park, 1992.

3. Deborah Tannen's *Talking from 9–5*, Virago Press, London, 1994, has provided an interesting analysis of the differences in conversational styles between men and women and how this affects who gets heard, who gets credit and what gets done at work.

4. *Washington Post*, produced in cooperation with *Yomiuri Shimbun*, 29 September 2000, p. 9.

5. G. Fontaine, 'Managing intercultural effectiveness', *Australian Journal of Communication*, vol. 18, no. 1, 1991, pp. 52–65.

6. T. Larkin, 'Communicating customer service', *Australian Journal of Communication*, vol. 17, no. 1, 1990, pp. 43–63. Another useful source that you can use to learn about employee attitudes is *Communicating change* by T. J. and Sandar Larkin, McGraw-Hill, New York, 1994.

7. G. Fontaine, 'Managing intercultural effectiveness', op. cit.

CHAPTER 3 PERSUASIVE STRATEGIES

1. K. Burke, *A rhetoric of motives*, University of California Press, Berkeley, 1969.
2. The text of this speech is extracted from *Asian Business Review*, November 1992, pp. 19–22.
3. P. Kelly, broadcast interview, *Lateline*, Australian Broadcasting Corporation, 31 May 1993.
4. A. Alda. This speech is reprinted here with kind permission of the Columbia University's College of Physicians and Surgeons. It was the 1979 commencement address and first appeared in *P&S Journal* (the journal of the Columbia University College of Physicians and Surgeons), vol. XXIV, no. 2, Summer 1979.
5. H. Simons, *Persuasion*, McGraw-Hill Inc., New York, 1986, pp. 58–60.
6. Ibid, pp. 127–34. This technique is also reported in M. P. Zanna & C. P. Herman, *Social influence: The Ontario symposium*, vol. 5, p. 170, 1987, Lawrence Erlbaum Assoc., Hillsdale, N. J.
7. The workings of the modern mind have been explored by Nicholas Rose, *Governing the soul: The shaping of the private self*, Routledge, London, 1989.
8. A. Maslow, *Motivation and personality*, New York, Harper, 1954.
9. The following is adapted from Kenneth Burke, *A rhetoric of motives*, University of California Press, Berkeley, 1969, and D. Stacks, M. Hickson III & S. R. Hill Jnr, *Introduction to communication theory*, Holt, Rhinehart & Winston, Orlando, Florida, 1991.

CHAPTER 4 PREPARING TO PRESENT

1. A. Mehrabian & M. Williams, 'Nonverbal concomitants of perceived and intended persuasiveness', *Journal of Personality and Social Psychology*, vol. 2, 13(1), 1969, pp. 37–58.
2. Quoted in C. Turk, *Effective speaking: Communicating in speech*, E. & F. N. Spon, London, 1985, p. 45.
3. J. Humes, *The language of leadership*, The Business Library, Melbourne, Australia, 1991, p. 29.
4. Our thanks to Gillian Palmer for the use of this material. Professor Gillian Palmer was keynote speaker for the International Accountants' Convention at the Gold Coast, 1991.
5. Cited in P. Tomkins, 'Translating organisational theory: Symbolism over substance', in *Handbook of organisational*

communication, eds F. Jablin, L. Putnam, E. Roberts & L. Porter, Sage, Newbury Park, CA, 1987.

6. J. Humes, *The language of leadership*, op. cit., p. 159.
7. R. J. L. Hawke, *The Hawke memoirs/Bob Hawke*, William Heinemann Australia, Port Melbourne, 1994, pp. 211–12.

CHAPTER 5 STRUCTURING FOR LISTENERS

1. J. Humes, *The language of leadership*, The Business Library, Melbourne, Australia, 1991, p. 45.
2. This headline appeared in *The Australian* on 18 August 1994.
3. T. Dusevic, 'Population boom hits poorest countries', *The Australian*, 18 August 1994, p. 2.
4. A. H. Monroe & D. Ehninger, *Principles and types of speeches*, Scott, Foresman & Co., Glenview, 1967, pp. 264–89.
5. Louise Milligan, *The Australian*, 5 September 2001, p. 1.
6. Humes, *The language of leadership*, op. cit., p. 41.
7. Quoted in *The international thesaurus of quotations*, George Allen and Unwin Ltd, London, 1970, p. 467.
8. A. Alda, 'A reel doctor's advice to some real doctors', reprinted with permission from the Columbia College of Physicians and Surgeons.
9. Quoted in P. Thompson, *The secrets of the great communicators*, ABC Enterprises, Sydney, 1992.

CHAPTER 6 USING LANGUAGE

1. J. Humes, *The language of leadership*, The Business Library, Melbourne, Australia, 1991, p. 53.
2. Ibid., p. 69.
3. This speech was reported in *The Australian*, 13 September 1993.
4. Both of these quotes were found in *The international thesaurus of quotations*, George Allen and Unwin Ltd, London, 1970. This book is a wonderful resource for all speakers.
5. Quoted in J. Humes, *The language of leadership*, op. cit., p. 70.
6. Quoted in P. Lyneham, *Political speak*, An ABC Book, Sydney, 1991, p. 6.
7. This presentation was devised and written for National Secretaries' Day by Pam Byde, lecturer in the School of Communication at the Queensland University of Technology 1995.

8. Reported on A.M., Radio National, Australian Broadcasting Corporation, May 1995.
9. R. Moss Kanter, *When giants learn to dance*, Simon & Schuster, New York, 1989.
10. Democratic National Convention, reported in *Daily Yomiuri*, 18 November 2000.
11. ABC TV Great Debate, *Is Football stupid?* 22 September 1995.
12. This quote from Dr Frank Carrick, of the Department of Zoology at the University of Queensland, was reported in *Veto voice: One voice—one victory*, vol. 2, no. 4, June 1994.
13. G. Palmer, 'Human resource development in the public sector: New developments'. Professor Gillian Palmer was keynote speaker for the International Accountants' Convention at the Gold Coast, 1991.
14. The text of this speech is extracted from *Asian Business Review*, November 1992, pp. 19–22.
15. Our thanks to Lynda Davies for allowing us to use this material. At the time she was an Associate Professor in the School of Computing and Information Technology at Griffith University, Brisbane, Australia.

CHAPTER 7 USING NON-VERBAL LANGUAGE

1. Quoted in A. Van Kesteren, 'Theatre, video, and incompetence', in E. Hess-Luttich, ed., *Multimedial communication vol. II: Theatre semiotics*, Gunter Narr Verlag, Tubingen, 1982, pp. 204–31.
2. B. Appleyard, 'Of mice and men and Microsoft', *The Weekend Australian: Review*, 12/13 November 1994 p. 1. This article originally appeared in the *Sunday Times Magazine*, London, 21 October 1994, and this section is reprinted here with their kind permission.
3. J. Burgoon, D. Buller & W. Woodall, *Nonverbal communication: The unspoken dialogue*, Harper and Row, New York, 1989, p. 9.
4. R. Schechner, *Performance theory*, Routledge, New York, 1988, p. 265.
5. J. Corner & J. Hawthorn, *Communication studies: An introductory reader*, Edward Arnold, 1980, p. 23.
6. P. Thompson, *The secrets of the great communicators*, ABC Enterprises, Sydney, 1992.

7. N. Wapshott & G. Brock, *Thatcher*, Macdonald, London, 1983.
8. M. Atkinson, *Our masters' voices*, Methuen, London, 1984.
9. N. Wolf, *The beauty myth: How images of beauty are used against women*, Vintage, London, 1991.
10. K. Dutton, *The perfectible body*, Allen & Unwin, Sydney, 1995, p. 213.
11. P. Davies, *Your total image: How to communicate success*, Piatkus, London, 1990.
12. Reported on the *Sunday* program, Channel Nine, Sydney, 20 May 2001.
13. Ibid.
14. From personal correspondence relating to this book from our colleague Jeff Kinghorn, University of Houston, USA.
15. J. Molloy, *Dress for success*, Warner Books, New York, 1975, and J. Molloy, *The woman's dress for success book*, Follett, Chicago, 1977.
16. Burgoon, Buller & Woodall, *Nonverbal communication*, op. cit., p. 253.
17. John Lyons, 'The new word is: you are what you wear', *Australian Financial Review*, 12 June 2001, pp. 110–11.
18. A. Mehrabian & M. Williams, 'Nonverbal concomitants of perceived and intended persuasiveness', *Journal of Personality and Social Psychology*, vol. 2, 13(1), 1969, pp. 37–58.
19. Burgoon, Buller & Woodall, *Nonverbal Communication*, op. cit., p. 253.
20. *Hamlet*, Act III, Scene 2.
21. Nick Morgan, 'The kinesthetic speaker—putting action into words', *Harvard Business Review*, April 2001, pp. 113–20.
22. *The 7.30 Report*, ABC Television, 4 November 1991.
23. G. Myers & M. Myers, *Communicating when we speak*, McGraw-Hill, New York, 1978, p. 63.
24. Geoff Elliot reports, *The Weekend Australian*, 19–20 May 2001, p. 33.
25. For an informative account of cultural differences in communication, see C. Gallois & V. Callan, *Communication and Culture*, John Wiley & Sons, Chichester, 1997.

CHAPTER 8 GETTING TO KNOW YOUR VOICE

1. *King Lear*, Act V, Scene 3.
2. Jill Margo, 'Listen up! Your voice is giving you away', *Australian Financial Review*, 7 June 2001.

3. B. Hutchings & S. Fisher, 'Women pitch lower for success', *The Australian*, 9 December 1993.
4. P. Rodenburg, *The right to speak*, Methuen, London, 1992. This is an excellent book to help you develop a good set of speech exercises. It will also be useful to help you to understand the aspects of voice and speech more fully.
5. C. Gallois & V Callan, *Communication and culture*, John Wiley & Sons, Chichester, 1997.
6. This is the title of another very useful book by one of the well-known voice experts of recent times. K. Linklater, *Freeing the natural voice*, Drama Book Specialists, New York, 1976.
7. P. Rodenburg, *The right to speak*, p. 5.
8. *The Scotsman*, Saturday, 30 June 2001, p. 5.
9. P. Rodenburg, *Well-tuned women*, Women's Press, London, 2000, pp. 96–109. See the chapter titled 'Powerspeak'.
10. S. Eisenstein, *The film sense*, translated and edited by Jay Leyda, Faber, London, 1986.
11. P. Rodenburg, *The right to speak*, op. cit., p. 118.
12. C. Turk, *Effective speaking*, Methuen, London, 1985, p. 4.

CHAPTER 9 SPEAKING ACROSS CULTURES

1. Robert Phillipson, *Linguistic imperialism*, Oxford University Press, Oxford, 1992.
2. Our thanks to Chris Hannan and Christy Cox, interpreters employed by conference consultants, Redcontur, Santander, Spain, and Professor Murata, Director of the International Study Centre, Sonoda Women's University, Japan, for sharing their knowledge and experience with us.
3. Fons Trompenaars & Charles Hampden-Turner, *Riding the waves of culture*, Nicholas Brealey, London, 1997 (2nd edition).
4. Ibid.

CHAPTER 10 USING TECHNOLOGY

1. This is a quote from Marshall McLuhan and Quentin Fiore's now classic book on technological innovation and its effect on society: *The medium is the massage*, Penguin, Hammondsworth, Middlesex, 1967.
2. M. McLuhan, *Understanding media: The extensions of man*, Ark, London, 1964.

3. This speech was delivered on 1 September 1993, and reported in *The Courier Mail*, 3 September 1993, p. 9.
4. This description was used by Mark Furness in *The Australian*, 3 September 1993, p. 28.
5. This research was reported at a trade exhibition and workshop on new technologies conducted by Software Publishing Corporation at the Bardon Professional Development Centre in Brisbane in 1991.
6. T. Iggukden, 'Power play', BOSS *Financial Review*, July 2001, p. 51.
7. This song was recorded by Australian singer Judy Small on her album *Ladies and Gems*.
8. Robin White of The Presentation People provided us with the opportunity to speak with the organising team.
9. The interview was conducted with Gerrard Gosens, a paralympian medallist.
10. Brendan Burkitt, an amputee, who has previously won a gold medal for Australia, delivered the poem.
11. The information for this case study was gathered with the generous collaboration of Brisbane community activist David Engwicht.
12. We conducted an interview with David Engwicht, organiser of the group, to understand how he went about designing the presentation.

CHAPTER 11 SELLING YOUR IDEAS

1. Neil Flett, CEO of Rogen International, speech consultants to the Sydney 2000 Olympic Bid.
2. This incident was reported in C. Sharpe, 'You never get a second chance', *Marketing*, March 1992, pp. 48–50.
3. We refer you to an invaluable guide for developing such proposals: P. Anderson, *Technical writing: A reader-centered approach*, Harcourt-Brace Jovanovich, New York, 1991. It has strongly influenced our thinking about making good proposals in business.
4. Neil Flett, *Pitch Doctor*, Prentice Hall, Sydney, 1996, p. 112.
5. Ibid., p. 62.
6. Ibid., p. 244.
7. Our thanks to Steve Wynne for the use of this material. This speech, presented by Steve Wynne, was the winning speech

in the Dean's Seminar Competition in 1993. This competition, organised by the Alumni of Engineering, Architecture and Surveying at the Queensland University of Technology, was sponsored by BHP Engineering in that year. It was judged by a panel of expert speakers and business people. Caroline Hatcher represented QUT. She was joined by representatives of BHP Engineering, the Department of Environment and Heritage, and the Queensland Electricity Commission.

CHAPTER 12 HANDLING THE MEDIA

1. R. Hart, *Seducing America: How television charms the voter*, Oxford University Press, New York, 1994, p. 9.
2. Our colleague Bernie Murchison, Senior Lecturer in Public Relations at the Queensland University of Technology, Brisbane, is responsible for this helpful advice.
3. Maxine McKew, *The Bulletin*, 28 August 2001, pp. 42–4.
4. Errol Simper, 'Subdued Powell torpedoes bluster', Media, *The Australian*, 10 October 2001, p. 4 (media section).
5. Reported on CNN, 11 September 2001.
6. Ibid., 20 September 2001.
7. Our ideas and experience on training for the media were recently confirmed by some important new research by Professor More: E. More, 'Crisis management and communication in Australian organisations', *Australian Journal of Communication*, vol. 22, no. 1, 1995, pp. 31–47.
8. M. Seymour, 'Crafting a crisis communication plan', *Directors and Boards*, vol. 15, no. 4, 1991, pp. 26–9.
9. I. Mitroff, 'Crisis management: Cutting through the confusion', *Sloan Management Review*, vol. 29, 1988, pp. 15–20.
10. D. Sturges, 'Communicating through crisis', *Management Communication Quarterly*, vol. 7, no. 3, February 1994, pp. 297–316.
11. P. Lagadec, 'Communications strategies in crisis', *Industrial Crisis Quarterly*, vol. 2, no. 1, 1988, pp. 19–26.
12. *Daily Yomiuri*, 18 November 2000.
13. This story was related by Joan Kirner during Naomi Wolf's *Fire with fire* speaking tour in 1994.
14. Our increased knowledge of these case studies is due to the expertise of our work colleague, Bernie Murchison, Senior Lecturer in Public Relations at QUT, who has always been

prepared to share his considerable knowledge of public relations practice.

15. This study is from the *PR Reporter*, 12 July 1993, and is quoted in P. Jackson and A. Center, *Public relations practices: Managerial case studies and problems*, Prentice Hall, New Jersey, 1995, pp. 440–6.
16. Ibid., p. 441.
17. Ibid., p. 442.
18. More details of case studies of this sort can be found in O. Bafkin & C. Arnoff, *Public relations: The profession and the practice*, Wm. C. Brown, Dubuque, 1992.
19. Reported in *The Weekend Australian*, 15–16 September 2000, p. 4.

CHAPTER 13 DEVELOPING LEADERSHIP THROUGH SPEAKING

1. J. Humes, *The language of leadership*, The Business Library, USA, 1991, p. 14.
2. G. Wills, *Lincoln at Gettysburg: The words that remade America*, Simon & Schuster, New York, 1992, p. 36.
3. Humes, *The language of leadership*, op. cit., p. 63.
4. Max Markson, 'Cashed-up Clinton has faces for both sides of the coin', *The Weekend Australian*, 8–9 September 2000, p. 2.
5. Our thanks to Associate Professor Satoshi Hamashima of Sonoda Women's University, near Osaka, for his contribution to this case study.
6. P. Keating, broadcast interview, *Meet the Press*, Channel Ten, 1992.
7. The following information is taken from P. Keating, *Labor Party policy launch*, ABC Television, 24 February 1993.
8. There is a detailed analysis of the policy launch in P. McCarthy, 'The men and their messages: Election 93', *Australian Journal of Communication*, vol. 20, no. 2, 1993, pp. 14–27.
9. Information for this case study was drawn from reports in *The Courier Mail* and *The Australian* of 3 September 1993. An edited version of the speech was published in *The Courier Mail* of that date, p. 9.
10. M. Atkinson, *Our masters' voices*, Methuen, London, 1984.

Index

263